A Family Matter

A Family Matter

Citizenship, Conjugal Relationships,
and Canadian Immigration Policy

MEGAN GAUCHER

UBCPress · Vancouver · Toronto

27 26 25 24 23 22 21 20 19 18   5 4 3 2 1

Printed in Canada on FSC-certified ancient-forest-free paper (100% post-consumer recycled) that is processed chlorine- and acid-free.

Library and Archives Canada Cataloguing in Publication

Gaucher, Megan, author
A family matter : citizenship, conjugal relationships, and Canadian immigration policy / Megan Gaucher.

Includes bibliographical references and index.
Issued in print and electronic formats.
ISBN 978-0-7748-3642-5 (hardcover). – ISBN 978-0-7748-3643-2 (pbk.). –
ISBN 978-0-7748-3644-9 (PDF). – ISBN 978-0-7748-3645-6 (EPUB). –
ISBN 978-0-7748-3646-3 (Kindle)

1. Canada – Emigration and immigration – Government policy. 2. Immigrants – Family relationships – Canada. 3. Immigrants – Government policy – Canada. 4. Citizenship – Canada. I. Title.

| JV7233.G38 2018 | 325.71 | C2018-900988-8 |
| | | C2018-900989-6 |

Canadä

UBC Press gratefully acknowledges the financial support for our publishing program of the Government of Canada (through the Canada Book Fund), the Canada Council for the Arts, and the British Columbia Arts Council.

This book has been published with the help of a grant from the Canadian Federation for the Humanities and Social Sciences, through the Awards to Scholarly Publications Program, using funds provided by the Social Sciences and Humanities Research Council of Canada.

Printed and bound in Canada by Friesens
Set in Zurich, Univers, and Minion by Apex CoVantage, LLC
Copy editor: Robyn So
Proofreader: Kristy Lynn Hankewitz
Indexer: Margaret de Boer
Cover designer: David Drummond

UBC Press
The University of British Columbia
2029 West Mall
Vancouver, BC V6T 1Z2
www.ubcpress.ca

Contents

Acknowledgments

It feels like an impossible task to fully express my gratitude to all those who influenced this book in some way, as it is the culmination of ten years of research and writing. Whether part of the process from the very beginning, a friendly face on the annual conference circuit, or a source of support in the latter stages of finishing this manuscript, my relationships with all of you were vital to seeing this project through and for that, I thank you.

Margaret Little was instrumental in helping me turn an idea I had into a scholarly reality, and wholeheartedly embraced the interdisciplinary nature of my research. Abbie Bakan and Janet Hiebert provided me with invaluable support throughout this process. Both went above and beyond their expected duties and continue to enthusiastically inquire about my research projects when I'm lucky enough to run into them and catch up over a glass of wine. Thanks also to Miriam Smith, Catherine Krull, and Grant Amyot.

While I am unable to mention names, I am forever indebted to my interview participants, whose insights informed every aspect of this project. I commend your courage to share your experiences and hope that in some way, I did your personal narratives justice. Thanks also to the staff from the Access to Information Office at Citizenship and Immigration Canada for their assistance with putting my dataset together, and to Library and Archives Canada for helping me sift through countless boxes of records.

To the team at UBC Press who patiently guided me through the publication process – thank you for your wisdom and support. Emily Andrew believed in this manuscript from the very beginning and, as such, was instrumental in its early stages. Randy Schmidt took over as editor near the end and provided me with the support needed to complete this project. Thanks to Ann Macklem and Robyn So for your editing genius and to my anonymous reviewers who, without a doubt, improved this manuscript in so many ways.

I am incredibly fortunate to have had support, personally and professionally, from a fantastic group of scholars. It was not until I stepped into Paul Saurette's and Kathryn Trevenen's classrooms as a third-year undergrad at the University of Ottawa that I realized political science could be an appropriate home for my academic pursuits. Paul's and Kathy's approaches of kindness and genuine interest in their students is something I have taken with me into my own academic career. To Lois Harder, my academic spirit animal – thank you for being such a generous mentor and friend. Thanks to Elizabeth Goodyear-Grant, Kathleen Lahey, Martha Bailey, Sean Rehaag, and Beverley Baines for providing feedback at various stages, and to Vuk Radmilovic, Alexandra Dobrowolsky, Christina Gabriel, Betty de Hart, Alana Cattapan, Marg Hobbes, May Chazan, and Leah Levac for your thoughtful commentary on pieces that I have presented over the years. Finally, to the Department of Migration Law at Vrije Universiteit Amsterdam, specifically Sarah van Walsum, Thomas Spijkerboer, Jess Lawrence, and Juan Amaya-Castro: thank you for your constructive feedback on the early stages of this project and for welcoming a politics student into your legal studies world.

Life as an academic can be extremely solitary and the long periods of isolation required to complete this manuscript were manageable in large part due to a fantastic group of friends who over the years continue to remind me there is life away from this computer. Many thanks to Derek Antoine, Katie Bausch, Laurel Besco, Randy Besco, Andrea Collins, Gabe Eidelman, Aaron Ettinger, Kelly Gordon, Rachael Johnstone, Edward Koning, Emmett Macfarlane, Matthew Mitchell, Nisha Nath, Marcel Nelson, Daisy Raphael, Leigh Spanner, and Ethel Tungohan for consistently making the not-so-fun aspects of academia actually enjoyable and sometimes downright hilarious. A special shout-out to my West Coast posse, Rémi Léger and Lucia Salazar; to Erin Tolley, for your intellectual generosity, witty commentary, and always being game for a catch-up over pints which has amusingly morphed from evening outings as grad students into afternoon happy hours with our little ones; and to Alexa DeGagné, for being my daily connection to the outside world. Finally, much love to Tricia and Nick Albright, Hilary and Leigh Boynton, Marissa Schroder, and Andrea Hopkins for your constant support for so many years.

To Mom, George, Leah, Dan, and Shelby – thank you for your unconditional support and for always keeping things real. To my Goodman family – thank you for your support, for newspaper clippings, and for engaging debates around the kitchen table. To Erin – thank you for your continued enthusiasm over my research, for celebrating each step of the publishing process with me, and for indulging my all-too-frequent bouts of nerding out over your daily work happenings.

While my life looks drastically different now compared to when I started this project ten years ago, one thing has remained constant. Whether driving to Kingston to make sure I was still a functioning human being, forcing me to vacate the windowless den and interact with other humans during the final stages of the dissertation writing process, or taking care of things on the home front so that I could finish the final edits while on maternity leave – Brad has been a consistent source of encouragement and patience. While this book will most definitely not fund his early retirement plan, I share this accomplishment with him and am truly appreciative beyond words. Finally, to my Ruby, who came along at the end of this process, which is probably for the best because I am positive I would have chosen hanging out with her over writing this book every single time. Thank you for teaching me what a work-life balance actually looks like, for unknowingly taking the sting out of the more trying aspects of this profession (and life in general), and for the time being, thinking it is cool to "be like mama" and sit at a desk and read. I will take it while I can get it.

A Family Matter

Introduction

"Immigration control is not just a power symbol of nationhood
and people, but also a means to literally construct the nation and
the people in particular ways."

– EITHNE LUIBHÉID

In March 2013, Immigration, Refugees and Citizenship Canada (IRCC)
launched its "Fraud Prevention Month" specifically to generate social
awareness on the issue of marriage fraud. Contending that abuse of Canada's
current family reunification program had reached a crisis point, the Harper
government introduced a series of initiatives for fraud prevention and
penalization, with then minister of citizenship, immigration and multiculturalism Jason Kenney stating, "Canada's doors are open to the vast
majority of newcomers who are hard-working and follow the rules, but
Canadians have no tolerance for anyone who tries to jump the immigration
line to gain entry to Canada or acquire permanent residency or citizenship
through fraudulent means" (*National Post* 2013).[1] The target of Fraud
Prevention Month was therefore the undesirable immigrant falsely using
family to obtain Canadian citizenship. As such, reforms focused on further
restricting what constitutes family for the purposes of reunification, establishing a role for the state to critically assess the intimate details of one's
conjugal relationships in order to protect Canadian citizens and the immigration system from perceived external threats.

Campaigns like Fraud Prevention Month have called into question the state's role in our intimate lives, a historically contentious issue. Then minister of justice Pierre Trudeau's assertion in 1967 that what was done in private between consenting adults should not concern the state – "there's no place for the state in the bedrooms of the nation" – assumed that our private lives should be impermeable to state influence. Fast-forward fifty years, Canadian law and policy have undergone a significant transformation with respect to relationship recognition, with the legalization of common-law and marital relationships for both opposite-sex and same-sex couples. Ironically, the extension of benefits to common-law and same-sex couples has solidified to a more permanent place for the state in the families – and ultimately the bedrooms – of the nation. While the state's view of marriage has been altered, this extension of protections and benefits occurs within a pre-existing framework, one that favours conjugality. State governing of our personal relationships transpires within a framework where conjugality continues to define the norms and limits of permissibility. As a result, not only does the state dictate which actions in the bedroom are acceptable and, consequently, which actions are not; it also establishes the conjugal family unit as the primary space for relationship recognition.

This intertwining narrative of family, citizenship, and security – front and centre in the Harper government's Fraud Prevention Month – was not an isolated incident; rather, similar narratives have been prominent in multiple immigration policy initiatives and actions taken by various federal governments. In 2002, Barthélémy Angba, a permanent resident from Côte d'Ivoire, was accused by IRCC of providing "false declarations to obtain his permanent residence" and was subsequently deported (Touzin 2006). His ex-wife, a Canadian citizen, sponsored Angba in 1992 after they married, and before they divorced in 1996, accused him of polygamy – he was simultaneously married to a woman in Côte d'Ivoire, an illegal practice in Canada – and applied to have his sponsorship revoked. In his defence, Angba claimed that he assumed his first wife was dead and, as such, believed he was single at the time of his second marriage. Complicating this particular situation, Laetitia Angba – Barthélémy's daughter whom he sponsored three years after receiving permanent residency – had her citizenship status called into question by IRCC in 2005 as a result of her father's polygamous activity, despite having lived here for over ten years.

The precariousness of her citizenship status in Canada was a direct result of her father's failure to adhere to the conditions of acceptable immigrant family practice. Simply put, in order for the Canadian state to maintain a particular definition of the conjugal family unit used to reinforce its physical borders, both Barthélémy and Laetitia had to be "excluded from the (socio-cultural) intimate space of legal citizenship" (Rambukkana 2015, 42). This case garnered a significant amount of media attention in Québec, resulting in government intervention and Laetitia Angba receiving permanent residency when she turned eighteen.

Also in 2002, IRCC imposed a lifetime ban on the sponsorship of family members who had not been declared and subsequently interviewed by an immigration officer when the sponsor immigrated to Canada. As a result, undeclared family members are excluded from IRCC's definition of family class and fail to qualify for sponsorship. In doing so, IRCC constructed a category of legal turned illegal family members, ultimately reinforcing a particular definition of family for the purposes of obtaining citizenship. Critics argue that this ban simultaneously punishes those who knowingly attempted to cheat the system and those who either misunderstood application protocol or opted to leave family members off their applications for legitimate reasons (e.g., unknown children, fear of claim refusal, cultural shame) (Canadian Council for Refugees 2007; Liew 2016; Liew, Balasundaram, and Stone 2017). This sponsorship ban ultimately delineates the parameters of an immigrant's family – both those already in Canada and those seeking access – and prohibits any flexibility with respect to familial composition, a privilege awarded to Canadian-born citizens.

The Harper government's *Zero Tolerance for Barbaric Cultural Practices Act,* aimed at "protecting Canadians from barbaric cultural practices such as child, forced, or polygamous marriages and gender-based family violence" (Alexander 2014), included an amendment, Bill S-7, 41.1(1), in the *Immigration and Refugee Protection Act* (IRPA) that renders all permanent residents or foreign nationals inadmissible on grounds of practising polygamy. As such, the act authorizes immigration officers to deport permanent residents and noncitizens suspected of engaging in polygamy without a Criminal Code conviction or finding of misrepresentation and to refuse sponsorship to applicants believed to be polygamous. Framing this as an initiative to protect women and children from harm, then

'zenship and immigration Chris Alexander stated, "Our
'omen and girls in Canada deserve the full protection of
ʌn law. When people try to bring these barbaric cultural prac-
ʌere, our Conservative govermnent has one response: that is not our
Canada" (Alexander 2014). In framing polygamy as both foreign and
culturally specific, a narrative of the polygamous family as the non-
Canadian family emerged (Gaucher 2016). Moreover, it solidified the
monogamous conjugal family as a marker for citizenship for immigrant
families both prior to and after obtaining permanent residency.

Most recently, in honouring its pledge to welcome twenty-five thousand
Syrian refugees to Canada in November 2015, the Trudeau government
limited admittance to women, children, and families (Barton 2015). A
response to ongoing security concerns regarding unaccompanied men
seeking asylum, particularly following the terrorist attacks in Paris earlier
that month, the privileging of female refugees reinforces the gendering of
refugee camps as "feminized charitable environments" that rarely frame
female refugees as a threat to the "global relations of inequality" (Strong-
Boag 2015). As a result, single male migrants are portrayed as potential
terrorists, the absence of family acting as an indicator of threat to the
Canadian state. Historically, single male migrants have benefitted from
Canada's immigration programs; male temporary foreign workers were
framed as "desirable" because they were assumed to be less likely to establish
permanent roots once their labour was no longer needed, and skilled
worker programs favoured male-dominated areas of work and education.
Post-9/11, however, the single male migrant of colour is now labelled a
security threat (Strong-Boag 2015). In this particular instance, the absence
of family no longer acts as an access point for citizenship for the single
male refugee, and "young male Syrians, Iraqis, and others captured on
today's newscasts, loom as simultaneously undeserving and threatening"
(Strong-Boag 2015).

What ties these examples together is that this normalization of acceptable family practice in policy discourse highlights the ways in which the
privileging of conjugality is intertwined with discussions of state power
and citizenship. How the state defines family determines who has access
to certain benefits and privileges reserved for those in relationships deemed
legitimate by the state.[2] Through limited access, individuals are able to

realize their rights as conjugal citizens to the exclusion of those whose familial arrangements fail to uphold this ideal. Moreover, this book examines how this narrative quickly became an integral part of the Harper government's immigration mandate. In power from 2006 to 2015, the Conservative Party of Canada – under former prime minister Stephen Harper – initiated a series of reforms to Canada's immigration, refugee, and citizenship programs.[3] The party's focus on family members as potential queue jumpers and system cheaters simultaneously established foreign families as threats (in comparison to the nonthreatening Canadian-born family) and the use of family as a clear access point to Canadian borders. Therefore, while the discursive intertwining of family, citizenship, and security was not unique to the Harper government, their use of this narrative was arguably more blatant and aggressive.

Scholars taking up the question of Canada's ever-restrictive family class have typically relied on two frameworks: a neoliberal explanation that frames the family as an undesirable grouping of dependents (Abu-Laban and Gabriel 2002; Richardson 2005; Luibhéid 2005; Abu-Laban 2009; Harder 2009a; Dobrowolsky 2013; Gabriel 2017) and a framework focused on security, explaining restrictions to the family class as an extension of border control post-9/11 (Dhamoon and Abu-Laban 2009; Salter 2013; Fleras 2015). Generating a remarkably coherent form of citizenship (Richardson 2000), the neoliberal state is defined by its population's ability to be economically self-sufficient citizens. Considering the family unit is composed of undesirable dependents, conjugality becomes a marker of privatized interdependency. Applying strict restrictions to spousal sponsorship and support obligations thus highlights the push for the self-sufficient migrant. For those using a security framework, family class migration has become part of a securitization project aimed at protecting Canada's borders, both physical and ideological. Migration has become increasingly securitized post-9/11, and therefore states have adopted various border controls to keep undesirable migrants out (Dhamoon and Abu-Laban 2009; Watson 2009; Salter 2013; Côté-Boucher 2015). Narratives framing restrictions to family class migration as being motivated by security concerns analyze this particular policy shift as one in a long list of shifts aimed at protecting Canada's borders from potential security threats.

While both of these frameworks have obvious utility, underlying them is the state's desire to construct "good" citizens through membership. As Jenson and Papillon explain, "The state plays an essential role in delimiting the boundaries of belonging and the result of such process is to create a political identity, based on the distinction between members and non-members" (2001, 12). In dictating the rights and responsibilities of citizenship, who has access to state institutions and public services, and ultimately who belongs to any given political community, the state creates members and nonmembers. Moreover, the parameters that delineate membership are in constant flux. State treatment of the family class not only dictates which migrant families are desirable as potential members, but also, more importantly, which ones are not. Citizenship, through the privileging of conjugality, is awarded to those who develop their personal relationships in a manner consistent with state views on relationship recognition – "It is kinship rules rather than consent that determine state membership" (Harder 2010, 204). Political societies are reproduced generationally, establishing rules of kinship as both "the product of state law and definitive of the state itself" (205; see also Stevens 1999). As such, what constitutes good citizenship involves state-defined expectations of "civility and good behaviour among individuals" (Jenson and Papillon 2001, 5). While changes to Canada's immigration and refugee program are motivated by economic prosperity and security concerns, these frameworks fail to fully account for the complexity of what Jenson and Papillon refer to as a "citizenship regime" (13) and how a specific version of family is used by the state to construct the parameters of this regime and, ultimately, political membership.

More often than not, family is absent from mainstream debates about Canadian citizenship. This is largely attributed to the fact that citizenship discourse in Canada relies on the individual as the primary unit of analysis. Though varied in their normative positions, Canadian citizenship theorists broadly claim that the equal treatment of citizens relies on state acknowledgment of individual difference. Relying solely on the individual, however, disregards the role of family and family construction in the provision of citizenship. Whether the family is welcome or unwelcome, an individual's conjugal relationship status results in the provision of certain state protections and the withdrawal or refusal of others. Conjugality therefore acts as an access point for Canadian citizens, challenging the individualist nature of citizenship discourse.

This focus on the individual in Canadian citizenship scholarship is compounded by the popular position that citizenship, a public mechanism of state governance, and the private domain of the family are separate. Often framed as the antithesis to political society, the family unit is typically conceptualized as apolitical. The assumption here is that family structure plays no role in the provision of citizenship, as it exists outside the parameters of state power. The conceptualization of these spheres as distinct negates the fact that the very drawing of a line between what constitutes the public sphere and, consequently, the private is a political act. Moreover, this position is tenuous, as it ignores the reality that even when the government claims there is "no place for the state in the bedrooms of the nation," the state's position within the private sphere is solidified through its privileging of conjugality. By using an individual's conjugal status to determine access to certain state protections, the line between citizenship and family is blurred.

Family class immigration continues to provide a steady source of immigrants for Canada, spousal/partner sponsorship having the highest rate of admittance (Immigration, Refugees and Citizenship Canada 2017b). It is important to note, however, that state monitoring of one's personal relationships is not limited to the family class. Regardless of an applicant's immigration category – family class, skilled worker, or refugee – immigration officers work under the assumption that successful applicants will apply to sponsor their immediate family members in the future. Moreover, for specific categories of refugees, the presence or absence of a relationship pattern is used by the state to legitimate one's claim of persecution. Family therefore influences multiple areas of migration policy development. The prominence of family migration is a simultaneous force of stability and instability for the Canadian state; reunification allows the state to reproduce the nuclear family unit while subjecting the "Canadian family" to perceived threats of otherness. State treatment of family reunification, particularly its reliance on the conjugal family unit, therefore warrants continued attention. If we are to continue relying on family reunification as a primary source of immigration, then we need to be cognizant of the state's inconsistent and unfair expectations for those seeking access to the Canadian state, both present and future.

In this book, I argue that the Canadian state relies on the conjugal family unit as a point of access in its immigration and refugee program, ultimately creating distinctions between families with Canadian citizenship and immigrant families seeking reunification. In the case of family reunification, it is not simply a case of individuals sponsoring individuals; it is about the state producing and maintaining the ideal family unit through the provision of citizenship. Immigrants and refugees are conceived of as citizens-in-waiting and, as such, the ways in which we define them as individuals, family members, and conjugal beings has important implications for their interactions with the Canadian state.

My primary claim is that the Canadian state has had and continues to have a vested interest in the privileging of conjugal families for immigration purposes. Moreover, the perceived purpose the conjugal family unit fulfills has differed across successive federal governments and is contingent on a party's political agenda. While conjugality continues to define the terms of accessibility to state protections for families living with Canadian borders, these terms are increasingly flexible depending on what is at stake. For those living outside Canadian borders, state treatment of conjugality is inconsistent; however, it is clearly used to demarcate families as legitimate and illegitimate and citizens as ideal and not ideal. In doing so, a specific understanding of the Canadian nation is maintained both within Canadian borders and abroad, one that is premised on the conjugal family unit. With respect to Canada's immigration and refugee program, what is therefore at stake is the fear of threat that foreignness presents for normalized assumptions about family, conjugality, and the Canadian nation.

Framing the Book

While the term *conjugal* has traditionally been used in reference to the relationship between husband and wife, a conjugal relationship in Canadian law and policy has been extended to include unmarried cohabiting couples with the *Modernization of Benefits and Obligations Act*, in 2000, and same-sex couples with the *Civil Marriage Act*, in 2005. Conjugal therefore refers to state-recognized conjugal relationships including both married and common-law and both same-sex and opposite-sex. Moreover, legal interpretations of conjugality over the past thirty years have recognized the complexity of conjugal relationships (an argument I develop further in

Chapter 2), understanding conjugality as being composed of multiple levels of interdependency (sexual, economic, emotional, etc.). In assessing the role of conjugality in determining immigrants and refugees' access to citizenship, I account for the multifariousness of the term conjugal and examine its role in a way that both embraces and critiques the state's "more inclusive" approach toward the conjugal family unit.

This book focuses on three specific areas of Canada's immigration and refugee program: the role of relationship history in the state's assessment of sexual minority refugee claimants; spousal sponsorship processes for married and common-law couples; and the Harper government's anti-marriage fraud campaign. Combined, these three areas effectively highlight the state's inconsistent treatment of conjugality as a mechanism to distinguish between the "good" and "bad" immigrant and refugee. Furthermore, the cases draw attention to the reality that the ways in which family acts as an access point for Canadian citizenship are not solely restricted to the family class. The breadth of influence that family has in state governance varies across and within policy domains, and its impact on the immigration and refugee program is no exception. While the assessment of all immigrants and refugees is impacted by the possibility of future reunification, these three cases capture current challenges the Canadian state's understanding of conjugality presents for those seeking access.

Comparatively speaking, Canada provides an intriguing case for analyzing the relationship between family, citizenship, and security. For Canada, the normative status of being an immigrant-receiving nation has resulted in a model of migration management premised on the belief that our society is both defined and enhanced by immigrant admittance (Alboim and Boyd 2012; Fleras 2015). Indeed, the facilitation of migration and a commitment to immigrant settlement and integration through multicultural policies is integral to Canada's national imaginary. Canada's leadership in many areas of immigration and refugee laws and policies places Canadian scholars at the forefront of immigration and citizenship debates taking place in political science (Kymlicka 1995; Abu-Laban and Strong-Boag 1998; Carens 2000, 2003, 2013; Abu-Laban and Gabriel 2002; Dhamoon 2007, 2009; Dhamoon and Abu-Laban 2009; Harder 2009a, 2015); legal studies (Macklin 2002, 2007; Dauvergne 2005, 2016); labour studies and social movements (Arat-Koç 1989, 1997; Macklin 1992, 1996;

Bakan and Stasiulis 1997, 2005, 2012; Gabriel and Macdonald 2007; Gabriel 2011; Tungohan 2012, 2013; Tungohan et al. 2015); and sociology (Satzewich 1993, 2015; Bernhard, Landolt, and Goldring 2009; Goldring and Landolt 2013; Fleras 2015). It is against this backdrop that I examine how the Canadian state, specifically under the Harper government, took up the notion of family as a potential security threat and, as such, an access point for citizenship. Such an analysis will prove to be useful for other immigrant-receiving countries asking similar questions.

The contributions of this book are, therefore, threefold. First, this book provides a much-needed mapping of the Canadian state's approach toward relationship recognition, focusing not only on immigration practices, but also on Canadian law and policy more generally. Second, it thoroughly examines connections between family, citizenship, and security, ultimately providing a novel approach to understanding long-standing debates surrounding Canadian citizenship. Finally, it provides an empirical foundation for analyzing and understanding the role of conjugality in the assessment of incoming immigrants and refugees. In the end, this book provides an innovative methodological approach, linking normative discussions of citizenship with empirical assessment of Canada's immigration policy and practice. The result is an interdisciplinary account of the state's treatment of family as an access point for citizenship and the implications this presents for current and future immigrants and refugees.

Using an interpretive policy analysis approach, the research – derived from a combination of discourse analysis and qualitative interviews – focuses on the "work" of Canadian immigration and refugee policy. The actual wording of immigration and refugee laws and policies provides us with insufficient information regarding application and enforcement, as actions undertaken by decision makers (immigration officers, ministers, courts, etc.) are susceptible to an "enormous scope for discretion and political intervention" (Macklin 2002, 220). Moreover, the execution of immigration and refugee laws and policies often conveys contradictory messaging, suggesting a neutral, bias-free system that in reality remains quite restrictive (Macklin 2002; Thobani 2007; Dhamoon 2009). In addition to examining policy as it is written, an interpretive policy approach involves exploring the very creation of these policies (Yanow 2000). This methodological combination therefore highlights the language of policy, as well as the motivations behind that language. The book relies on a thorough analysis of Canadian immigration policy documents, examining how discourses of family, citizenship, and security are used to construct the access-seeking immigrant and refugee. While other methodologies are occupied with understanding social reality as it exists, discourse analysis questions the production of that reality (Wood and Kroger 2000; Phillips and Hardy 2002). These policy documents include policy briefs, government manuals, immigration officer training manuals, and government-initiated studies.[4] My analysis of policy documents and legal decisions is complemented by news coverage of significant changes to the IRPA under the Harper government, as well as by twenty-nine interviews: eight with former and current policy analysts and immigration officers from Immigration, Refugees and Citizenship Canada, two with former members of the Law Commission of Canada, two with immigration lawyers and former Immigration and Refugee Board of Canada (IRB) members, and seventeen with a collection of common-law and married couples – both same-sex and opposite-sex – who successfully applied for spousal sponsorship.[5]

Outline of the Book

Although the individual is the primary unit of analysis for mainstream Canadian citizenship scholarship, I propose a family-based lens. It is not dismissive of this body of literature; rather, it is important to examine how and why this approach has evolved and the logic that drives these individualist approaches toward understanding citizenship. Chapter 1 elaborates on the state of citizenship discourse in Canada, focusing on its reliance on the individual as the primary unit of analysis. From there, I establish a theoretical starting point for incorporating family into discussions of citizenship, using critical citizenship literature to highlight the role that the conjugal family unit plays in the provision of Canadian citizenship.

Domestically, Canadians generally have the freedom to construct their familial units as they see fit; however, this elasticity is not replicated in our immigration and refugee policy program. If anything, what constitutes family has become increasingly restrictive, used to enact stricter regulations on reunification. In Chapter 2, I examine how this differentiation in treatment creates two versions of the conjugal family – the inside family (families living within Canadian borders) and the outside family (families living outside Canadian borders) – and how the construction of inside and outside families shapes our understanding of the noncitizen seeking access. In addition to examining the evolution of these two categories in Canadian law and policy, this chapter explores the ways in which the Harper government's use of this distinction differed from governments past. Restrictive immigration programs were not unique to the Harper government; however, changes to the IRPA after the Conservative Party of Canada took power in 2006 were framed in a discourse of security that distinguished this government from its predecessors. This chapter thus focuses on the construction of inside and outside families in Canadian law and policy and how the Harper government used this distinction to shape our understanding of good and bad families and, consequently, desirable and undesirable citizens.

Chapters 3 to 5 delve into the three selected areas of immigration and refugee policy: an examination of the Canadian state's treatment of conjugality in the assessment of sexual minority refugee claims (Chapter 3); an assessment of common-law couples seeking spousal sponsorship (Chapter 4); and the government's anti–marriage fraud campaign (Chapter 5). These three cases highlight how the use of conjugality as a point of access for Canadian citizenship is both ambiguous and contradictory, ultimately calling into question its effectiveness. Moreover, it suggests that the state's targeting of certain groups reinforces a narrative of family premised on a normalized conception of the conjugal family unit, an understanding that cuts across lines both defined and reinforced through sexism, racism, heterosexism, and colonialism. These chapters reinforce my central claim that the Canadian state has a vested interest in privileging the conjugal family unit in its immigration and refugee program.

In Chapter 6, I propose several policy frameworks in which conjugality no longer holds primacy in state-recognized relationships. Through an examination of these frameworks, this chapter aims to take stock of theoretical debates surrounding the state of conjugality in policy development and to provide a starting point for future discussions on immigration, family, and citizenship. This is complemented by a discussion of several tensions in need of address should the execution of these frameworks be extended to immigration. This chapter establishes a space for discussing the potential of an immigration system in which conjugality no longer dictates the terms of permissibility for those seeking access.

1

The Invisibility of Family in the Canadian Conversation

"The study of the idea of citizenship, and of the multiple practices and institutions and experiences that the term is used to represent, are fundamentally inseparable."

– LINDA BOSNIAK

As it currently stands in Canada, citizenship suffers from an identity crisis. It is defined as a fixed set of rules, an ever-changing dynamic, a way of being, a source of social disunity, the answer to national unity – the list goes on. The multifariousness of citizenship presents challenges for policy development; the way citizenship is framed shapes policy development and, conversely, public policy reflects and reinforces the values inherent in our understanding of citizenship. It is therefore imperative that we recognize the complexity of citizenship, as it simultaneously dictates who is in and who is out – "Citizenship both alienates and assimilates, ostracizes and 'equalizes' ... It is a highly problematic, contested, and contestable category, composed as much of negative as positive content, of absence as much as presence especially for members of the uncountable demographics who find themselves other-than-naturalized" (Fleischmann, van Styvendale, and Maccaroll 2011, xx). Conceptualizing citizenship therefore requires accounting for both its inclusive and exclusive properties, as both a status and a practice premised on a system of "differentiated universalism" (Lister 1997a, 42).

At its most basic level, citizenship involves the construction of insiders and outsiders (Jenson and Phillips 1996, 114). In addition to establishing criteria for legally crossing Canadian borders, citizenship shapes the treatment of immigrants once they have arrived in Canada through access (e.g., passports, political institutions, and public services), a system of rights and responsibilities between the state and its citizens as well as between citizens, and identity (e.g., community belonging, participation in economic and social life, state support when needed) (Jenson and Papillon 2001; Joppke 2010). On one hand, the way citizenship is defined informs immigration officers of the type of citizens the state wants, while on the other hand, immigrants have successfully challenged citizenship frameworks to be more inclusive. The interconnectedness between migration, citizenship, and nation building therefore warrants attention, as our immigration program manages access to both formal and substantive aspects of Canadian citizenship (Thobani 2007, 74).

This is not to suggest that citizenship and immigration are interchangeable concepts; the *Immigration and Refugee Protection Act* and *Citizenship Act* are separate pieces of legislation. Moreover, the *Citizenship Act* applies to all Canadian citizens, not to just those who come to Canada through our immigration and refugee program. While not substitutable, immigration and citizenship have multiple connections. Canada's immigration and refugee program establishes guidelines dictating which individuals not born on Canadian soil are potentially eligible for access to the state's borders and citizenship. As such, discriminatory immigration laws are grounded in discriminatory citizenship laws (Luibhéid and Cantú 2005; Fleras 2015). These acts also shape the familial composition of those non/partial citizens seeking entry, as they contain "ethno-normative and heteronormative logics that profoundly structure what types of intimate subjectivity Canadians are allowed to have as citizens and as families/what types of intimate subjects and families are allowed Canadian citizenship" (Rambukkana 2015, 39).[1] Both concepts are therefore crucial to this study because combined, they command which migrant families are worthy of admittance to the Canadian state and the Canadian family.

In 2015, 65,490 immigrants arrived in Canada through the family class, 71 percent being sponsored spouses/partners (Immigration, Refugees and Citizenship Canada 2015b). Prior to 2012, all sponsored family members received permanent residency upon arrival. Between 2012 and 2017, all sponsored spouses were required to fulfill a two-year residency requirement prior to obtaining citizenship, a policy that has since been reversed by the Trudeau government. Whereas sponsorship of parents, grandparents, older children, and extended family has slowed due to a combination of changes in government objectives and bureaucratic backlog, spousal/partner sponsorship has remained relatively consistent since 2009.[2] With respect to processing times, spousal/partner sponsorship remains the quickest way to acquire status; sponsorship applications involving a spouse, common-law partner, or dependent child are processed in approximately twelve months while those involving a parent or grandparent take approximately forty-seven months (Immigration, Refugees and Citizenship Canada 2017a). The challenge lies in proving that your relationship is, in fact, legitimate to the satisfaction of specific gatekeepers. Canada's immigration and refugee program relies on a strict definition of conjugality that awards citizenship to those families deemed legitimate. Therefore, how we frame citizenship is particularly important for our understanding of how current migration policy shapes family construction.

Despite its role in the provision of citizenship, family is rarely taken up in Canadian scholarship on citizenship and state power. While this body of literature is impressive, its reliance on the individual as the primary unit of analysis renders analysis of family in Canadian citizenship discourse less complete. This is concerning because how we frame citizenship implicates migrants and their families. The definition of family used in Canada's immigration and refugee program not only influences who immigrates as part of the family class but also who becomes a citizen. When it comes to family reunification, the "ideal" family is in many ways determinative of the "ideal" citizen. This raises the question: "How have rules that address individual claims to belonging to both family and nation been reconciled with the trend toward individualization and what changes do they reflect in the ongoing tension between individual, family, and state?" (van Walsum 2008, 13). In the case of family reunification, it is not simply a case of individuals sponsoring individuals; it is about the state producing and reproducing a desirable familial form through the provision of citizenship.

Canada's *Citizenship Act* is not structured according to any definition of the family. It is therefore inaccurate to suggest that citizenship determines family construction because technically, the definition of family does not directly preclude people from becoming citizens. This book situates family within Canadian citizenship circles and examines the type of family our immigration and refugee program recognizes. Furthermore, it makes a case for acknowledging that in citizenship discourse, family acts as an organizing principle of the state. While I recognize that sponsored family members and refugees are not automatically awarded full citizenship, the implications of citizenship are not limited to full citizens, as the effects of citizenship vary among those with full status, partial status, or no status (Thobani 2007; Dhamoon 2009; Fleischmann, van Styvendale, and Maccaroll 2011).

Current citizenship frames in Canadian scholarship therefore limit our understanding of the relationship between immigration, citizenship, and family, resulting in an incomplete picture of Canadian citizenship. Family reunification remains a primary means by which migrants come to Canada and, as a result, the way in which we define family plays an important role in the construction of citizens (van Walsum 2003, 223). This chapter proposes a new frame for theorizing citizenship, one that accounts for the role that family plays in citizenship projects. In doing so, this frame allows for a discussion about the role conjugality plays in family reunification processes and, consequently, the impact this has not only on state treatment of immigrants and refugees, but also on the production of citizens, a conversation that is currently incomplete when using a more individual-oriented framework.

Revisiting the Canadian Conversation

Labelled the "Canadian conversation" by Kernerman (2005), the theorization of citizenship in Canada has been the focal point of much academic rigour from liberal theorists (Webber 1994; Tully 1995; Ignatieff 2000; Carens 2000, 2003, 2013) and critical theorists (Razack 1998; Bannerji 2000; Day 2002; Abu-Laban and Gabriel 2002; Arneil 2007; Thobani 2007) alike. For Kernerman, the Canadian conversation is not solely defined by its content but also by its perennial tension, that being deep-founded contentions between questions of unity and the accommodation of diversity. This site of political contestation – what Kernerman refers to as "multicultural nationalism" – is an ambiguous zone of Canadian political thought, as those involved in this conversation are "all multiculturalists, nationalists, and not least liberals" though are "unlikely to understand themselves (or their various opponents) in these terms" (2005, 5).[3] While these theorists situate themselves along liberal and critical lines, there are normative parallels across these positions. Visions of Canada reliant on an equality-as-sameness approach seem incompatible with those promoting an equality-as-difference rhetoric; however, the objective of both is to define the Canadian political community. Moreover, while both visions promote the idea of a unified nation, they accomplish this at the cost of recognizing certain identity-based groups and disregarding others. The perceived polarization of the Canadian conversation is, therefore, misleading, as dividing lines between competing positions are not as well defined as the literature suggests.

For Kernerman, the focus should not be on resolving these tensions but rather on the logics that cultivate these positions (2005, 5). This section will do exactly that, focusing on how specific logics of family, immigration, and citizenship foster certain positions within the Canadian conversation and the implications this has for family reunification, commencing with an examination of a liberal-critical dialogue between two Canadian citizenship scholars: Will Kymlicka and Rita Dhamoon. Kymlicka's and Dhamoon's work effectively captures the perennial tension inherent in the Canadian conversation, providing an appropriate starting point to discuss the absence of family in this body of scholarship. Kymlicka challenges the perceived incompatibility between differentiated citizenship and national unity, claiming that multicultural states require a framework that accounts for differentiation in cultural needs in order to maintain unity (establishing parameters of the state) and manage diversity (recognizing the need for space for recognition of cultural differences). Alternatively, Dhamoon criticizes Kymlicka's reliance on culture as the sole site of individual self-capacity, arguing that the politics of identity requires us to focus on multiple relationships of power at play in citizenship discourse and advocating for an account of meaning-making that allows us to conceptualize the role of power in the production and reproduction of difference, the very foundation of citizenship. While these two scholars arguably frame citizenship from competing positions, both represent an ongoing conversation in Canada concerning the interconnectedness of identity and citizenship and, furthermore, the normative implications this presents for full citizens, partial citizens, and noncitizens.

Inherent in the approach of the so-called Canadian School to framing citizenship is the belief that a single uniform framework for citizenship claims is inadequate.[4] The Canadian state's commitment to multiculturalism requires a framework that recognizes differentiation in citizens' needs, what Carens coined a "contextual" understanding of citizenship (2000, 2).[5] According to the Canadian School, liberal democracies have (and should have) overarching principles to guide the provision of citizenship; however, these values require a degree of flexibility with respect to claims for cultural autonomy, as how we interpret citizenship has different implications for different cultural groups. This framework challenges classic liberal theorizations of citizenship grounded in the belief that membership is awarded with a single set of individual rights that guarantee the equal treatment of all members of a given society. Citizenship, according to the Canadian School, is therefore responsible for establishing the parameters of the state while accounting for the need for space to recognize cultural differences.

Labelled a "major architect of the liberal multicultural approach" (Dhamoon 2009, 3), Kymlicka contends that a theory of justice grounded solely in universal individual rights is insufficient, as it fails to account for the differentiated needs of citizens living in multicultural states, and a "comprehensive theory of justice in a multicultural state will include universal rights, assigned to individuals regardless of group membership, and certain group-differentiated rights or 'special status' for minority cultures" (1995, 6). In light of this, Kymlicka prescribes a liberal theory of minority rights, justifying how the accommodation of differentiated rights fits within a liberal democratic framework that champions individual liberty and social justice. Recognizing that the development of a single theory of minority rights is impossible, Kymlicka argues that we need to make certain types of generalizations, "identifying at least certain common patterns of dynamics of state-minority relations, and trying to make sense of their underlying normative logic" (2009, 373). Appealing to both normative theory and social practice, Kymlicka frames citizenship in multicultural states as twofold: it establishes an overarching normative framework responsible for upholding common liberal democratic values, and it allows for differentiation in the provision of rights themselves so that citizens have access to cultural self-autonomy.[6]

Kymlicka contends that due to its multinational and polyethnic composition, the Canadian state has a moral responsibility to adopt and encourage an understanding of citizenship that is multifaceted in its approach. When it comes to accommodating Canada's "newer" citizens, realization of this moral duty requires two primary considerations.[7] First, as previously mentioned, citizenship is differentiated. The terms of differentiation are informed by the source of culture as well as the nature of the rights in question. Kymlicka distinguishes between two sources of culture – multinationalism (multiple nations coexisting within state borders) and immigration.[8] States with high levels of immigration and a commitment to allowing immigrants to practice certain aspects of their culture publicly are what Kymlicka refers to as "polyethnic" states. What distinguishes multinationalism from polyethnicism is the fact that immigrant groups are not considered nations; as Kymlicka points out, contrary to nations, the distinctiveness of immigrant groups is accommodated primarily through their private lives (e.g., family, voluntary associations) and does not hinder institutional integration (1995, 14). While immigrant groups have a claim to cultural accommodation, these claims are usually made within the context of pre-existing institutions of the dominant culture; the aim of polyethnic rights is typically to encourage integration into society at large.

Kymlicka's attachment to liberalism's compatibility with minority rights stems from his belief that a rich cultural structure is a necessary condition for one's conception of the good life; cultural survival cannot depend on shared values alone. Shared institutions are required as well. According to Kymlicka, the link between culture and one's conception of the good life is this: individuals need the freedom and resources to lead their lives from the inside; however, they also need the freedom and capacity to question their beliefs. Culture provides the space to explore these options in a way that makes them meaningful – "People can stand back and assess moral values and traditional ways of life and should be given not only the legal right to do so, but also the social conditions which enhance this capacity" (Kymlicka 1995, 92). Group-differentiated citizenship creates cultural structures for individuals to develop identities and beliefs that are integral to one's conception of the good life, a fundamental principle of liberal thought. Therefore, the emphasis should not be on deciding which cultures should be recognized and consequently which ones should not; rather, attention should be paid toward developing a fair approach to supporting all cultures.

An important caveat here is that Kymlicka's citizenship framework applies only to those living within Canadian borders. A consequence of this is that the processes used to determine who is granted access exist outside Kymlicka's framework. The ways in which citizens-in-making are constructed have no bearing on the liberal state's approach to acknowledging rights claims put forth by polyethnic groups – the focus of differentiated citizenship is on those who have or do not have access to mainstream institutions rather than on those who have access to the state itself. While the implications of this will be discussed later in this chapter, the primary focus for Kymlicka is not how citizens become citizens but, rather, the degree of access to integration awarded to already established citizens.

Dhamoon's work focuses on the limits of liberal multiculturalism by recognizing the simultaneous production and reproduction of difference through citizenship. Taking issue with Kymlicka's reliance on culture, Dhamoon questions the utility of framing culture as the dominant social identity for citizenship. While culture is not irrelevant, it should not be the primary category of analysis in citizenship discourse. Ultimately, Dhamoon advocates the importance of identity-difference politics in framing citizenship and argues that "it is necessary to make an analytic shift away from the current preoccupation with culture as an explanatory framework through which to grasp conflicts of difference to a critical examination of how meanings of difference are produced, organized, and regulated through power, and the effects of these meanings on socio-political arrangements" (2009, 2).[9] For Dhamoon, this is a shift away from the liberal multicultural politics of culture to a *critical politics of meaning-making*. This frame explores how power creates and recreates difference and, further, how these differences shape institutions, values, beliefs, and practices.

Dhamoon's matrix of meaning-making informs her framing of citizenship, as she recognizes that membership inevitably involves social relations of difference. Like Kymlicka, Dhamoon advocates for differentiated citizenship; however, this differentiation must go beyond one's cultural identity. A reliance on culture as the sole characteristic of one's identity for the purposes of citizenship assumes that culture is static. Culture from a liberal multiculturalist perspective adopts features of stability, formal structure, and longevity (Dhamoon 2007, 31). It implies a predetermined set of characteristics that groups must embody in order to be viewed by the state as a genuine cultural group. This is of concern, as it privileges one set of differences over others; cultural identity takes precedence over identity shaped by racism, sexism, ableism, capitalism, and heterosexism (Dhamoon 2007, 32). Furthermore, it favours certain aspects of culture over others. Narrowly defining culture in these terms renders differences between, as well as within, cultural groups invisible.

Liberal multicultural theory uses culture to identify non-Western cultures that seek inclusion within Western institutions. This understanding of culture therefore depends on a process of *othering* – the other desires recognition of their cultural differences so that they are able to integrate while the state portrays an image of tolerance and accommodation by recognizing the other. Interpreting culture as fixed overlooks the reality that as the boundaries of cultural recognition shift, so too does the other; if new boundaries are drawn, new others are created (Arneil 2007). Culture is therefore in constant flux and to suggest otherwise "ignores the reality that cultures are composed of multiple modes of interaction beyond nationality, ethnicity, and linguistic differences" (Dhamoon 2009, 23). Relying solely on culture depoliticizes relationships of power that continuously produce and reproduce the cultural other. If identity is difference, then we must recognize that difference is not unidimensional, and not all differences are considered equally significant.

Dhamoon believes there to be analytical utility in culture; however, it cannot be viewed as the primary process of identity formation – "We should not weigh culture differently or make it more fluid ... instead we should work from a position that does not champion or dismiss culture, a position that understands culture within a matrix of power" (2009, 46). In order to accomplish this, Dhamoon outlines four questions posed by a politics of meaning-making:

- How are meanings of difference constituted relationally through discourse?
- How do forces of power constitute subjects differently and differentially?

- How are meanings of difference constituted in different historical contexts, and how do these play in social-political arrangements?
- How are the penalization/privileging of these meanings of difference disrupted? (2009, 49)

An account of meaning-making attempts to answer these questions by highlighting various processes that produce and reproduce difference. Furthermore, it explores the social aspect of identity formation, particularly the ways in which certain relationships of power are normalized. The politics of meaning-making works from the assumption that identity is not pure – "Identities are located through multiple arrangements of power in which most people are insiders and outsiders by virtues of intersectionality" (Dhamoon 2009, 39).[10] From there, difference is understood in a manner reflective of its multidimensionality, accounting for the reality that when it comes to relationships of power, the amount of privilege one has varies depending on the context. When theorizing citizenship, it is imperative that we understand one's position within this matrix in order to highlight how multiple relationships of power shape not only who we are, but also, stemming from that, how they impact our interactions with the state.

As a result, the adoption of a citizen/noncitizen binary is insufficient. Through immigration, the state constructs a discourse of desirable and undesirable citizens. Cutting across lines of race, religion, sexuality, gender, class, sexual orientation, physical ability, and colonialism, this discourse becomes the foundation for rules that dictate how an outsider (those applying for immigration or refugee status) can become an insider (those who receive immigration or refugee status). Dhamoon uses the example of race to highlight the internalization of whiteness in Canadian immigration policy – "Whiteness works to make citizens out of subjects and subjects out of citizens" (2009, 78).[11] It is essential to deconstruct discourses of whiteness in order to contextualize how categories of white, semiwhite, and nonwhite vary across time and space. In addition, variation does not solely exist within the category of noncitizen; it also exists among those recognized as Canadian citizens. Processes of meaning-making produce understandings of the immigrant as "strange" and "strangers" while the host nation is perceived as benevolent – "The immigration system is a means of further distinguishing outsiders from insiders through a policy that is made by 'us' but applies to 'them'" (Dhamoon 2009, 78). This suggests that citizenship is not a uniform status equally applied to all; there remain implicit and explicit distinctions between Canadian-born citizens and immigrant citizens. A politics of meaning-making therefore examines the meanings of difference that highlight these distinctions between citizens, potential citizens, partial citizens, and noncitizens. If citizenship is about status, then immigration and refugee policies are about exclusion.

Finally, while Kymlicka focuses on those who have obtained citizenship, Dhamoon takes a broader approach by examining how meanings, values, and beliefs shape our immigration policy and vice versa. The institutional makeup of immigration policy directly affects not only the development of policy but the ideals of citizenship as well (Dhamoon 2010). In this light, Dhamoon frames citizenship as a mechanism of security. Challenging Kymlicka's view of security and multiculturalism as oppositional, Dhamoon contends that multicultural citizenship is part of a securitization project aimed at "regulating various degrees of difference" (2010, 256). Security is therefore an integral component of this discourse of meaning-making that frames our understanding of citizenship. Formally establishing a distinction between insiders and outsiders, citizenship furthers Canadian nation-building projects of territory (legitimizing defined territorial boundaries), identity (securing the notion that Canada is accommodating of diversity), whiteness (intentionally or unintentionally reinforcing distinctions between white and nonwhite bodies), and economic development (establishing a space for Canada in the global economy). Citizenship and security are therefore "co-implicated in reiterating processes of normalization and Otherness that consolidate unequal relations of power" (Dhamoon 2010, 257).

Kymlicka endorses group-differentiated citizenship; however, his arguments remain tied to liberal understandings of the individual in that while cultural groups may receive rights, these rights are justified as providing the space for meaningful individual self-realization, the good of cultural membership. Similarly, Dhamoon's focus on the relationship between power and identity construction encourages us to avoid making any type of group-based generalizations; rather, we should understand the construction of citizenship as taking place within broader systems of power. While their approaches differ in terms of where citizenship begins, focus is on the position of the individual citizen with respect to liberal conceptions of the good (Kymlicka) or intersecting processes of privilege and oppression (Dhamoon).

Framing citizenship around the individual has obvious utility, as thousands of individual immigrants and refugees are welcomed into Canada every year; however, relying solely on the individual disregards the role of family, a significant source of immigration in Canada and in the construction of citizens – "The discourse of migration is shaped by an array of variables such as relationship to family and kin" (Stychin 2000, 604). With migration patterns becoming increasingly complex, individualist framings of citizenship are becoming less theoretically and analytically appealing (Janoski 2010; Samers 2010; Fleras 2015). How we frame citizenship presents consequences for family reunification. The way in which family reunification is structured influences who can immigrate and ultimately become a citizen; the state is not creating only citizens, but families as well. When it comes to reunification, the ideal citizen is therefore synonymous with the ideal family type.

Scholars have attributed minimal attention paid toward family in citizenship discourse to the general perception that the family unit, located in the private sphere, is positioned outside the parameters of state control (Lister 1997a, 1997b; Brodie 1997, 2008; Dobrowolsky and Jenson 2004). In the case of immigration, conceptualizing the family as private suggests that family class migration is secondary to entry determined by the point system (Hathaway 1994, 6). This is misleading, as the family serves both a social and an economic function, a site for "the social and physical reproduction required to sustain the market citizen, traditionally furnished by the unpaid labour of women in exchange for material support" (Macklin 2002, 240–41). This blurring between the public and private spheres challenges the perceived neutrality of the family unit and calls for state accountability for its role in using the family – a private institution – to achieve its objectives.

Labelling family as private therefore allows the state to bypass certain responsibilities; however, as Macklin contends, state determination of what constitutes private is "partial, selective and inconsistent" (2002, 221).

Moreover, state involvement with the family unit crosses policy domains, challenging the commonly held assumption that the family is free from state influence. It is imperative that we acknowledge "family as a key locus for state power and domination over immigrants" (Luibhéid 2004, 229). This is echoed by Pessar: "The common claim that the immigrant family is an adaptive social form ... diverts our attention from the important task of analyzing legislation and government policies that effectively block or limit the formation, unification, and material well-being of immigrant families" (1999, 583–84). Thus, in order to understand the relationship between family and citizenship, we must re-conceptualize this traditional logic of the public/private divide.

Although Dhamoon's framework focuses on the individual as the primary unit of analysis, this matrix of meaning-making provides a theoretical opportunity. The family acts a site of reproduction for certain meanings, values, and beliefs that, in turn, contributes to the unequal distribution of power across populations. The ways in which the state defines family through law and policy ultimately shape the individual's interaction with the state. Thus, this poses the question: How should family be situated within Dhamoon's matrix of meaning-making? Moreover, what are the implications for our understanding of citizenship if family is recognized as a source of inequality and injustice? In order to answer these questions, Dhamoon's framework needs to be expanded to include discussions concerning the work of governing that family performs and the impact this has on identity formation.

Enhancing the Canadian Conversation

The work of critical citizenship scholars provides a useful starting point for analyzing the connections between citizenship, family, and conjugality, and for addressing some of the limitations of Dhamoon's matrix of meaning-making. Citizenship has long been a component of sexual politics – "All citizenship is sexual citizenship, as citizenship is inseparable from identity, and sexuality is central to identity" (Bell and Binnie 2000, 33). Citizens are constantly "sexed" (Weeks 1998; Bell and Binnie 2000; Richardson 2000; Plummer 2003; Puar 2007) through a variety of legal and legislative measures including, but not limited to, age of consent laws, conjugal rights and responsibilities, family tax credits, and the prohibition of nonmonogamous sexual practices. These measures permit the state to regulate the bodies of its citizens, producing a normalized narrative of sexual responsibility. Those deemed responsible in their sexual endeavours represent desirable sexual citizens. Sexual citizenship thus becomes a tool of nation building; the state seeks control over the sexual nature of its members in the name of protecting "national values" (Pryke 1998, 540). This narrative of sexual responsibility permits states to simultaneously discipline sexual behaviour and enforce a particular conceptualization of national identity. The creation of good and bad sexual citizens results in unequal access to claims for citizenship rights, therefore shaping sexual identities through processes of membership, compromise, and exclusion.

In drawing attention to the vested interest that states have in our intimate lives, the work of sexual citizenship scholars poses a new way of understanding the public/private divide – "The sexual citizen makes a claim to transcend the limits of the personal sphere by going public, but the going public is, in a necessary but nevertheless paradoxical move, about protecting the possibilities of private life and private choice in a more inclusive society" (Weeks 1998, 37). Claims for sexual citizenship use the public sphere in order to obtain a private space for the individual. The "space of intimacy" is a "public-private realm that defines multiple forms of human relationship and acts a crucial space of mediation between our selves and our worlds" (Rambukkana 2015, 28). Intimate space is, therefore, disputed space, and in this contention lies criteria for social membership "produced by personal acts and values, especially acts originating in or directed through the family sphere" (Berlant 1997, 5). While the language of rights predominantly focuses on the rights and responsibilities of the individual citizen, there exist citizenship rights that are granted on the basis of relationships, specifically the rights to consent to sexual practice, freely choose one's sexual partners, and have public recognition of one's sexual relationships (Delphy 1996; Richardson 2000). With some exceptions, the conjugal couple is typically considered the norm against which the worthiness of obtaining these rights is gauged. In order to exercise the right to make decisions about our intimate relationships, the state must deem our actions sexually responsible; it is through this public claim for state recognition that our private lives are protected. In challenging the public/private divide, sexual citizenship theory troubles traditional understandings of the family as a single universal entity; rather, this framework proposes that family ought to be interpreted as a "subjective reflection of contemporary re-imaginings," recognizing that there is "no simple continuum of public to private" for familial recognition (Sempruch 2011, 162).

In addition to regulating the intimate relationships of those living within a state's borders, narratives of sexual responsibility also shape the access-seeking immigrant. Honig (2001) explores the intersections between sexuality and xenophobia in citizenship discourse that frame the sexual values of certain immigrant populations as threatening to the national population. Immigration produces "foreignness," which for Honig is a simultaneous source of stability and instability for the nuclear family. On one hand, family reunification enables the state to "create hetero-patriarchal relations for the recruitment and socialization of labour," therefore reproducing specific state values through the provision of access (Reddy 2005, 103). On the other hand, while some immigrant groups are prone to adopt conservative values with respect to familial makeup (Soroka et al. 2011; Harell 2013; White, Bilodeau, and Nevitte 2015), otherness is framed as a threat to traditional family practice. The Canadian state encourages migrants to migrate but then frames these same migrants as a potential threat to the Canadian family and society at large. Immigration control is not solely about securing the state from potential threats; initiatives aimed at protecting a population from foreignness also act as mechanisms for "constructing, enforcing, and normalizing dominant forms of heteronormativity while producing figures as supposed threats" (Luibhéid 2008, 296). Ultimately, the state ascribes membership to those whose sexual values correspond with national values, excluding certain groups located both within and outside a state's borders from narratives of belonging.[12]

In addition to examining the provision of citizenship within state boundaries, we must also account for interactions between states. As our world becomes increasingly globalized, citizenship shapes not only the relationships between citizenship and the state, but also relationships between states. It is therefore imperative that examinations of citizenship recognize that the "power relations that underlie national citizenship are not confined to dynamics within the nation-state and instead reflect and reinforce global relations of power such as the hierarchy of states in the overarching world system of states, and the increasingly transnational character of resistance in civil society" (Bakan and Stasiulis 2005, 13). In this light, citizenship takes the form of a negotiation monitored by *gatekeepers* – both state and nonstate actors – who establish and reinforce mechanisms for determining access.[13] It is through these negotiations that foreignness is both produced and regulated, as states alter definitions of who gets in, in order to further a specific agenda (Honig 2001; Luibhéid 2008; Dhamoon and Abu-Laban 2009).

One such agenda is protecting the institution of marriage. While conjugality has not always been of primary interest to the state, it has become a means of reinforcing social, economic, and political structures through ritual (e.g., dowries, patriarchal division of labour) and active exclusion (e.g., refusal of access based on race, class, religion, sexual orientation). These structures exist because there is a perceived social need for them. The idea that conjugality is crucial to the maintenance of the state becomes internalized, generating norms that are not only produced and reproduced by state actors, but by nonstate actors as well. The power of conjugality as a tool of governance highlights the influence of "one of the great instruments of power" – normalization (Foucault 1979, 184). While marriage in Canada has been extended to include common-law and same-sex couples, conjugality remains normalized through institutional and social practice. Through normalization, conjugality becomes a way to "document the judgement, that the practice of marriage is general or at least widespread in the dominant strata of the population" (Foucault 1988, 74).

Conjugality, therefore, becomes a system of knowledge through which individuals simultaneously experience belonging and excluding those who do not belong. For Foucault, there are two concurrent discourses at play – a discourse that regulates state alliance and a discourse that aims to discipline behaviour. These discourses amalgamate within the family, "the site where state power has penetrated into the most intimate domains of modern life, producing a society in which the population is governed by the individual governing the self" (van Walsum 2008, 20–21). The conjugal family therefore acts as an organizing principle of the state through processes of normalization – "Foucault's framework suggests that immigration-control practices, down to their most mundane procedural details, produce and naturalize these identities" (Luibhéid 2002, xxii). Family is then integral to understanding citizenship, as it is a prominent site for the production and reproduction of state power.

Situating Family in the Canadian Conversation: Important Caveats

Developing a theory of Canadian citizenship capable of recognizing the role of family reveals several prominent tensions in discussions of what constitutes family. These tensions include the mislabelled apolitical nature of the family unit, perceived inflexibility of family composition, the relationship between care and family form, and the notion of public stake in private family life.

Political Nature of the Family Unit

Understanding the relationship between citizenship and family recognizes that one has implications for the other. Stevens (1999) examines how the public/private dichotomy is often synonymous with a kinship/political society dichotomy in political science scholarship, with kinship relegated to the private sphere and political society to the public. Traditionally, labelling something as "public" suggests that a relationship of power exists; therefore, by consequence, kinship and family are concepts perceived to be impermeable to state influence and, as a result, are power free. Distinguishing political society and kinship in this way is misleading because it assumes kinship to be pre-political. Moreover, the conceptualization of these spheres as distinct negates the fact that the very drawing of a line between what constitutes the public sphere and, consequently, the private is a political act. Echoing Stevens, I argue that these concepts are political and play an influential role in state development by shaping rules of affiliation.

Perceived Inflexibility of Family Composition

In addition to abandoning traditional understandings of the public/private divide, this reframing of citizenship must also account for the fact that family composition is not static. Answers to the question, "What constitutes family?" vary across ideological lines; as a result, justifications for protecting the nuclear family primarily manifest themselves in three ways: childrearing, economic survival, and monogamous intimacy. First, while the composition of the conjugal family unit has been altered, an attachment to a two-parent childrearing model remains (F. Kelly 2011). The belief that healthy families breed healthy children has become part of a common-sense rhetoric imbued with cultural and nationalist undertones. Butler discusses how the nuclear family as the primary site of social reproduction is tied to Western claims of cultural survival: "The belief is that culture itself requires that a man and a woman produce a child and that the child have this dual point of reference for its own initiation into that symbolic order, where the symbolic order consists of a set of rules that order and support our sense of reality and cultural intelligibility" (2002, 29). Conjugality is therefore assumed to be a relatively straightforward way to organize familial affiliation.

Second, feminists have argued that conjugality is essentially used by the state to privatize the dependency of women and children on men (Fineman 2001, 247). Historically, the law made it impossible for women to be economically self-sufficient, undermining their ability to be independent. Marriage, as Pateman explains, was "[women's] only hope at a decent life," establishing marriage as "nothing more than the law of the strongest, enforced by men in contempt of the interests of weaker women" (1988, 158). While the legal system, as well as the institution of marriage more specifically, has undergone challenges to rectify gender discrimination, the continued unequal economic status of women – as compared to men – reproduces cycles of dependency (Little 2011).

Finally, the normalization of marriage relies on an affective narrative of love and romance; however, the state is uninterested in the presence or absence of romantic love. According to Cott (2000), romantic love was initially viewed as an impediment to the higher virtues of political reality, religious devotion, and a strong work ethic; it was not until the nineteenth century that love was accepted as normal and almost universally attainable. Love was therefore never the original purpose of state-recognized marriage. When love is considered by the state, it is assessed in relation to other characteristics of state-defined marriage (e.g., cohabitation, monogamy, children, economic interdependency).

The traditional nuclear family is claimed to be under threat by modern changes in family dynamics. Conservative scholarship has attributed a perceived rise in social ills (e.g., crime, same-sex rights, teen pregnancy) with the deterioration of the traditional nuclear family. Social conservatives in Canada and the United States oppose the extension of marital rights to cohabiting and same-sex couples, arguing that this shift reduces heterosexual marriage to a personal relationship between individuals. This reduction represents a "fundamental reinterpretation of the core social purposes of marriage" (Cere and Farrow 2004, 13). The loss of the heterosexual conjugal unit has been labelled the catalyst for the deterioration of the nuclear family, sparking pro-family movements focused on the re-entrenchment of the nuclear family model. While the American pro-family movement has enjoyed more success than its Canadian counterpart – a result attributed to variations in their political institutions – Canadian pro-family activists continue to warn of the consequences this deterioration holds for society at large (Fetner and Sanders 2011).

Critics argue that this connection between the nuclear family and societal destruction is embellished and question the very existence of this family unit as a nostalgic starting point. Coontz examines how advocates of the pro-family movement "continue to filter our changing family experiences and trends through the distorted lens of historical mythologizing about past family life" (1992, xi). The challenge with this is that it becomes difficult to pinpoint exactly what constitutes the traditional family. Even if we agree that the traditional family refers to the heterosexual married couple with two and a half kids and a dog, that very unit has undergone significant transformation. From a feminist perspective alone, this unit has shifted from an inherently patriarchal environment to one reflective of increasing women's rights both inside and outside the home. In addition, family dynamics have been altered along the lines of class, race, and sexual orientation. This return-to-a-traditional-family rhetoric is therefore void of substance, as the idea of a single traditional family unit is ultimately a myth. Furthermore, the inability to agree on a single point of reference in this debate complicates claims that families are changing for the worse (Coontz 1992, 14). In order to understand the role of family, it is important that we "get past abstract nostalgia for traditional family values and develop a clearer sense of how past families actually worked and what the different consequences of family behaviours and values have been" (22).

In reality, the state of the family is in constant flux, reflected in a growing body of literature focused on the changing nature of family along racial

(Razack 1998; Bakan and Stasiulis 2005; Thobani 2007), economic (Sapiro 1990; Mink 1990; Lahey 2001; Hymowitz 2006; Little 2011), and queer lines (Butler 2002; Plummer 2003; Stacey 2004; Rayside 2008). This, in turn, has sparked discussions concerning the relevance of conjugality (Warner 1999; Cott 2000; Brook 2002, 2007; Lyndon-Shanley 2004) and the legal treatment of relationship recognition more generally (Cossman 1994; Cossman and Ryder 2001; Law Commission of Canada 2001; Bailey 2004; Barker 2006; Polikoff 2008). Theorizations of family composition have gone beyond focusing on blood and marital ties to explore how kinship is increasingly defined by alternative relationships of care (Weston 1991; Smart and Neale 1999; Smart 2000; Roseneil and Budgeon 2004; Weeks, Donovan, and Heaphy 2004). Whether the family is now considered a "pure relationship" in which sexual and emotional equality has been achieved (Giddens 1992, 2), a postfamilial entity that recognizes that antiquity of obligations/relationships in families past (Beck-Gernsheim 1998), or a personal community distinguishing between given and chosen relationships (Pahl and Spencer 2004), the ways in which individuals develop and nurture these relationships are multiple. In theorizing the role of the family in (re)producing citizens, it is therefore imperative we recognize that the family is not a single homogeneous unit and, more importantly, never has been.

Relationships between Care and Family Form

We are now in a position to recognize that the politics of care does not necessarily dictate a specific family form. While traditionally the family unit was seen as an automatic source of support (financial, emotional, personal, etc.), it has become evident that individuals quite often look for support outside these networks (Finch 1989; Smart and Neale 1999). In their study of alternative interdependent relationships in the United Kingdom, Roseneil and Budgeon (2004) conclude that family is not defined by marital or blood ties; rather, it is interpreted as systems of interdependency – "There was a high degree of reliance on friends, as opposed to biological kin and sexual partners, particularly for the provision of care and support in everyday life" (146). Therefore, I propose we understand family as "vital social structures made up of specific individuals with specific interests who together generate their own normative registers concerning social responsibility" (van Walsum 2003, 223). This framework reflects Sempruch's position that "if care, in its full complexity, is to be understood as a set of social relations that shape and are shaped by access to variously defined citizenship rights, such as sexual, socio-cultural, and political citizenship, then all three aspects must be targeted simultaneously" (2011, 167). The complexity of care requires adequate attention in citizenship discourse; it is essential that we avoid reproducing a one-size-fits-all approach.

Public Stake in Private Family Life

Finally, I borrow Carens' three normative principles for family reunification policy in liberal democratic states to guide this exploration of the relationship between family, immigration, and citizenship:

- Family reunification is currently about the moral claims of insiders, not outsiders;
- In addition to their interest in family life, people also have a deep and vital interest in being able to continue living in a society where they have settled and established roots;
- No one should be forced by the state to choose between home and family. (2003, 96–99)

Making a case for justifiable moral limits to immigration policy, Carens challenges the perceived neutrality of family reunification and advocates for moral checks on states' determination of who receives access. This conflict between moral guidelines and state sovereignty reflects "tension between an approach to the definition of family that is open to analogies, cultural variability, and functional equivalents and an approach that is fixed and relies on criteria from the dominant culture" (Carens 2003, 98). The assumption here is that when it comes to family reunification, there is public interest at stake. The right to family reunification is a moral good, essential to individual well-being – "We are bound to our family members through a more richly complex web of relationships, a mixture of love and dependence, than we share with any other people ... To deprive someone of these relationships is to deprive him[/her] of his[/her] richest and most significant bonds with other human beings" (Meilaender 2001, 182). This book builds upon these assumptions and expands liberal understandings of family through a discourse of citizenship. In bridging the gap between liberal and critical theoretical tensions, it echoes liberal rhetoric of morality and public good but is critical of current state frameworks used to translate this dialogue into actual policy practice.

As a disciplinary institution, family can complement state objectives; however, it can also frustrate them (van Walsum 2003, 223). Citizenship is no exception. Family is defined through immigration policies and programs, but it also challenges them to be more inclusive as family dynamics continue to shift. Despite its role in creating citizens, the family remains largely absent in Canadian citizenship literature. As subsequent chapters demonstrate, a transformation in familial composition in Canadian law and policy has brought relationship recognition to a crossroads – either maintain the current privileged state of conjugality or re-evaluate policy recognition of adult interdependent relationships. Both options require reframing citizenship in order to account for the role family plays in the construction of the nation-state. We need to take these connections seriously in order to develop a richer, more robust theorization of Canadian citizenship.

2

Inside/Outside Families: The Politics of Relationship Recognition in Canadian Law and Policy

"We are taking action to strip citizenship and permanent resident status from people who don't play by the rules and who lie or cheat to become a Canadian citizen."

– JASON KENNEY, FORMER MINISTER OF
CITIZENSHIP AND IMMIGRATION

It is no secret that the institution of marriage in Canada has been dramatically altered over the past hundred years. Used as a tool of colonial settlement, the heterosexual monogamous marriage model, in the view of the Canadian nation's architects, protected against the unstable and potentially harmful relationship practices of Indigenous communities, non-British immigrant groups, religious-based polygamists, and their American neighbours (Carter 2008). The success of the national project was therefore seen as reliant on the Christian marital unit as the core of prosperous family life. In addition to fending off perceived challenges to national strength, marriage was used to privatize women's dependency. Pateman contends that due to their unequal position in society, women were deprived of the capacity to be independent; since marriage was the only chance at an economically sustainable future, women were obligated to enter into a marriage contract (1988, 158). Wary of Pateman's narrative of women as a monolithic group, critical race feminists highlight the racialization of dependency that marriage performs as well (Davis 1981; Collins 1993; Beale 2008; Johnson and Loscocco

2015). Marriage has been used by the Canadian state to civilize Indigenous women according to colonial standards (Carter 2008), justify the denial of immigrant status to Asian women during the first half of the twentieth century (Reddy 2005), and privatize cultural differentiation within the marital unit through the establishment of a universal marital narrative. Marriage was, therefore, solidified as the white, patriarchal, heteronormative life for two.

Today, marital rights have been extended to common-law couples (those in a cohabiting conjugal relationship), as well as to same-sex couples. Feminist mobilization has successfully challenged the male-breadwinner model in certain respects; while women continue to make less than men, marriage is no longer a necessary condition for economic survival. In addition, state use of marriage as a mode of racial and cultural purification has been deemed inconsistent with the human rights ideology that shapes our legal and political frameworks. While the institution of marriage is not without flaw, marriage in Canada has become less of an obligation and more of a choice. Census data highlights the changing nature of conjugality: the number of common-law couples is increasing at a faster rate than the number of married couples; the number of same-sex families and lone-parent families (predominantly female-headed) continue to increase; and childless family units are becoming increasingly common (Statistics Canada 2017). Family dynamics are constantly shifting, and governments in Canada have worked to extend the definition of conjugality in order to accommodate these changes.

Domestically, Canadians generally have the freedom to enter and exit intimate relationships as they see fit, a result of flexibility in the state's approach toward conjugality within its borders. Conjugality continues to be privileged, but citizenship is not on the line, and, as a result, the level of intrusion into the conjugal nature of Canadian citizens' relationships is different. In addition to a lag between court decisions on changes in relationship recognition and implementation of those changes in immigration processes, current immigration policy continues to rely on a more rigid definition of conjugality. With spousal sponsorship currently the primary form of family reunification, the state's treatment of conjugality dictates the type of family granted access. This differentiation in treatment therefore creates two versions of the conjugal family – the inside family (families within Canadian borders) and the outside family (families outside Canadian borders).

Relationship Recognition within Canadian Borders: Creation of the Inside Family

While Parliament's influence on judicial behaviour has been studied, scholarship on the *Canadian Charter of Rights and Freedoms* has predominantly focused on the judiciary's role in public policy development. Critics maintain that the bestowal of power on unelected judges allows them to pursue their own agendas through undemocratic means (Morton and Knopff 1992, 2000; Manfredi 2001). Others contend that the courts' influence is inflated, arguing that legislators should internalize judicial review when developing and debating policy (Kelly 1999; Hiebert 2002). Either way, the Charter plays an important role in the legislative process – "Legal considerations have become as important as fiscal considerations for policy development" (Dawson 1993, 55). In addition to their impact on public policy, court decisions affect political discourse; decisions involving Charter rights have altered public opinion on specific rights-based issues (Matthews 2005; Macfarlane 2008). While judges are not expected or desired to be legislators, their influence is inherently political; as Macfarlane asserts, "Judicial policy making is not an accidental by-product of the Court's adjudicative function" (2013, 5). The politics of relationship recognition in Canada is no exception; the extension of conjugal benefits to unmarried, cohabiting heterosexual couples and homosexual couples is a culmination of legal and legislative change. Canadians have used the courts to challenge the limited definition of spouse, and these decisions have informed policy changes. An examination of the legal treatment of conjugality is therefore crucial to understanding state recognition of relationships in Canada, as the courts have influenced several significant policy changes.

The extension of rights to unmarried cohabiting couples is an iconic illustration of the Canadian state's reluctant efforts to develop policy reflective of changes in social reality. An increase in unmarried cohabitation in the sixties sparked voluntary incremental changes with respect to the rights and obligations associated with conjugal relationships (Holland 2000, 119). Heterosexual common-law relationships therefore started receiving state recognition through the legalization of support obligations in the seventies and division of property in the eighties; these modifications focused on outlining the terms of relationship dissolution. By recognizing that unmarried, cohabiting heterosexual relationships involved varying elements of interdependency, federal and provincial governments incorporated this familial arrangement into discussions of support obligations, the objective being to protect vulnerable parties as well as the state itself. While the federal government regulated cohabitation for its own reasons, the regulation of domestic partnerships is a provincial responsibility. As a result, legalization of common-law relationships involved a whole host of responses that occurred at different times with distinctive rationale.

Our narrative begins with *Molodowich v Penttinen* establishing the functional equivalence test to legally determine the existence of a conjugal relationship.[1] Predecision, courts used the subjective equivalence test – premised on the assumption of a consensual economic commitment until death do us part – to distinguish between conjugal and nonconjugal relationships (Cossman and Ryder 2001, 283). Taking issue with restricting the definition of *spouse* to married couples in the *Ontario Family Law Act*, Tena Molodowich sought spousal support following the dissolution of her longstanding, nonmarital, childless relationship with Lauri Penttinen. Having lived together off and on for several years, Molodowich claimed that this arrangement took place with what she thought was the intention of a permanent relationship. Describing her relationship with Penttinen as spouse-like, Molodowich highlighted several elements characteristic of a state-recognized conjugal relationship including cohabitation, sexual intimacy, economic support, emotional interdependency, and the division of daily tasks (e.g., meal preparation, household chores).

This case challenged the subjective equivalence test in two ways. First, it confronted the assumption that the act of getting or not getting married is always a choice and that marriage is not a necessary condition for interdependency. The element of choice in conjugal relationships was discussed further in *Walsh v Nova Scotia*, a decision involving the dissolution of an unmarried cohabiting relationship.[2] In the dissenting opinion, Justice L'Heureux-Dubé concluded:

> To recapitulate, the decision of whether or not to marry is most definitely capable of being a very fundamental and personal choice. The importance

actually ascribed to the decision to marry, or alternatively *not* to marry, depends entirely on the individuals concerned. For a significant number of persons in so-called 'non-traditional' relationships, however, I dare say that notions of 'choice' may be illusory. It is inappropriate, in my respectful view, to condense the forces underlying the adoption of one type of family unit over another into a simple dichotomy between 'choice' and 'no choice.'[3] (emphasis in original)

The language of choice is, therefore, a slippery slope, as it ignores the multitude of motivations for relationship development. The subjective equivalence test interpreted conjugality as a consensual decision between a man and a woman to officially commemorate their economic interdependency through marriage. Alternatively, those couples who chose not to do so consciously made a decision not to be financially responsible for each other. Molodowich claimed that even though they had never discussed marriage, she considered herself to be Penttinen's wife – "I felt like a married person even though I had no certificate or ring. I felt secure and never expected the relationship would end."[4] On the other hand, Penttinen did not view their association in the same way, often downplaying the relationship by referring to Molodowich as "my friend" or "Tena." The presence or absence of a formal conjugal relationship is, therefore, not necessarily by choice. Despite having conflicting interpretations regarding the conjugal nature of their relationship, the reality was that the two were interdependent. Ultimately, conjugal relationships can develop in the absence of a consensual decision made between two people; choice is not a necessary condition for the existence of interdependency.

The second way *Molodowich v Penttinen* tested the boundaries of the subjective equivalence test was by challenging economic interdependency as the primary characteristic of a conjugal relationship. In addition to proving economic interdependency, Molodowich used evidence of emotional intimacy between the two in order to strengthen her claim of spousal qualification, including long-distance telephone bills, correspondence, photos, family visits, shared meals, vacations with friends, and testimonies from friends and neighbours confirming community perception of their relationship. In light of this evidence, Justice Kurisko acknowledged that the law's strict reliance on economic interdependency was troublesome, as it neglected additional moments of intimacy that separate conjugal from nonconjugal relationships: "Marriage involves a complex group of human inter-relationships – conjugal, sexual, familial and social as well as economic. In more than the romantic sense, cohabitation and consortium are regarded as basic elements of marriage. It would be wrong to say that these elements are not present when persons, not legally married, live together as husband and wife."[5]

The court's response was the functional equivalence test, extending the definition of conjugality to include a broader range of relationship characteristics; conjugality would now be determined by the "objectively observable features of the relationship rather than the stated subjective understandings of the parties" (Cossman and Ryder 2001, 287). The newly adopted test recognized the complexity of conjugal relationships and required that a series of factors be taken into consideration when attempting to assess the legitimacy of a conjugal relationship, ultimately recognizing that "marital equivalence is situated within a bundle of factors that together indicate the existence of an emotionally and economically interdependent relationship" (283). Proof required now went beyond the subjective claims of the participants involved.

The functional equivalence test consists of several attributes presumed capable of capturing the level of personal commitment required for nonmarried couples to qualify as conjugal. While not all of these attributes need to be present in order for a relationship to be deemed legitimately conjugal, courts require convincing that a combination of these characteristics sufficiently exists. These attributes comprise the following:

- Shelter – cohabitation, sleeping arrangements, other roommates
- Services – meal preparation, chores, household maintenance
- Social – participation in community activities, familial interaction
- Societal – community perception of the relationship
- Support – financial arrangements, property
- Children – attitude/conduct concerning children
- Sexual/Personal behaviour – sexual relations, fidelity, emotional intimacy, care

These attributes highlight how conjugal relationships are measured against characteristics believed to be part of the ideal marriage. Conjugality thus became synonymous with marriage or, more specifically, "how judges imagine marriage ought to be" (Cossman and Ryder 2001, 290). Moreover, the attributes reveal that conjugality is not determined by economic interdependency alone. What separates economic partnerships from conjugal relationships is the assumed presence of intimacy as narrowly defined by sexual relations, fidelity, and care (Bala 2003, 94). It is this assumption of intimacy as defined by the functional equivalence test that now steers court assessment of conjugality. *Molodowich v Penttinen* set the tone for legal recognition of intimate relationships in Canada by conflating cohabitation and interdependency in order to guide governments when differentiating between legitimate (conjugal) and illegitimate (nonconjugal) relationships.

While *Molodowich v Penttinen* recognized the possibility of conjugal living without a marriage certificate, it took several years for the category of common-law to be placed on the legislative agenda. This was in response to a series of Charter challenges aimed at drawing attention toward the discriminatory nature of restricting conjugal benefits to married heterosexual couples, combined with census data confirming the increase of heterosexual common-law households in Canada. A consequence of using the Charter to advance claims for common-law recognition was that issues of discrimination were addressed on a case-by-case basis and not necessarily in a logical fashion (Holland 2000, 119). Examining these Charter decisions highlights the piecemeal nature of relationship recognition, for example, division of property (*Gostlin v Kergin* 1986), access to insurance policies (*Miron v Trudel* 1995), and widower relief legislation (*Fitton v Hewton Estate* 1997). This is not to suggest that governments were necessarily resigned to a reactive role, but federal and provincial treatments of common-law relationships have typically been in response to court decisions. Combined, these decisions shaped a principle of "conjugal relationship equality," challenging the legitimacy of legal distinctions between the married and unmarried for economic protections (Cossman and Ryder 2001, 275). It was not until the passing of the *Modernization of Benefits and Obligations Act* in 2000 that the federal government recognized unmarried cohabiting couples beyond the context of pension and taxation law (276). Under the act, the legislative landscape of relationship recognition in Canada was altered, as unmarried cohabiting couples now enjoyed identical rights as married couples in all federal legislation.[6]

Molodowch v Penttinen established a judicial precedent capable of recognizing the flexibility in conjugal and conjugal-like relationships. What remained untouched was the gender composition of the conjugal unit; relationship recognition remained focused on the opposite-sex model. As a result, same-sex couples were denied the symbolic and material benefits reserved for heterosexual couples (both married and unmarried). With the construction of the Charter came the promise of a legal mechanism for homosexuals to challenge the discriminatory nature of policy with respect to sexual orientation. Despite intense lobbying, sexual orientation was not included in the original drafting of section 15 – the section responsible for protecting equality rights; however, the drafters assured that the section's open-ended language would protect sexual minorities (Lahey 1999, 30). This assurance appeared suspect, as discrimination based on sexual orientation remained invisible, forcing queer claims for Charter inclusion to emphasize discrimination based on sex. Courts continuously avoided questioning whether sex included sexual orientation through the following reasoning – discrimination against homosexuals was on the basis of sexual orientation instead of sex, but sexual orientation was not mentioned in the Charter and, as such, it did not prohibit this type of discrimination (Lahey 1999, 31). Furthermore, the Charter's framers insisted that even if the Charter did prohibit discrimination on the basis of sexual orientation, Charter rights are individual rights, rendering them inapplicable to relationships (Lahey 1999; Wintemute 2004). When the three-year moratorium on section 15 was lifted in 1985, not a single piece of federal or provincial legislation had been passed to address the unequal treatment of sexual minorities.[7] Priority was thus given to questioning the silencing of sexual orientation in discussions of sexual equality, and the challenge lay in the courts' ability to justify its continued invisibility.

The significance of *Egan v Canada* lay in the Supreme Court's contribution to a number of cases that ruled section 15 prohibited discrimination on the basis of sexual orientation.[8] James Egan and John Nesbit, a same-sex couple in a long-term relationship of almost forty years, were denied spousal allowance under the *Old Age Pension Act,* as the act's definition of *spouse* did not include same-sex partners. Egan and Nesbit claimed this was an infringement of their right to equal protection and equal benefit of the law (section 15) and that this infringement was discriminatory on the basis of sexual orientation. The Court ruled four to one that the distinction the act created between spouse and nonspouse was nondiscriminatory because it had nothing to do with sexual orientation. More importantly, however, dissenting judges argued that the distinction had everything to do with sexual orientation and was therefore discriminatory:

> It may be correct to say that being in a same-sex relationship is not necessarily the defining characteristic of being homosexual. Yet, only homosexual individuals will form a part of a same-sex common-law couple. It is the sexual orientation of the individuals involved which leads to the formation of the homosexual couple. The sexual orientation of the individual members cannot be divorced from the homosexual couple. To find otherwise would be as wrong as saying that being pregnant had nothing to do with being female. The words 'of the opposite sex' in the definition of 'spouse' specifically exclude homosexual couples from claiming a spousal allowance.[9]

Despite the Court's dismissal of the appeal, the case was considered a success among gay and lesbian rights activists because of the unanimous stand among dissenting judges that sexual orientation was, in fact, an analogous ground under section 15 and was therefore a prohibited form of discrimination. This recognition, however, provided no insight as to the extent to which courts would interpret this ruling.

Following *Egan v Canada,* the lobby for same-sex relationship recognition continued along a similar path used by heterosexual common-law couples, choosing to focus on obtaining economic protections included in state recognition before challenging the definition of the conjugal family unit itself. Denial of spousal support to same-sex couples was discriminatory, as it implied that "same-sex couples are judged to be incapable of forming intimate relationships of economic interdependence as compared to opposite-sex couples" (Wintemute 2004, 1155). By demonstrating their ability to participate in economically interdependent relationships, same-sex couples were entitled to protections awarded to state-recognized heterosexual common-law couples. In *M v H*, the court ruled that the omission of same-sex couples from the *Ontario Family Law Act* (FLA) violated section 15 on the basis of sexual orientation, and the infringement was not deemed a reasonable limit under section 1.[10] This decision was instrumental because it was the first time the Supreme Court recognized that same-sex cohabiting couples should be entitled to those protections awarded to opposite-sex couples. For Cossman, this was achieved because M. and H. had cohabited in an economically interdependent relationship – "The Court recognized that a same-sex couple may, after years together, be considered to be in a conjugal relationship and should therefore receive the same economic rights as opposite-sex couples" (2002, 490). The allocation of relationship rights to same-sex cohabiting couples was legally confirmed with the *Modernization of Benefits and Obligations Act* and the legalization of same-sex marriage with the *Civil Marriage Act*.[11]

In theory, state extension of conjugal benefits to common-law couples suggests a transformation in how family is defined. The court's ruling in *Molodowich v Penttinen* that the existence of a conjugal relationship is not solely dependent on a marriage certificate demonstrated that interdependent relationships exist outside the traditional marriage model. Recognizing the complexity of conjugality, courts would now approach conjugality as being composed of a series of factors. While supportive of expanding the legal definition of family to include common-law couples, several prominent legal scholars took issue with the state's definition of common-law. The Ontario Law Reform Commission accused the courts of continuing to interpret a conjugal relationship as a marital relationship, "placing considerable emphasis on the existence of economic dependency, a sexual relationship, and the parties being identified in public as a couple". While functional similarities exist between marital and common-law relationships, critics were concerned by the courts' continued reliance on the conjugal relationship as defined by "a stereotypical model of marriage that fails to account for the existing diversity of marital relationships" (Ontario Law Reform Commission 1993, 62). Contrary to the theoretical expansion of conjugality to include common-law couples, the actual application of this expanded family unit continues to have implications for unmarried cohabiting partners (Lahey 1999). Instead of revisiting pre-existing legislation, the federal government took a one-size-fits-all approach, simply adding in "common-law partner" anywhere that married partners were mentioned. As a result, the differences between unmarried cohabiting and married couples remain unaddressed; according to the state, common-law couples are essentially married without a marriage licence. The conflation of common-law and marriage under the legislative umbrella of conjugality therefore has significant implications for common-law couples.

The common-law relationship is now clearly established as a popular familial option among Canadian couples. Census data confirms a steady increase in the number of common-law couples in Canada from 1,142,415 in 2001 to 3,510,265 in 2016 (Statistics Canada 2017). Between 2006 and 2016, the number of same-sex common-law couples increased 61 percent (Statistics Canada 2017). Provincially and territorially, common-law cohabitation constitutes around 20 percent of Canadian couples, with Newfoundland and Prince Edward Island below average (12 percent) and Quebec, Yukon, Northwest Territories, and Nunavut above average (34 percent, 29 percent, 34 percent, and 42 percent respectively). With the exceptions of Alberta and Quebec, common-law couples are defined as unmarried conjugal couples who meet the cohabitation requirement, conjugal being defined by characteristics outlined in *Molodowich v Penttinen*.[12] On paper, common-law status is therefore perceived as a combination of cohabitation and conjugality.

In practice, however, a common-law relationship in Canada is primarily defined by cohabitation. Legal precedent highlights the scrutiny relationships have undergone when couples have sought legal recognition for the purpose of obtaining conjugal protections; couples had to prove that a relationship actually existed. When it comes to applying for government benefits as a common-law couple, however, cohabitation alone is generally sufficient. While requirements vary across governments, couples typically qualify for common-law status after living together for a period of one to three years.[13] State reliance on cohabitation as the primary indicator of common-law status is also consistent across levels of government. The Canada Revenue Agency defines a common-law partner in its *General Income Tax and Benefit Guide* as someone who is **not your spouse** (emphasis added) but someone you have been living with in a conjugal relationship for at least twelve continuous months. What qualifies as conjugal, however, is not outlined in the guide. Common-law couples who opt to name each other on their tax returns are not obliged to prove that their relationship is conjugal in nature. Moreover, couples do not have to prove they are, in fact, cohabiting; filing as common-law simply requires couples to check the "living with a common-law partner" box on the form. This reliance on cohabitation is evident in provincial common-law relationship regimes as well. For the *Adult Interdependent Relationships Act* (Alberta), *Common-Law Partners' Property and Related Amendment Act* (Manitoba), and *Civil Unions Act* (Quebec), the primary qualification is conjugal cohabitation without having to prove the conjugal part. In practice, common-law couples are therefore primarily defined by their living arrangements. Cohabitation has become the default method of assessment for assigning common-law status in Canada and, as such, the state uses cohabitation as a proxy for the imposition of conjugal support obligations.

From redefining conjugality in *Molodowich v Penttinen* to the *Civil Marriage Act*, courts have played an influential role in defining the parameters of conjugality in Canadian law and policy. Moreover, legislators have often looked to the courts to deliberate questions concerning state treatment of conjugality, questions legislators have been unable or unwilling to address. While changes in the courts' interpretation of conjugality have resulted in various legislative measures, the execution of these initiatives has varied across legislatures and policy domains. As a result, state treatment of conjugality remains inconsistent; legislatures and courts are not necessarily always on the same page. These policy incongruities, therefore, warrant further attention.

Inconsistent Treatment of Conjugality within Canadian Borders

In current domestic policy frameworks, relationship recognition rights are available to both opposite-sex and same-sex common-law and married couples in all provinces and territories. This does not suggest that the treatment of conjugality is universal across governments. Policy asymmetry is not unusual in federal systems; the Canadian state has been built on a series of intergovernmental exchanges, shifting policy power across federal, provincial, and municipal governments (Milne 2005). In this light, both federal and provincial levels of government have demonstrated a degree of flexibility in their treatment of conjugality in domestic policy (Cossman and Ryder 2001). While examples of these inconsistencies are numerous, I have chosen three: *Falkiner v Ontario* – a decision involving the definition of spouse in Ontario's social assistance legislation; *R v Labaye* – a Supreme Court decision that discussed the parallels between such activities as group sex and swinging in a Montreal nightclub with Canadian values of personal autonomy and liberty; and *Reference Re Section 293 of the Criminal Code of Canada* – a Supreme Court of British Columbia decision involving an examination of the constitutional validity of polygamy's illegality.[14]

Falkiner v Ontario (2002)

After the *Ontario Family Law Act* was amended in 1995 to include non-married cohabiting couples in the definition of spouse, individuals living together who were denied benefits because their relationships were now considered conjugal appealed the interpretation and constitutional validity of the new definition. The reformulated definition of spouse included persons of the opposite sex living together who had "a mutual agreement or arrangement regarding their financial affairs," meaning that once two people of the opposite sex were living together, their relationship was assumed to be conjugal unless they provided evidence to the contrary. Ultimately, the new definition of spouse was extensive enough to "include relationships that lacked the meaningful financial interdependence that characterizes spousal relationships" (Bailey 2004, 158). This new definition – referred to as the "spouse in the house" rule – was at issue in these appeals. *Falkiner v Ontario* involved two such appeals, both of which involved unmarried women with dependent children who were in trial relationships with men for less than a year. The definitional change of spouse in 1995 resulted in these women suddenly becoming ineligible for social assistance as a "sole support parent."[15]

The respondents claimed that the revised definition of spouse was an infringement of section 7 (individual autonomy and personal legal rights) and section 15 (equality rights) under the Charter. Defending the legislation, the Harris government contended that the intention of the new legislation was to ensure equality between married and common-law couples, as well as to provide social assistance to those most in need. For the respondents, the new legislation captured relationships that were not considered conjugal; furthermore, it unfairly distinguished between social assistance recipients and nonrecipients, as well as between single mothers on social assistance and others on social assistance. These distinctions, they contended, discriminated on the basis of sex and reinforced long-standing distinctions between the deserving and undeserving poor (Little 2003). The Ontario Court of Appeal ruled in favour of the respondents, Attorney General Michael Bryant commenting that "it's not the business of government to decide when a family is a family" (CBC News 2004). While the spouse in the house rule has been removed, welfare policies in Canada continue to interpret conjugality and family in a way that furthers the dependency of single mothers on others (Little 2011).

What is interesting about this particular decision is that while conjugality is typically used to exclude individuals, the Harris government was using the definition of spouse to include as many individuals as they could in order to reduce dependency on the state. Pushing the conjugal model onto nonconjugal couples allowed the state to privatize dependency; individuals would be increasingly reliant on each other with the removal of social assistance. In this sense, state use of conjugality was consistent with the desire to privatize economic interdependency and simultaneously inconsistent with legal discussions concerning the composition of interdependence.

R v Labaye

In this decision, the Supreme Court ruled that group sex and swinging activities that took place in a Montreal nightclub were consistent with Canadian values of personal autonomy and liberty. Jean-Paul Labaye was charged under section 210(1) of the Criminal Code for owning a club where couples who pay a membership fee can engage in sexual activities. Distinguishing the activities taking place at this club from sex work, Labaye contended that all activities were consensual and that members paid fees to the club in lieu of paying for sex. The majority opinion focused on determining whether the activities taking place qualified as indecent, arguing that morality was no longer a sufficient way to assess indecency. Using past indecency cases, the court wrote that indecency is measured according to what Canadians are able to socially accept; therefore, the indecency in question must be proven harmful to certain people.[16] For the majority, harm was the only appropriate measure for indecency in Canadian law.

Using a harm-based approach, the court understood indecency in Canadian law as something that endangers one's freedom, subjects one to something undesirable, compels one to perform a transgression, or hurts someone while engaging in a specific act. While the court recognized that there are sexual acts capable of constraining autonomy, the majority ruled that Labaye was not guilty of indecency because he facilitated participation in these activities for willing individuals. Furthermore, the court wrote that when assessing harm in sexual conduct, it is imperative that the threshold be high; certain kinds of sexual conduct should not be deemed impermissible simply because some Canadians are not in favour. The court thus concluded that the seriousness of harm in *R v Labaye* need not be considered, as there was no evidence of harm – "Consensual conduct behind locked doors can hardly be supposed to jeopardize a society as vigorous and tolerant as Canadian society."[17] Dissenting opinion criticized the majority's dismissal of social morality, arguing that legislation regarding sexual conduct is not created in a vacuum. In the end, charges against Labaye were dropped, as the acts in his club were considered private and not of harm to the participants.

R v Labaye contributes to our understanding of the Canadian state's inconsistent treatment of conjugality in two ways. First, it highlights that while monogamous conjugal privilege shapes Canadian law and policy, the state's approach toward monogamy does not necessarily entail the expectation of a lifelong relationship between two people. For couples living within Canadian borders, serial monogamy is permissible. The relaxing of divorce laws in Canada has made it easier for individuals to enter into and exit from conjugal relationships; it is not uncommon for one to engage in several conjugal relationships over the course of a lifetime. Furthermore, it is important to remember that the clients of this particular establishment were conjugal couples looking to enhance their sex lives. The court ruled that while some Canadians would disapprove of these couples' decisions to engage in these activities, social condemnation does not necessarily warrant persecution. A second and related contribution of this decision is its discussion of consent. According to the court, couples came to the club as willing, consenting participants; this private decision made between individuals was therefore not considered a matter of the state. State involvement with matters pertaining to the private sphere is, therefore, selective. In the case of *Labaye,* couples were awarded privacy; however, the luxury of privacy is not an automatic assumption of the state. Ultimately, state allowance of sexual activities that challenge traditional understandings of conjugality are an exception to the rule.

Reference Re Section 293 of the Criminal Code of Canada

Established in 1946, the polygamous community of Bountiful, British Columbia, consists of two sects of Mormon fundamentalists who migrated from the United States (Cott 2000, 105). While polygamy's illegality is enshrined in Canada's *Criminal Code* (section 293), actual prosecution of those engaging in polygamy has been rare.[18] In fact, prior to the investigation into Bountiful that commenced in 2005, no Canadian had been indicted for polygamy in over sixty years (Carter 2008). In 2007, special prosecutor Richard Peck was appointed by the provincial government of British Columbia to investigate the activities of those living in Bountiful. Peck concluded that there lacked enough evidence to substantiate sexual abuse or exploitation charges and recommended that the constitutionality of section 293 be reviewed. In response, the Supreme Court of British Columbia upheld section 293 in 2011, Justice Bauman stating that the law's objective is to prevent "harm to women, to children, to society, and to the institution of monogamous marriage."[19] Winston Blackmore and James Oler, former leaders of Bountiful, were convicted of practising polygamy in 2017, Supreme Court of British Columbia Justice Sheri Ann Donegan opting to focus on whether the accused did in fact have multiple wives rather than examining the constitutional implications of the current ban.[20] The investigation of this particular polygamous community sparked national discussion regarding the "realities of polygamous living" in Canada. While polygamy is technically illegal, polygamous families have resided and continue to reside in Canada without state recognition but, at the same time, with minimal state interference (O'Malley 2007; Javed 2008a, 2008b).

This decision sheds light not only on the inconsistent treatment of polygamy in Canada, but also on the state's asymmetrical approach to monogamous conjugality. Support for polygamy's continued illegality has typically relied on the assumption that polygamous arrangements reproduce deep-rooted gender imbalances harmful to women and children (Campbell 2005, 2010; Status of Women Canada 2005; Baines 2012). If the criminalization of polygamy continues to be justified as a way to protect women and children from harm, how do we account for this lack of criminal accountability with respect to Bountiful and other polygamous arrangements within Canadian borders?[21] This is not to suggest that polygamous relationships exist in abundance in Canadian society; however, minimal usage of section 293 calls its effectiveness and relevance into question.

Despite Bountiful being a Canadian community, this narrative of polygamy and harm is further complicated by discussions of foreignness. Polygamy has historically been labelled anti-Canadian, a familial arrangement that undermines the institution of marriage, the Canadian family, and society at large (Campbell 2010, 347). The framing of polygamy as a foreign practice was evident in the reference decision, Justice Bauman claiming that easing polygamy laws could result in the "rapid production of certain immigrant groups."[22] Bauman contended that the current ban on polygamous immigration, pre-act, lacked the legislative muscle to protect Canadian borders from such an increase. Considering that Bountiful was able to exist without legal intervention for close to fifty years (Campbell 2010), along with the state's low prosecution record of polygamous offences more broadly (Carter 2008), it appears that the state has been relatively lax on the issue of polygamy until it became possible that specific groups of immigrants might import this familial practice, a narrative made more prominent with the Harper government's passing of the *Zero Tolerance for Barbaric Cultural Practices Act* in 2015.

The adoption of a narrative of foreignness therefore accomplishes two things. First, it allows the state to incorporate monogamy into discussions of Canadian national identity; the betterment of the nation relies on a system of monogamous privilege (Denike 2014; Lenon 2015; Rambukkana 2015). Second, this narrative permits a focus on polygamous groups rather than on the practice of polygamy itself. While Bountiful consists of Christians living within Canadian borders, polygamy is framed as an external threat. As such, polygamy is framed as deviant non-Western behaviour that good

Canadians would not engage in and as an external threat to Canadian livelihoods. It appears then that the Canadian state has a vested interest in protecting this system of monogamous privilege that goes beyond protecting vulnerable parties from harm.

This asymmetrical treatment of conjugality in Canadian law and policy demonstrates that state privileging of conjugality in domestic policy is both inconsistent and dependent on political agenda. While not all relationships are recognized by the state, Canadian policy is generally flexible when it comes to the relationships of most inside families. Outside families, on the other hand, are unable to enjoy this same level of flexibility; applicants who are unable to prove – or to at least satisfy doubts – that their conjugal relationships are genuine are denied entry. Immigration policy provides minimal flexibility on the question of conjugality. An examination of Canada's immigration and refugee program highlights the increased importance conjugality has in shaping the state's understanding of family.

Canadian Immigration Policy and Conjugality

Canada's immigration and refugee program has been significantly restructured under multiple governments, Liberal and Conservative alike; however, immigration scholars have agreed that one constant underlying these amendments is the desire to stimulate economic growth by admitting desirable classes through a system of selective migration (Bauder 2008; Basok and Bastable 2009; Fleras 2015). In this light, family reunification has always been "a problematic area of immigration management" (Hawkins 1989, 85). Familial sponsorship is instrumental to immigration policy in Canada, not only with respect to the family class specifically, but also for refugees and skilled workers. Immigration officers must account for the possibility that applications are not typically restricted to the applicant alone – "You're [immigration officers] left with the issue of as soon as you bring a person in, it is not one person, it is potentially a group – almost nobody has nobody" (Interviews). This is why applicants must provide immigration officers with a list of dependents (e.g., spouse, parents, children) regardless of whether they intend on sponsoring them in the future.[23] Irrespective of the type of applicant, familial sponsorship – both actual and potential – plays a role in all areas of immigrant application assessment.

While continuously identified as a priority by politicians in electoral rhetoric, family reunification has received minimal substantive policy attention, generally being treated as an afterthought. Consensus among interviewed former policy analysts from Immigration, Refugees and Citizenship Canada (IRCC) was that while aware of the flaws in the system, "no one wanted to bring that [changes to the family class] forward, no one wants to bring legislative change forward" (Interviews). For past governments, the issue has not necessarily been with immigrants wanting to sponsor their family members; rather, the challenge lay in establishing the parameters of family reunification, particularly with respect to how many and who one wants to sponsor (Hawkins 1989).[24] This presents challenges for IRCC, primarily in the areas of agenda-setting and policy development. IRCC's agenda-setting is informed by the values of the government of the day, public opinion, and bureaucratic capacity to address anticipated roadblocks. While target projections of admitted immigrants are not necessarily fixed, they establish guidelines for those responsible for application assessment. The challenge of familial sponsorship is that when it comes to controlling the number of applications, target projections only go so far. Considering that immigration officers work under the assumption that all immigrants will apply to sponsor family members at some point, it becomes difficult for IRCC to accurately predict what the projection in any given year will look like. As one former IRCC policy analyst explained:

> In Canada, we have an ever-expanding family class. Let's say you want 250,000 immigrants, and you say, okay, what share of that population should be family class, what share should be skilled workers, and what share should be refugees ... it is impossible to control the family class and it squeezes out the other classes. You cannot make policy saying a strict number for family class because you can't control it. (Interviews)

This is not to suggest that there are no control mechanisms in place to filter the number of immigrants coming to Canada; Canada is a country of regulated immigration. It becomes difficult, however, for Canada and other immigrant-receiving countries to fully predict levels of demand for familial sponsorship.

Prior to the implementation of the point system in 1976, the ability to sponsor one's family members was a privilege of certain ethnic groups. Immigration officers were granted considerable discretion to refuse entry based on a variety of circumstances including nationality, citizenship, ethnicity, country of origin, "peculiar" customs, and suitability for integration (Hawkins 1989; Kelley and Trebilcock 2000; Abu-Laban and Gabriel 2002; Thobani 2007). The evaluation of relationship credibility as a method of immigrant assessment is nothing new. Indeed, questions of credibility have played an integral role in family sponsorship determination processes, specifically for nonpreferred immigrant groups, over the past century. Legislative measures, including the Head Tax (1885), Continuous Passage requirement (1908), the inclusion of race as a category of immigrant assessment in an earlier version of the *Immigration Act* (1910), the migration of "picture brides" (early 1920s), and the *Chinese Exclusion Act* (1923), drew clear distinctions between preferred and nonpreferred races of immigrants – "European immigrants were actively and aggressively recruited to replenish the nation" (Thobani 2000, 36). By permitting nonpreferred males as temporary foreign workers, yet excluding women from those same ethnic groups, the state aimed to guarantee the temporariness of these male workers, assuming they would return to their country of origin once their labour was no longer needed. In doing so, the white European nuclear family was established as the Canadian family (Thobani 2007). Critics took issue with the blatant racist and sexist underpinnings of this program, calling for a more neutral and balanced admission system.

The 1976 *Immigration Act* established three categories of immigrants – independents (retirees, entrepreneurs, self-employed), refugees, and family class. Included in the act was the point system (established in 1967), a method of assessment that assigns a score according to one's skills and education. Exempt from the point system, family class applicants are individuals sponsored by family members who are either Canadian citizens or permanent residents. Also new to the Canadian immigration system, family class sponsors were obligated to financially support their sponsored relatives for ten years. Under the previous system, sponsors only had to publicly ensure that their family member would not be a burden on the state. This had proved ineffective, as sponsors failed to meet their financial obligations, and their immigrant family members ended up on social assistance. The new system attempted to minimize the responsibility of the state by legally enforcing sponsor accountability. Missing from this initiative, however, was a lack of adequate enforcement mechanisms capable of guaranteeing these promises were kept, as it is difficult to keep track of immigrants once they have arrived in Canada (Kelley and Trebilcock 2000, 402). Furthermore, there was minimal incentive for the federal government to track both sponsors and the sponsored because integration is the responsibility of provincial and municipal governments. Following the 1976 *Immigration Act,* amendments were added to include the sponsoring of parents, dependent children, and adopted children under the age of nineteen.

While the language of the point system is technically neutral, there remain gendered implications specifically for female migrants (Abu-Laban and Strong-Boag 1998; Abu-Laban and Gabriel 2002). A reliance on formal education and financial contribution, compounded by the failure to account for unpaid domestic work, means that the point system typically favours male migrants from certain countries and, as such, female migrants are more likely to come to Canada as dependent spouses through the family class program; in 2015, 58 percent of sponsored spouses were women (Citizenship and Immigration Canada 2017). Sponsored spouses are obligated to rely on their sponsor for economic and social support. By reinforcing the heterosexual nuclear family form, where the "man is the main breadwinner and his wife's main contribution to the family was through her role as mother, carer, and housewife, rather than a wage earner," both the point system and the family class program maintain gendered dynamics of dependency (Luxton 1997, 12–13).

In addition to the family class being inherently gendered, the definition of family in this program embodies heterosexist and racist undertones as well. Same-sex spousal sponsorship was not permitted until 2002; between 1952 and 1976, homosexuals were identified as "undesirable migrants" and were denied access to Canadian borders (Abu-Laban and Gabriel 2002, 53). Moreover, the state's reliance on the nuclear family fails to account for the fact that what constitutes family cuts across ethnic (e.g., racial) lines – for many, family goes beyond one's spouse and children to include grandparents, aunts, uncles, cousins, etc. While the family class program continues to permit the sponsoring of some extended family members – primarily parents and grandparents – it has become increasingly difficult to sponsor nonnuclear family members.[25] Privileging the nuclear family breadwinner model in our point system and family class program continues to implicitly reproduce specific understandings of the nuclear family that cut across sexist, racist, and heterosexist lines; more importantly, the connection between the point system and the family class program reinforces Hawkins' argument that the parameters of the family class are secondary to the migration of independent migrants.

It was not until Mulroney's Conservative government took power in 1984 that the topic of immigration became a highly politicized issue (Hawkins 1989; Abu-Laban and Gabriel 2002). Claiming that immigration promoted economic growth, Mulroney framed immigration reform as a solution to the ongoing recession. Interestingly, the focus was not solely on skilled workers coming to Canada through the point system, but also on the family class. In fact, while unemployment rates continued to rise, the Mulroney Conservatives "kept the family-class category proportionately higher than the others, partly in the hopes of winning voters from minority communities, partly of their feeling that immigration was good for the economy" (Abu-Laban and Gabriel 2002, 47).[26] In several interviews, former IRCC policy analysts mentioned that the Mulroney government was surprisingly committed to weakening barriers for family class migrants. One interviewee commented, "We had a prime minister [Mulroney] at the time who for personal reasons that I have not figured out, besides the fact that his wife's family were immigrants, was committed to immigration" (Interviews). This demonstrates that immigration reform is largely dependent on the government of the day and, as such, approaches to reform are not necessarily party-specific.

In constructing family as a desirable migrant class, the Mulroney government prioritized family as a key component of Canada's immigration program; rates of migrants arriving through the family class continued to increase while independents decreased (Hawkins 1989). The simultaneous increase in migration and unemployment rates resulted in public opposition toward Mulroney's more open immigration program (Palmer 1996); national opinion polls stated that 30 percent (1988), 45 percent (1993), and over 50 percent (1994) of Canadians agreed that there were too many immigrants in Canada and that the government should take more restrictive measures (Abu-Laban and Gabriel 2002, 47). In 1992, prior to introducing Bill C-86, involving significant amendments to the 1976 *Immigration Act,* IRCC conducted a series of intensive national consultations. Accumulated research concluded that Canadians were more accepting of immigrants if they felt that their own personal financial stability was not at stake (e.g., immigrants were not taking their jobs) and if they had personal experiences with immigrants. Those who were wary attributed it to their seeing immigrants do bad things; instead of being exposed to success stories, they witnessed "stories of shootings in major cities, gang violence, queue jumpers, living off the welfare system, etc." (Interviews). Through these consultations, it became evident that participants were generally receptive to the state accommodating more immigrants so long as they believed that the government was going to control for the "bad eggs" (Interviews). Immigration policy analysts must therefore maintain a balance between easing admission restrictions in the name of fairness and appeasing public opinion, a balance made difficult by the lack of control over exact application projections. Bill C-86 attempted to mediate public concern, producing a more restrictive immigration program that ultimately returned the family class to a less desirable group.

In their 1995 annual report to Parliament, IRCC focused on family class immigrants' reliance on Canada's social welfare system. The report estimated the social welfare cost of default in sponsorship obligation in 1993 as close to $700 million (Citizenship and Immigration Canada 1995). *Sponsorship breakdown* was identified as a primary concern in need of immediate attention.[27] The proposed solution involved several initiatives including a revised sponsorship agreement, new financial standards, enforcement mechanisms, and enhanced federal-provincial cooperation (Citizenship and Immigration Canada 1994, 39–41). Sponsorship breakdown was and continues to be an impetus for improvements to family sponsorship policy, particularly with respect to spousal reunification. It frames discussion about sponsors/the sponsored as a language of winners and losers with minimal reference to state responsibility. The federal government conceptualizes the category of intimate partners in a way that recognizes the interdependent nature of these relationships. The more economically stable the relationship is perceived to be, the more legitimate the claim for family class status.

This focus on immigrant self-sufficiency and the subsequent privatization of the family class is reflective of broader ideological changes in Canadian public policy development in the 1990s; immigration and citizenship reforms highlighted a commitment to global neoliberal discourses of economic competitiveness, privatization, and cost recovery (Abu-Laban and Gabriel 2002; Harder 2009a; Dobrowolsky 2013). While Chrétien's Liberal government, elected in 1993, agreed with Mulroney's position that immigration positively impacts economic growth, it was hesitant to extend this mentality to all immigrants (Interviews). Rather, in order for Canada to compete on a global scale, "the 'best' immigrants, and by extension prospective citizens, are those whose labour-market skills [would] enhance Canada's competitive position in a world economy" (Abu-Laban and Gabriel 2002, 62). As such, the family class reclaimed its position as an undesirable group considering its very composition was that of dependents. The ideal immigrant was one who did not have to depend on the state for support, and if that immigrant came with a family, the family would not make demands on the state either. In privatizing dependency, the financial burden of integrating into Canadian society was now downloaded onto the individual sponsoring their family members. This was echoed in IRCC's *A Broader Vision: Immigration and Citizenship Plan 1995–2000* – "the balance between economic, family, and other immigrant components will place greater emphasis on attracting those with the capacity to settle quickly in Canada" (Citizenship and Immigration Canada 1995, 13). Amendments to the immigration program resulting in the reduction of admittance to noncontributors – those not selected using the point system – reinvigorated gendered narratives of dependency and framed immigrant women and families as potential drains on the welfare state.

Consistent with domestic relationship recognition, recognized interdependency among immigrant families was awarded solely to heterosexual married couples prior to the *Modernization of Benefits and Obligations Act* (2000). Common-law couples were only considered under humanitarian and compassionate grounds, and same-sex applicants were obligated to apply as independents under the point system. It was only when they failed to qualify as independents that they could make a case on humanitarian grounds. This came under fire in an immigration legislative review, the report proposing that the sponsorship program reflect the ruling in *Canada (AG) v Mossop* that "it is the social utility of families that we all recognize, not any one proper form that the family must assume" (Ministry of Public Works and Government Services Canada 1997, 46). Critical of the state's reliance on the traditional family model, the report concluded that the traditional heterosexual family form does not guarantee interdependency.

The proposed solution was a three-tiered family class system, believed to be reflective of the varying degrees of interdependency inherent in intimate relationships. The first tier, "those included in the most intimate family core" – spouses and dependent children – was the closest thing to automatic acceptance (Ministry of Public Works and Government Services Canada 1997, 46). The second tier was reserved for fiancé(e)s, parents, and grandparents (only when one's parents are deceased), recognizing the need for stringent sponsorship guidelines to avoid the increasing reliance of aging immigrants on social services and health systems. Finally, the third tier was to account for "individuals who form strong emotional bonds with persons who are not their intimate partners or spouses, nor their biological partners, nor even blood relatives" (47). This tier was conceived to be inclusive of anyone ranging from a same-sex or common-law partner to a best friend. While this tiered system was criticized for its reduction of same-sex relationships to friendships, the report pre-emptively compensated by recognizing that the Canadian state was in the process of providing more sensitive treatment of same-sex relationships and was advocating that immigration policy should eventually be reflective of these changes as well. The federal government chose not to adopt the proposed system; however, the report ignited a short-lived conversation concerning reliance of the Canadian immigration system on the traditional nuclear family (Interviews).

With the passing of the *Immigration and Refugee Protection Act* in 2001, family reunification was identified as one of the primary objectives of Canadian immigration policy (LaViolette 2004). The act expanded the category of family class to include spouses (married persons) and common-law partners (cohabiting in a conjugal relationship with a Canadian citizen), and it reduced the sponsor financial obligation to three years. Due to their inability to marry in most countries, same-sex couples were obligated to apply as common-law partners. Attempting to develop a definitive method for same-sex couples to prove the conjugal nature of their relationship was difficult, as the cohabitation requirement failed to account for the persecution of gays and lesbians, "making it impossible for them to collect the documentation required to demonstrate a legitimate partnership" (LaViolette 2004, 982). Furthermore, the category of common-law partner was inconsistent with the definition of conjugality outlined in *Molodowich v Penttinen* and *M v H*, which accounted for the various characteristics that constitute a conjugal relationship, characteristics including but not limited to cohabitation. Highlighted in *Alfonso v Canada,* the claimant was denied permanent residency on the grounds that the couple failed to meet the cohabitation requirement despite having lived together – both inside and outside Canada – for over three years.[28] In response, an amendment was added promising couples unable to cohabit due to persecution or penal control that they would be considered common-law for the purposes of a visa. Ultimately, increased focus on family reunification in the 2001 act established a more prominent role for conjugality in the processing of family class applicants; with more relationships qualifying as conjugal, the state now had the power to assess the legitimacy of relationships in the absence of a marriage certificate.

There has generally been a lag between changes to the familial unit in domestic policy and those changes being implemented in immigration policy. The inclusion of same-sex couples in the category of spouse is no exception. Same-sex marriage was legalized in 2005; however, married couples were unable to sponsor each other until 2007. The category of spouse continues to be restricted to those same-sex couples married in a country where same-sex marriage is also legal, significantly minimizing the number of potential applicants.[29] More important than the delay in changes to the family unit between areas of policy, the inconsistent treatment of conjugality domestically does not cross over to immigration. The federal government explicitly privileges conjugal relationships in their immigration program, and as remaining chapters will demonstrate, the definition of conjugality has not changed to the same extent with the incorporation of more relationships into the category of family class.

Changes to the IRPA post-2001 symbolize a return to the replacement of family reunification with economic progress as the driving force behind Canadian immigration (Abu-Laban and Gabriel 2002; Walton-Roberts

2014; Fleras 2015). In their 2005 annual report to Parliament, then minister of citizenship and immigration Joe Volpe identified immigration as an integral component in maintaining "labour force growth and the necessary skilled labour supply in different sectors and regions across the country" (Citizenship and Immigration Canada 2005, 7). This commitment to labour force growth was continuously identified as a top priority of the Harper government by both former minister of citizenship and immigration Jason Kenney (2012) and Harper himself – "We have traditionally just been a country that passively accepts applications. We are now trying to go out and shape those immigration applications and process those in a way that will serve the labour force holes that are emerging" (Campion-Smith 2012). Focusing on the recruitment of "designer immigrants," the Conservative government favoured migrants with the language and work skills to obtain a job upon arrival and the financial resources to support themselves until then (Simmons 2010, 85). The construction of three categories of designer immigrants – labour market – ready (those who have employment lined up or will be able to obtain employment soon after arriving), labour market – preference (those with "ethnic capital"), and provincial nominees (recruitment of workers for regional economies) – combined with a reliance on a demand-driven temporary worker program highlights the then government's continued focus on neoliberal ideals of productivity, cost recovery, and immigrant self-sufficiency (Fleras 2015). While the Conservative government upheld and even bypassed the number of accepted immigrants in certain categories compared to previous Liberal governments, the Conservatives managed immigration "on their own terms" (Jeffrey 2015, 225).

This continued focus on economic growth produced changes to immigration policies one could consider to be antifamily reunification, an example being the increasing prominence of the Temporary Foreign Worker Program (TFWP). Versions of temporary foreign worker programs have existed in Canada since 1966; however, the total number of migrants coming to Canada through these programs had been relatively low prior to 2006 (Lenard and Straehle 2012, 7). Since 2006, over five hundred thousand temporary foreign workers have come to Canada, the product of a more expeditious application process implemented by the Harper government in 2007 (Harper 2014; Wingrove 2014). Labelling these workers "temporary" reinforces the expectation that once there is no longer a need for specific types of labourers, they will return to their country of origin. As such, those who come to Canada through this program are unable to apply for permanent residency and to sponsor family members.[30] This is not to suggest that the TFWP is inherently antifamily; rather, it is to highlight that in a return to focusing primarily on encouraging temporariness, there is less demand for reunification, as temporary foreign workers are denied the ability to make such claims. In relying on the TFWP as a primary source of immigration, the Harper government therefore accomplished three things: the government's priority of economic prosperity was reinforced (Patten 2013), a system of expiration date immigration was fostered, and the pool of landed immigrants able to potentially seek reunification was limited.

In addition to a continued focus on economic prosperity, subsequent changes to the IRPA allowed for enhanced ministerial autonomy, giving the minister of citizenship and immigration undisputed authority over determining the parameters of access. The passing of *Protecting Canada's Immigration System Act* (Bill C-31) in 2012 allowed the minister to establish and edit the safe country list, determining which countries can produce potentially legitimate refugee claimants. Similarly, the minister had the authority to revoke citizenship in situations of fraud and terrorism and to reinforce mandatory residency requirements for permanent residents and sponsored spouses following the passing of the *Strengthening Canadian Citizenship Act* (Bill C-24) in 2014.[31] What is interesting about these two bills is that while family class migration no longer held primacy in Canadian immigration policy, the Harper government continued to implement restrictions on family reunification. Moreover, legislative changes created a system in which the minister could single-handedly define the role of conjugality in determining access for immigrants and refugees, both current and future. In 2017, the Trudeau government's bill to amend the *Citizenship Act* (Bill C-6) was passed, reversing several primary citizenship changes enacted under the Harper government specifically related to citizenship revocation, language requirements, and children's rights (Zilio 2017).

These policies highlight a "consistent pattern in Canada's contemporary approach to border control, in which rights-restrictive policies have been used to limit the ability of individuals, interest groups, and the courts ... to challenge state control measures through the promotion of the rights of non-citizens" (Anderson 2013, 1). The production and reproduction of foreignness has, therefore, been a longstanding characteristic of Canada's immigration and refugee program regardless of which party is in power. What distinguished changes to Canada's immigration and refugee program under the Harper government from those of previous governments was its simultaneous support for immigration as an economic booster and introduction of program restrictions to appease the party's social-conservative base – "While economic advantage drove the pragmatism that caused the Conservatives to support immigration, their political need to respond to the ideological concerns of their social-conservative base led them to impose a number of extreme sanctions on various categories of 'offenses'" (Jeffrey 2015, 226). Sanctions including the detainment of refugee passengers on the MV *Sun Sea* (2010),[32] the attempted passing of the *Preventing Human Smugglers from Abusing Canada's Immigration System Act* (2010), the elimination of health care coverage for refugee claimants (2012), a nationwide crackdown on "marriage fraud" (2011), the creation of a national tip line to report "fraudsters" (2011), the *Faster Removal of Foreign Criminals Act* (2012), the elimination of 280,000 immigration applications in order to relieve "backlog" (2012), the *Protecting Canada's Immigration System Act* (2012), the *Strengthening Canadian Citizenship Act* (2014), the refusal of Syrian refugees (2015), the *Anti-Terrorism Bill* (2015), and the *Zero Tolerance for Barbaric Cultural Practices Act* (2015) highlight an agenda of moral regulation aimed at recruiting and naturalizing a specific version of the Canadian immigrant and/or refugee. In this light, immigration is good for the economy so long as it is the right type of immigrant; contrary to past Canadian neoliberal immigration programs, what constituted the right type of immigrant for the Harper government went beyond economic self-sufficiency.

Here, it is worth mentioning the individual efforts of Jason Kenney; while his cabinet portfolios included citizenship, immigration, and multiculturalism (2008–13); employment, social development, and multiculturalism (2013–15); and national defence (2015), Kenney had a continued presence in the construction and execution of the party's immigration agenda. Prior to the 2011 federal election, Kenney appointed an "ethnic outreach team" tasked with targeting "socially and fiscally conservative immigrant groups whose values were deemed amenable to those of the Conservative Party" (Marwah, Triadafilopoulos, and White 2013, 107). Versions of Canadian conservative parties past – for example, the Progressive Conservative Party under Mulroney (1984–93) – had been pro-immigration; however, the decision of the Harper-led Conservative Party of Canada (CPC) to court the "ethnic vote" represented a shift in traditional electoral strategy adopted by the Reform and Canadian Alliance parties in Canada and conservative parties abroad (Marwah, Triadafilopoulos, and White 2013; Carlaw 2015; Omidvar 2016; Tolley 2017). While the CPC was not necessarily pro-immigration, the current electoral system and the reality that Canadian political parties overlap on multiple immigration-related topics made it difficult for any party to win a majority without appealing to immigrant voters, specifically in Canada's largest cities – "To be anti-immigrant in highly diverse Canada is tantamount to abdicating on the immigrant-rich ridings in and around metropolitan Vancouver, Toronto, Montreal and, increasingly, beyond" (Omidvar 2016, 182). Studies show that new Canadians vote at the same rate as Canadian-born citizens (Anderson and Black 2008, 56–57), making foreign-born citizens an important portion of the electorate – a portion largely monopolized by the Liberal Party from the 1960s to the early 2000s. As such, Harper and his team began to explore "what they have in common with immigrant voters," and, in doing so, establish a balance between garnering electoral support among immigrant populations and furthering an increasingly restrictive immigration and citizenship policy agenda (Marwah, Triadafilopoulos, and White 2013, 96).[33]

Nicknamed "Minister of Curry in a Hurry," Kenney became a social media regular, documenting his attendance "when it mattered at community events, festivals, parades, inners and national days of some two hundred nations all across the country" (Omidvar 2016, 185). In addition to community outreach, team tactics included targeted mailings, interviews with "ethnic" press outlets, a series of apologies for historical wrongdoings (e.g., Chinese head tax, the *Komagata Maru* incident, internment of Italian-Canadians during the Second World War), and policies aimed at establishing a conservative common ground on issues of law and order and traditional values (Marwah, Triadafilopoulos, and White 2013, 108–10).[34] Through his efforts, Kenney was successful at executing ethnic outreach while, at the same time, making citizenship more difficult to obtain and permanently precarious. Public opinion on Kenney varies depending on one's position on the political spectrum; however, it is difficult to deny the impact he had on the party's immigration agenda, specifically with respect to policing the family class (Fleras 2015; Carlaw 2016).

This agenda of moral regulation was compounded by the adoption of a post-9/11 discourse of security that identified immigration and citizenship policies as "key sites at which threats to the state must be addressed" (Harder 2010, 204). As a result, restrictive changes to Canada's immigration and refugee program have been justified as measures to protect Canadians from external threat. In *Securing an Open Society: Canada's National Security Policy*, the Privy Council Office called attention to the security threat migration presents for Canadian borders and applauded the government's use of security measures to "improve the screening of immigrants, refugee claimants and visitors and to enhance the capacity to detain and remove anyone posing a risk to Canada" (Privy Council Office of Canada 2004, 41). Conflating issues of immigration, terrorism, and border control into the same policy agenda post-9/11 has resulted in narratives of migration being securitized (Watson 2009; Bourbeau 2011; Salter 2013; Omidvar 2016). An example of this overlapping of departmental/policy agendas was when then minister of national defence Jason Kenney, addressing the need for additional screening mechanisms admitting Syrian refugees during the 2015 federal election, warned of the potential threat these migrants could present to the Canadian public – "I do not mean to suggest for a moment that all or most of the people in the camps are connected to terrorist organizations or constitute a security risk but it is plainly evident that some do" (Graveland 2015). While defining the parameters of our refugee program is historically not the responsibility of the Department of National Defence, framing certain migrants as a threat makes a space for discussions regarding the movement of people in national security policy programs. In this light, some migrants are considered safe while others are assumed to be dangerous, and the "legal entitlement to citizenship cannot interfere with the state's absolute right to protect itself" (Salter 2013, 151).

Calls for securitization rest on the assumption that a particular situation requires emergency action that goes "beyond normal parameters of political procedure" (Watson 2009, 26). The Harper government used this language of security to sell an agenda "based at least partly on fear, and even more on indignation about 'phony' refugees, 'queue jumpers,' 'part-time Canadians,' and other perceived malfeasance that required additional punitive measures" to both immigrant and nonimmigrant voters (Jeffrey 2015, 225). Restrictions to family reunification and sponsorship were framed as a way to protect our country from queue jumpers and maintain the integrity of a system that so many immigrants turned Canadian citizens have used to gain entry. In their framing of migration as an issue of security, the Harper government was able to change the national migration narrative:

> Though an audience may be generally convinced or unconvinced of a security claims, successful securitization is not an either/or proposition – securitizing claims may fully succeed, resulting in the institutionalization of the securitized relationship; they may fail, with the security claim categorically rejected; or they may produce an outcome in between, wherein the association of particular developments with insecurity becomes part of the general discourse, though emergency responses are not regularized in an institutional apparatus. (Watson 2009, 25)

The securitization of migration thus creates a frame for exploring questions of migration in a way that separates the desirable (safe) from the undesirable (dangerous) migrants, and, as such, the Harper government was able to construct meanings of difference that shaped the claims of those seeking access and justified enhanced state policing of these claims. In this light, the Harper government used conjugality as a tool to protect Canadian borders, both physical and ideological.

While family reunification continues to be less of a priority with the family class being reframed as an undesirable class, recent policy amendments to our family class program illustrate the desire to maintain a specific version of family – the conjugal nuclear family. In this light, foreignness is both an external and internal threat; those immigrants and refugees constructed as undesirable are a detriment not only to the security of our borders, but also to the security of the so-called Canadian family. When it comes to protecting the conjugal family unit, the internal foreigner is as dangerous as the one who has yet to be granted entry (Dhamoon and Abu-Laban 2009). Discourses of security, citizenship, foreignness, and family therefore intersect, establishing an immigration system that allows "only those that are permissible until such time as they too are deemed to be threatening to the nation, and keeping those as acceptable in line with national norms" (Dhamoon 2010, 261). As such, the Harper government's version of foreignness not only marked certain bodies as external threats, but also potentially stripped those of citizenship and belonging who were labelled an internal danger despite being previously granted access.

Changes in immigration policy concerning the parameters of conjugality have not been as extensively litigated as Canadian domestic decisions affecting conjugal relationships. This is largely attributed to two factors. First, the crux of immigration policy is state admission for noncitizens, meaning that the individuals primarily affected are those who have limited access to our political and legal institutions. Court challenges require substantive resources that are difficult enough for Canadian citizens to obtain (Interviews). For those seeking to immigrate, the difficulty in obtaining the appropriate resources is compounded by the fact they are noncitizens (Dauvergne 2013). It is therefore challenging for applicants to question assessment practices at the judicial level. Second, as Dhamoon (2010) suggests, governments generally enjoy more autonomy when it comes to developing stricter immigration policies, as this policy domain is intertwined with questions of security. Because changes in immigration policy are framed as initiatives aimed at further protecting Canadian citizens, legislators are often given a free pass. As a result, modifications to the immigration system are typically legislature-driven rather than responses to court decisions.

This is not to suggest that increasing Charter litigation of immigration decisions would necessarily challenge the state's current focus on conjugal relationships. Technically, legislators are expected to develop immigration policy in a manner consistent with judicial interpretation – family reunification is now available to common-law heterosexual and same-sex married and unmarried couples. Furthermore, judicial treatment of personal relationships remains fixed on the conjugal family unit; the extension of state recognition has transpired in a manner that upholds conjugal privilege. Policy incongruities are therefore not caused by a disconnect between judicial and legislative decisions affecting conjugal relationships; rather, the asymmetrical treatment of conjugality across policy domains is the direct result of both branches relying on a system of conjugal privilege and using this system – either intentionally or unintentionally – to maintain distinctions between inside and outside families.

There is no doubt that conjugality is the preferred adult personal relationship with respect to Canadian law and policy both inside and outside the state. The extension of conjugal rights to common-law and same-sex couples permitted the state to be more inclusive while maintaining a definition of family reliant on the conjugal couple. While conjugal relationships hold primacy, those living in Canada generally have the freedom to develop their own familial networks. This is a result of the flexibility in the state's approach toward conjugality within its borders. As this chapter demonstrates, domestic treatment of conjugality is inconsistent, as it is often paid only lip service (e.g., Bountiful) or taken to extremes (e.g., spouse in the house rules). As a result, our understanding of permissible relationships in Canadian law and policy is convoluted. This both helps and hinders individual decision making regarding the development of one's intimate relationships.

Despite the consequences of definitional elasticity, there is generally less flexibility in our immigration programs. While the parameters of conjugality have evolved in this policy domain as well, conjugal interpretation as a mechanism of border control warrants attention. Spousal sponsorship is currently the primary form of family class sponsorship; therefore, the conjugal unit demarcates the legitimate immigrant family. The Canadian state's inconsistent treatment of conjugality has established two versions of the conjugal family – the inside family (families within Canadian borders) and the outside family (families outside Canadian borders). Moreover, the Harper government used this inside/outside distinction to frame bad immigrants as a threat to our borders as well as to Canadian families. While the courts have had less influence on changes to immigration policy compared to domestic policy, both judicial and legislative interpretation of adult personal relationships relies on upholding a system of conjugal privilege. We must therefore account for the role conjugality performs in state practice and question the often silent power it holds in determining access to the Canadian state. Subsequent chapters will provide a more in-depth analysis of specific immigration and refugee policies, focusing on how conjugality produces and reproduces a very particular version of Canadian citizenship. While inconsistent treatment of conjugality has resulted in a complex understanding of acceptable personal relationships both inside and outside our borders, the remaining chapters aim to provide some clarity.

3

The Role of Relationships in Canadian Refugee Determination Process for Sexual Minorities

"The idea of establishing identity is an added burden and one that particularly, I would argue, most impacts queer and trans refugees."

– HARSHA WALIA

In 2006, a bisexual male from Brazil filed a claim for refugee status in Canada. Claiming to be in need of protection, the claimant testified he had been the victim of a violent attack in his neighbourhood and of discrimination at his place of employment, attributing both events to his sexual orientation. When questioned by Canadian officials about his relationship history, the claimant responded that while he had dated both men and women, he had never been in a long-term relationship; he explained that he had never felt safe enough to develop the type of long-term relationships he desired. While the assigned Immigration and Refugee Board of Canada (IRB) adjudicator accepted the applicant's claim that he was a victim of physical violence, they were unconvinced the claimant was bisexual and thus was skeptical that the physical violence was a direct result of his sexual orientation. The claimant's application was refused on the grounds that "the claimant has never resided with either a man or a woman, therefore, it is impossible to identify the claimant's true sexual identity" (TA5–07054, 5). The claimant's lack of long-term relationship pattern contributed to his claim being denied, the absence of conjugal living casting doubt on his claimed sexual orientation.

The ability to migrate between countries is both empowering and restricting. Canada's refugee program provides those who are either persecuted or fear persecution as a result of their sexual orientation with the opportunity to not return to their country of origin. As a refugee-receiving country, Canada has the highest acceptance rates for sexual minorities of any receiving country in the world, reinforcing our reputation as a protector of sexual minority rights worldwide (Millbank 2009). The benevolent nature of receiving refugees often glosses over power imbalances between the state that is welcoming refugees and the refugees themselves; the refugee is seen as the stranger seeking access while the host state is perceived as compassionate.

While the Canadian state has taken a progressive stance, comparatively speaking, on gay and lesbian rights, there remain issues with the assessment of refugee claimants who fear persecution as a result of their sexual orientation. These criticisms primarily focus on how some IRB adjudicators may find claims credible only if the claimant's narrative meets stereotypical or Western conceptions of sexuality and sexual orientation (Rehaag 2008; Janicek, Wong, and Lee 2009; Young 2010; LaViolette 2014; Hersh 2015; Murray 2015; Gaucher and DeGagné 2016). Further, the presence or absence of an intimate relationship is used to reproduce these stereotypes despite the fact that the refugee program is an individualized process. Refugees claiming persecution because of their sexual orientation are obliged to prove that they are, or are perceived to be, gay, lesbian, or bisexual, which may involve testimony about their relationship patterns. What is unsettling is that the IRB uses certain relationship characteristics (sex of partner, duration of relationship, public perception of relationship, etc.) to assess the validity of testimony. In doing so, a claimant's relationship pattern becomes influential in determining the legitimacy of the claimant's sexual orientation, which can in turn diminish the seriousness of the claimant's experienced or feared persecution. This is not to suggest that the conjugal nature of one's intimate relationships is the sole determinant in refugee assessment cases; however, conjugality does play a role in case assessment. As such, the problem is not that adjudicators assess the credibility of evidence, but whether they do so in a manner that is free of prejudice, stereotypes, and narrow conceptualizations of sexuality and sexual orientation. These trends present implications for those seeking refuge, as the Canadian state's understanding of sexuality and sexual identity shapes the type of claimant capable of gaining access.

This chapter explores the implications of IRB adjudicators' evaluations of relationship patterns for homosexual and bisexual refugee claimants, arguing that current trends in assessment of sexual minority refugee claimants highlight flaws both of the stereotypes that shape refugee policy and of the mechanisms used to assess claimant testimony.[1] After providing an overview of Canada's refugee program in order to outline the legal and political context for sexual minority claimant application assessment, I examine several trends currently taking place in the evaluation of homosexual and bisexual claimants. This discussion is grounded in an analysis of unpublished and published IRB and Federal Court decisions. While published decisions are publicly accessible, they fail to comprise a representative sample of all refugee determinations, as only a small fraction of Canadian refugee decisions are published.[2] The IRB is not obligated to publish positive decisions if there is no appeal, and decisions often selected for publication are those that "raise unusual fact situations or new approaches to issues" (Rehaag 2008, 70). To rectify this methodological challenge, unpublished decisions were also obtained from the IRB through a formal access to information request.[3] In total, 250 published and unpublished IRB decisions were analyzed, including 50 decisions involving bisexual claimants and 13 decisions involving female homosexual and bisexual claimants.[4] In analyzing these decisions, this chapter highlights several assessment trends that present implications for sexual minority refugee claimants.[5]

Sexual Minorities and the Canadian Refugee Program

Since 1989, the refugee determination process has been the responsibility of the IRB, an independent tribunal. The government of the day sets the immigration policy agenda and typically limits refugee flows through procedural obstacles rather than by altering either the definition of refugee or the assessment instructions for IRB members. As such, the IRB is expected to provide a nonpartisan, independent assessment of refugee claims but has limited powers to set any kind of policy agenda or alter refugee law. Since 1991, when the Canadian government allowed sexual minorities to claim refugee status, the IRB has processed thousands of persecution claims based on sexual orientation (LaViolette 2009, 440). The IRB's Refugee Protection Division (RPD) assesses claims brought forward by those seeking refugee status; the RPD is therefore responsible for deciding "whether they believe the claimant's evidence and how much weight to give to that evidence" (Immigration and Refugee Board of Canada 2017a). In this light, a well-founded fear of persecution requires both a subjective and an objective requirement.[6] Refugee claimants must possess a fear of persecution; however, that fear must be objectively evaluated in order to determine if a valid basis for that fear exists. This is typically achieved through independent country information consisting of governmental, nongovernmental, and media reports concerning conditions for sexual minorities.[7] As James Hathaway states, "It is clear that even the most fervently stated fear of persecution will not be enough if objective evidence tends to deny the existence of risk" (1991, 71). Objective evidence is therefore a compulsory and pivotal element in refugee claims.

The IRB is not bound by a Canadian definition of refugee; rather, Canada is internationally obliged to uphold the 1951 United Nations' *Convention Relating to the Status of Refugees,* defining a refugee as an individual "who, by reason of a well-founded fear of persecution for reasons of race, religion, nationality, membership in a particular social group or political opinion is outside their country of nationality and is unable or, by reason of the fear, unwilling to avail themselves of the protection of that country" (United Nations General Assembly 1951). It is important to note that adjudicators are not assessing cases with absolute discretion, as the court can review decisions for errors of fact and law. IRB decisions are subjected to judicial review either through the IRB's own appeal process, established in 2012, or through the Federal Court. Adjudicators do not operate under an explicit understanding of acceptable and unacceptable evidence; rather, they must be convinced that the evidence presented by the claimant is "probably so," what the IRB refers to as the "balance of probabilities" (Immigration and Refugee Board of Canada 2017a). The burden of proof is therefore placed on the claimant and the adjudicator must be persuaded that (a) the refugee claimant is a sexual minority; (b) the claimant has a well-founded fear of harm in their home country as a result of their being a sexual minority; and (c) the claimant's home country is either unable or unwilling to provide protection from that harm. While this vague approach to evidence is beneficial – as it recognizes that formal types of evidence (police reports, government documents, etc.) are not always attainable – discretion can be a double-edged sword. The capacity to entertain a broad spectrum of evidence also gives adjudicators the leeway to justify rejecting a broad spectrum of evidence. While refugees are legally obliged to provide proof that substantiates their claims of persecution, both feared and actual, this chapter problematizes the interpretation and assessment of that proof.

Because sexual orientation is not enumerated in the United Nations' definition of refugee, legal strategies to include sexual orientation are multiple and contested (LaViolette 1997; Millbank 2002, 2009; Rehaag 2008, 2009; Gitari 2011). For the most part, however, the IRB continues to rely on the understanding that sexual minorities are members of a particular social group defined by an innate or unchangeable characteristic (Interviews). *Canada v Ward* – a Supreme Court decision – made clear that sexual minorities qualify as a "particular social group" to which refugees could claim membership.[8] Interestingly, the case had nothing to do with sexual orientation; the appellant was a former member of the Irish National Liberation Army (INLA) who sought refugee status in Canada, claiming fear of persecution as a result of his affiliation and criminal actions with the INLA. For Justice La Forest, the issues here were the actual meaning of a "particular social group" and the relevance of state complicity, as "international refugee protection is to serve as surrogate shelter coming into play only upon failure of national support."[9] With respect to state complicity, the court ruled that well-founded claims of persecution do not solely rely on situations in which the state is an accomplice; persecution can take place in situations where states are simply unable to protect their citizens. Independent human rights documentary evidence confirmed that the appellant's home country was unable to protect its citizens from the actions of the INLA. This established a broader interpretation of state compliance, recognizing that state action as well as inaction (either voluntary or involuntary) contributes to instances of persecution.

In deciding what constitutes a particular social group, Justice La Forest identified three distinct types of social groups:

1) Groups defined by an innate or unchangeable characteristic;
2) Groups whose members voluntarily associate for reasons so funda-mental to their human dignity that they should not be forced to forsake the association; and
3) Groups associated by a former voluntary status, unalterable due to its historical permanence.[10]

Using this three-pronged approach, the court ruled that INLA members failed to qualify as a particular social group, and Ward was denied Convention refugee status. As previously mentioned, *Ward* had no direct connection to sexual persecution; however, sexual orientation was men-tioned in the court's offering of examples of these social group categories. Justice La Forest interpreted the first grouping – groups defined by an innate or unchangeable characteristic – as including "individuals fearing persecution on such bases as gender, linguistic background and sexual orientation."[11] Incorporating sexual minorities into this category suggests they are deserving of international protection because they are unable to change the personal characteristic for which they are being persecuted, that being their sexual orientation. The IRB's immediate adoption of this understanding of a particular social group produced positive results for gay men and lesbians seeking refuge in Canada. As LaViolette contends: "Panel decisions published since the 1993 Supreme Court decision no longer reveal a variety of views on whether gay men and lesbians constitute a particular social group for the purposes of the *Convention*'s definition of refugee. Nor do they disagree on the reasons why membership in a sexual minority can ground a claim of state persecution" (1997, 22). The court's decision in *Ward* resulted in the IRB's acceptance of sexual orientation as an immutable characteristic in need of state protection.

The categorization of homosexuality as immutable highlights a long-founded tension between determinists (homosexuality as natural) and social constructivists (homosexuality as socially constructed). Determinists suggest that sexual orientation should be understood as innate. Individuals do not choose to be gay; they just are and should not be persecuted for reasons that are beyond their control. On the other hand, social constructivists contend that sexual identities are socio-historical constructions. Challenging the perceived fixed nature of sexuality inherent in determinist conceptualizations, social constructivists interpret sexuality as fluid, context-dependent, and defined by ever-changing social, economic, and political dynamics (LaViolette 1997, 29). For social constructivists, culture, not human nature, defines sexual orientation, while determinist understandings of sexuality ignore the state's role in the production of sexual identities.[12]

While recognition of sexual minorities as a particular social group defined by an innate or unchangeable characteristic has been beneficial, it is not without consequence. By framing sexual orientation as biological and unchangeable, adjudicators might expect claimants to publicly recognize and act out this characteristic, ignoring the impact this expectation might have on claimants who struggle with their sexual orientation or who have not either engaged in same-sex relationships or relationships exclusively with same-sex partners. Moreover, it suggests that if our sexual orientations were chosen, we would avoid being homosexual (Cragnolini 2013). The suggestion that sexual orientation is immutable arguably eliminates the opportunity for sexual minorities seeking refuge to self-identify and experience their sexuality in different ways.

In addition, sexual orientation as an innate characteristic simultaneously simplifies processes for homosexuals seeking refuge and complicates processes for nonhomosexual queer-identified claimants. Rehaag (2008, 2009) contends that while sexual orientation is viewed as immutable, refugee determination and refugee law more generally fails to account for variation in sexual identity. Considering the sexual orientation, identity, and behaviour of those who identify as bisexual is not directed exclusively toward persons of one specific sex or gender, assessment trends suggest some adjudicators may believe that if you are bisexual, you can opt to be with a heterosexual partner and therefore avoid persecution. In this light, unlike homosexuals who are persecuted for something that is beyond their control, bisexuals possess the ability to avoid discrimination. Bisexuality therefore tests the state's interpretation of sexual minorities as members of a particular social group defined by an innate or unchanging characteristic. The court's framing of sexual minorities as constituting a particular social group – while producing positive results – has implications for how sexuality is legitimized and assessed with respect to refugees.

This interpretation of sexuality as innate is further complicated by two factors: claimant credibility and establishment of harm. Sexual minority refugee claimants often lack physical evidence to corroborate their claims of persecution, primarily as a result of the homophobic climate in their home country. As such, the determination process is often solely reliant on claimant testimony; issues of credibility present challenges for sexual minority refugee claimants due in large part to pre-existing prejudices about sexuality and sexual orientation (Millbank 2009). This is not to suggest that the issue of credibility is unique to sexual minority claimants, nor is it to imply that a claimant's credibility should not be assessed; rather, the chapter aims to explore the ways that this interpretation of sexuality and assumptions about sexuality and sexual orientation influence assessment of credibility for these specific claimants. Adding to the issue of claimant credibility, the state's reliance on exogenous harm makes it challenging for adjudicators to assess the claimed threat of persecution, especially in applications where physical evidence is absent. International courts have recommended that immigration tribunals account for the existence of endogenous harm – specifically, the affront to one's dignity as a human being – however, what constitutes endogenous harm remains under investigation (Hathaway and Pobjoy 2012, 333). Comparatively speaking, sexuality-based persecution claims constitute a small minority of refugee claims worldwide, yet the implications of these challenges manifest themselves differently for sexual minority refugee claimants.

Trends in Canadian State Treatment of Sexual Minority Refugee Claimants

While 202 of the 250 obtained decisions involved refused claims, studies conducted by Catherine Dauvergne and Jenni Millbank (2003) and Sean Rehaag (2008) conclude that "grant rates for refugee claims by members of sexual minorities are similar to the grant rates for traditional refugee claims" (Rehaag 2008, 61).[13] As such, this high refusal rate does not suggest that sexual minority claims are less successful than nonsexual minority claims. Grant rates for sexual minority and nonsexual minority refugees are comparable; however, bisexual refugee refusal rates are higher than those for homosexual refugees (Rehaag 2008, 2009). This has been attributed to the general invisibility of bisexuality in Canadian law and policy and to the IRB's reliance on an understanding of sexual orientation as immutable. The assumption that bisexuality is a choice and that bisexuals have access to heterosexual privilege construct what Rehaag refers to as the "bisexuality myth," putting bisexual claimants in the position of "having to substantiate their sexual identity to adjudicators who might not believe that bisexuality exists, and who do not have a sense of what bisexuals might look like if they do exist" (2008, 87).

It is for this reason that Federal Court decisions were included in my analysis, as the court often rectifies legal misinterpretations during a claimant's initial interaction with the IRB. I am aware of the limitations that a lack of positive decisions presents; the purpose of this chapter is not to suggest that these adjudicators' understanding of sexuality and conjugality leads to misjudged cases. It is impossible for me to decide whether a refugee should have been accepted based on the IRB decisions that are included in this study. Instead, I argue that the IRB's focus on relationship patterns in the current determination process for sexual minority refugee claimants reproduces sexual stereotypes and narratives that reinforce the notion of the good sexual citizen.

It is important to reiterate that because claimants must satisfy the IRB's doubts concerning the credibility of their testimony, there is no single formula for assessment. While all adjudicators assess applications within a framework dictated by international convention and court decisions – a framework that provides suggestions as to the type of evidence an adjudicator can request – how this evidence is weighted is within the discretion of the assigned adjudicator (Interviews). My review of decisions involving homosexual and bisexual refugee claimants in Canada highlights three assessment trends. First, adjudicators rely on stereotypes of sexual orientation and assumptions about sexuality and nonheterosexual relationships more generally to assess the credibility of sexual minority refugee claimants. A second and related trend is that the presence or absence of a conjugal relationship pattern is used to evaluate a claimant's rejection of the heterosexual nuclear family form, ultimately reproducing these stereotypes. Finally, this deviation is then often considered evidence when assessing whether a well-founded fear of harm exists. While conjugality is not necessarily the deciding factor in the refugee determination process, it noticeably influences adjudicators' assessments of claimant trustworthiness and therefore warrants attention.

Relying on Sexual Stereotypes

How adjudicators interpret "what (homo)sexuality is and how it is and ought to be expressed" informs the refugee determination process (Millbank 2002, 145). Claimants currently bolster their claims with a personal narrative of their experiences of persecution, a positive development for many scholars who contend that the sharing of personal narratives has the potential to give voice to those groups "whose marginality defines the boundaries of the mainstream, whose voice and perspective – whose consciousness – has been suppressed, devalued, and abnormalized" (Delgado 1989, 2412). In this light, a determination process based on individual narrative is beneficial for sexual minority claimants, as it arguably avoids the application of a single sexual minority template to all applicants. As Jenni Millbank concludes, however, adjudicators often have difficulty taking these narratives seriously when they fail to correspond with their preconceived assumptions about sexual identity and sexual orientation (2002, 177). This is evident in *PWZ v Canada* – a published decision – where the assigned adjudicator stated, "The claimant presents as an articulate, professional, well-groomed, and attractive young woman. Based on all of these considerations ... the panel cannot conclude that the claimant's sexual orientation would be physically obvious to intolerant and bigoted segments of Colombian society."[14] Or, similarly, as commented in *KQH v Canada* (2003):

> With the goal of determining whether ... the claimant is gay, the panel asked him about his social activities since arriving in Canada. We asked him if he went to the gay bookshop and he answered "no" ... We asked him if he went to gay bars or discotheques in Montreal ... The claimant explained ... that he went more often to the downtown bars. Because of his ... ignorance of the gay reality ... I find that the claimant is not credible.[15]

Comments about one's physical appearance have typically not been used to confirm a claimant's identity following the release of the United

Nations High Commissioner of Refugees' (UNHCR) *Guidance Note on Refugee Claims Relating to Sexual Orientation and Gender Identity* in 2008; however, adjudicators have been known to make the occasional negative comment, such as "no signs of being gay," "effeminate voice and manner," and "looked gay."[16] Personal narratives define the refugee determination process, and these narratives are measured against adjudicators' personal conceptions of sexual orientation and sexual identity. This places the sexual minority refugee claimant under heightened scrutiny, as personal narratives simultaneously become a site of legitimacy and illegitimacy.

This is further complicated by the IRB's reliance on documentary evidence. Claimant testimonies are assessed against existing country documentation; those narratives in conflict with this documentation are deemed suspicious. In a decision involving a gay male from Mexico, the assigned adjudicator questioned his testimony, as it contradicted documentary evidence highlighting positive steps the Mexican government had taken toward combatting homophobia. His claim was therefore refused on the grounds that "although the situation pertaining to homosexuals may not be perfect in Mexico, there has been significant progress made as well as many positive developments within the political and legal landscape" (MA5–02382).[17] This was echoed in the conclusion of the assigned member in a decision involving a lesbian woman from the Philippines seeking refuge:

> I find that if societal or governmental abuse amounting to persecution or to a risk to life or to a risk of cruel and unusual punishment against gays and lesbians was prevalent in the Philippines, human rights organizations such as Amnesty International, the Country Reports on Human Rights Practices or the International Lesbian and Gay Association would have informed the Refugee Protection Division. (TA5–11796, 5)

This suggests that country documentation can potentially trump claimant testimony should the two disprove each other. Claimant testimony is arguably considered well-founded so long as it corresponds with adjudicators' preconceptions of sexual orientation and external documentary evidence.

Upholding Sexual Stereotypes

The bolstering of sexual stereotypes with existing country documentation can make it challenging for sexual minority refugee claimants to provide testimony deemed legitimate by IRB adjudicators. Predetermined assumptions about sexual orientation and relationship tendencies are examples. Historically, Western culture has a habit of understanding sex as a destructive force – labelled "sex negativity" by Rubin (1984) – redeemable solely if used for the purposes of procreation within marriage. This, in turn, produces a hierarchy of sexual value; "good" sex is heterosexual, married, monogamous, private, and procreative, while "bad" sex is homosexual, unmarried, promiscuous, public, and non-procreative (13). As Rubin explains:

> Individuals whose behaviour stands high in this hierarchy are rewarded with certified mental health, respectability, legality, social and physical mobility, institutional support, and material benefits. As sexual behaviours or occupations fall lower on the scale, the individuals who practice them are subjected to a presumption of mental illness, disreputability, criminality, restricted social and physical mobility, loss of institutional support, and economic sanctions. (1984, 12)

It would be misleading to suggest that this hierarchy is fixed. The legalization of same-sex marriage in Canada has arguably made some homosexual sex (e.g., conjugal, monogamous homosexual sex) good sex at the expense of further shaming other types of homosexual sex, what Warner refers to as "selective legitimacy" (1999, 82). While the boundaries between good and bad sex are in constant flux, the linking of queer sexualities to assumed relationship patterns continues to reproduce sexual stereotypes, and these assumptions can influence adjudicators' assessment of claimant testimony. The longstanding heteronormative claim that homosexuals are naturally promiscuous and should therefore engage in multiple homosexual experiences often influences the assessment of claimant legitimacy, an example being when the assigned adjudicator took "the sum total of the claimant's homosexual experiences" into consideration when assessing the testimony of an Ethiopian gay male claimant (TA5–16633, 6). The claimant testified that he had engaged in two homosexual experiences, one as a teenager and one in his early twenties. For this particular adjudicator, two sexual experiences – despite taking place in a recognized homophobic country – were "hardly a pattern of homosexual activity ... that would lead someone to accuse the claimant of homosexuality" (TA5–16633, 9). This logic also pervades the assessment of bisexual claimants, resonant with stereotypes of bisexuals as "sexually voracious or pathologically promiscuous" (Rehaag 2009, 426). In a decision involving an eighteen-year-old bisexual female from Saint Lucia, the adjudicator found the claimant's lack of sexual activity during her time in Canada suspicious – "The claimant testified that she has not been sexually active [in Canada]. She [the claimant] says she is underage to go to gay clubs and she is busy with going to school. It is difficult to believe how a person sexually active with a male and two females from the age of 14 is living a celibate life now" (TA6–12910, 4). Stereotyping homosexuals and bisexuals as promiscuous can lead to inconsistencies between adjudicators' assumptions about relationship patterns and claimant testimony.

Interestingly, one's relationship pattern can also be assessed with regards to the degree of permanency. While claimant testimony is deemed suspicious when it fails to match heteronormative assumptions about queer sexual experience, long-term relationships – while contradicting reliance on the assumption of promiscuity – often lend an element of legitimacy to the claim. References including "a two-year homosexual relationship" (TA5–16134, 5), "She does not currently have a partner" (TA6–00989, 4) and "It was pointed out by the claimant in his oral testimony that he had a ten-year relationship" (TA6–02210, 4) suggest that the seriousness of the relationship factors into assessments of homosexual claimants. This is not to suggest that being in a long-term homosexual relationship automatically qualifies one for refugee status; however, it appears to strengthen the credibility that one is, in fact, a sexual minority. A lesbian woman from Nigeria was denied refuge on the grounds that she previously had a common-law heterosexual relationship that included children (TA6–00989). The type of relationship therefore plays an important role in proving one's sexual identity. Furthermore, it appears that being a sexual minority means consistently being a sexual minority, and consistently being a sexual minority means being unswervingly homosexual. These expectations place sexual minority refugee claimants in a double bind. Claimants who fail to meet preconceived assumptions about queer relationship patterns are questioned, while at the same time, long-term relationship patterns strengthen their claims. Indeed, sexual minority refugee claimants are potentially damned either way.

In addition to adjudicators examining claimants' relationships in their home countries, claimants who spend time in Canada prior to applying for refugee status are expected to develop relationships in Canada that lend legitimacy to their claimed sexual orientation.[18] Fearful of the homophobic climate in their countries of origin, claimants describe Canada in their testimonies as a place where they can be their true selves, free of violence and discrimination. As such, claimants are expected to prove their commitment to explore their newly acquired sexual freedom; failure to do so can call the claimant's sexual orientation into question. This was evident in a decision involving a gay male from Indonesia, the adjudicator commenting, "You [the claimant] had no homosexual relationships since you have been in Canada ... I find your actions after arriving in Canada are inconsistent with your comments that you make in your PIF [Personal Information Form], that you are here in fact to have an open gay lifestyle. I find that you are not a homosexual" (TA6–03304, 4). Similar grounds for refusal were used in a decision involving a lesbian claimant from China, the adjudicator stating he was "not convinced she [the claimant] was a homosexual because she had not entered into any homosexual relationships with anyone while in Canada" (TA6–03337, 3), and in a decision involving a gay male from Ukraine, another adjudicator concluding that the Board "could not ignore that the claimant had not participated in any homosexual relationships in Canada despite having been there for a year" (TA5–03780, 4). Assessment of sexual minority refugee claimants is therefore influenced by their relationships with others, both in their home countries as well as in Canada. As confusing and contradictory as this evaluation of relationship evidence appears, a claimant's sexual conduct with others impacts their claim of sexual minority status.

IRB adjudicators' focus on relationship patterns has implications specific to bisexual claimants as well. As indicated in IRB decisions involving bisexual claimants, the relationship pattern of the claimant is often used to assess whether the claimant is heterosexual or homosexual. For example, in a case involving a bisexual female from Iran, the adjudicator concluded, "The claimant arrived in Canada with a male companion ... In response to the question as to whether they were planning to get married, the claimant replied, 'So far, there is a commitment but officially we haven't signed a paper or anything' ... [The claimant's] actions are those of a heterosexual woman."[19] Likewise, the adjudicator ruled that a bisexual woman was not legitimately bisexual due to her heterosexual conduct at the time of application:

> A problematic part of the testimony is her reference to her being in a relationship with a man after the end of her lesbian relationship ... That finding of a relationship with a man was preceded by a reference to her own testimony that she was bisexual. A review of the transcript indicates that she seems to have moved, over time, from heterosexual, to lesbian, to bisexual orientation, ultimately questioning the credibility of the claimant's account.[20]

In both decisions, the seriousness of the relationship, as well as the biological sex of the participants involved, had an impact on the legitimacy of bisexual claimant testimony. This was made clear in *Gyorgyjakab v Canada*, where the assigned adjudicator cited evidence suggesting that at the time of application, the bisexual female claimant was living with her boyfriend;[21] and in another decision involving a male bisexual claimant, the adjudicator concluded:

> At the hearing, the claimant testified that he loved his wife and believed in women again, his wife did everything he wanted, and they had a variety of sexual activities, satisfied each other, and lived together as a family. When asked whether he saw himself as a man having a need for sex only with his wife, the claimant answered that it was the case at the moment ... The claimant's testimony ... supported the panel's conclusion that he did not establish his homosexuality or bisexuality with persuasive evidence. (TA1–28696)

Similar to homosexual claimants, bisexual claimants are also questioned about their lack of homosexual relationships upon arriving in Canada; in a decision involving a bisexual male from Chile, the adjudicator concluded,

"The claimant is not an active bisexual by choice, as he did not act upon his alleged bisexuality in Chile nor in Canada. Ultimately, there is no indication that he will practice it in the future" (MA5–04358, 5). The adjudicator assessing an application involving a bisexual male from St. Vincent made an analogous query stating, "The claimant stated he did not have a current partner and had not had any partner in Toronto since he arrived. The Board found this explanation to be unsatisfactory and believes the evidence regarding his homosexuality or bisexuality to be lacking in credibility" (TA5–01198, 4). Approaching sexual orientation as a homosexuality-heterosexuality spectrum, rather than recognizing bisexuality as a sexual identity unto itself, implies that adjudicators often attempt to pinpoint which end of the spectrum the bisexual claimant is closer to.

This treatment of bisexuality is troublesome for several reasons. First, it fails to take the reality of bisexual experiences seriously. One's sexual identity is generally determined by the gender of their current or recent sexual partner. As a result, bisexuality is not seen as a standalone sexual identity; rather, it is an identity that lends itself to either homosexuality or heterosexuality. Current treatment of bisexual claimants highlights how one's relationship patterns further complicate this, ultimately ignoring the possibility that bisexuals are capable of engaging in relationships with concurrent sexual partners or in long-term monogamous relationships – something that, coincidentally enough, heterosexuals and homosexuals do as well. Rhetoric used in bisexual refugee decisions suggests that bisexuality is a form of dabbling; individuals are either gay or straight and use the label "bisexual" when they choose to dabble in the other. This flippant attitude toward bisexuality erases experiences that are unique to those who identify as bisexual. If we understand sexual orientation and sexual behaviour as connected but not necessarily codependent, then it is unclear "in what respect evidence that a refugee claimant maintains a sexually exclusive relationship could plausibly be read as challenging the credibility of his or her asserted bisexual identity" (Rehaag 2009, 428).

Attempts to determine the "true" sexual orientation of a bisexual claimant in order to assess the degree of harm the claimant has had or could experience assumes that the homosexual aspect of bisexuality is the only side susceptible to harm. In an Australian case involving a bisexual claimant, the Refugee Review Tribunal noted that "the notion of a group defined as 'bisexuals' has been considered insofar as the homosexual side of bisexuals ... were an issue" (N95/07313). Similarly, the IRB ruled in *Re B.D.K.* – the first refugee decision in Canada involving a bisexual claimant – that the claimant qualified as a sexual minority because he was a "bisexual man who prefers men."[22] This suggests that refugee boards are willing to consider the possibility that bisexuals can qualify for refugee status so long as the experienced persecution is a result of their homosexual tendencies. As Rehaag points out, this is concerning for bisexuals as well as homosexuals; while this process minimizes bisexual identity, it also interprets homosexuality as "the absence or antithesis of heterosexual desire" (2009, 426). Bisexual claimants' relationship patterns can be used to quantify their homosexual and heterosexual tendencies and to assess which side is more prominent, constituting the claimants' true sexual orientation. In doing so, claimants in these decisions were evaluated on their ability to pass as heterosexuals, relieving the Canadian state of any obligation to provide protection.

Finally, assessing one's ability to pass as a heterosexual ignores the complexity of homophobia. Discourses of heteronormativity rely on a politics of passing; traditional interpretations of passing are extended to include certain sexual minorities capable of "fitting in" within a normalized heteronormative framework. It is evident in these obtained decisions that IRB members often assess bisexual refugee claimants on their ability to pass as heterosexual, for example, accusing a bisexual male claimant from Nigeria of "downplaying his heterosexual life in order to impress the Board about his homosexual life" (TA5–07252, 3), and commenting on a case involving a bisexual male claimant from Jamaica that "if he [the claimant] was having a relationship with a person of the opposite sex as a cover up for his homosexuality, then surely his second heterosexual relationship seems to be overkill" (TA5–10217, 4). This discourse of passing assumes that homophobia is not experienced by those deemed capable of fitting into the heterosexual world. One can experience homophobia on a multitude of levels, regardless of their ability to pass. Adopting a rhetoric of passing for the assessment of bisexual refugee claimants reinforces heteronormative privilege, as it attempts to push claimants who pass as heterosexual into a space where they are perceived to be immune to persecution.

The invisibility of bisexuality in Canadian law and policy has made it difficult for adjudicators to pinpoint what constitutes a well-founded claim of sexual persecution for bisexual refugee claimants. As a result, bisexuality is interpreted as a middle ground between homosexuality and heterosexuality, placing one's relationship patterns at the forefront of possible indicators to determine where one falls on the sexual orientation spectrum. The notion that relationship history sufficiently serves as proof of bisexuality is unsustainable, as an ambiguous understanding of bisexual identity directly translates into unfair assessment mechanisms for refugee claimants. By not taking bisexuality seriously, some adjudicators approach the relationship patterns of bisexual refugee claimants with unfounded skepticism.

Providing "Concrete Proof" of Queer Relationship Patterns

In addition to relying heavily on relationship patterns, trends in determination cases suggest that some adjudicators expect claimants to provide physical proof in order to corroborate their relationship narratives. In a decision involving a lesbian claimant from Nigeria, the adjudicator questioned the seriousness of the claimant's current relationship noting, "In spite of her close bond with her partner, she never received any correspondence from her while travelling abroad" (TA6–00989, 4). This was echoed in the assessment of a gay male claimant from Pakistan, the adjudicator drawing attention to the perceived suspiciousness of the claimant's nine-year relationship with another man:

> He [the claimant] was also asked during the nine-year period he and XXXX were together, whether they exchanged any letters or cards. The claimant relied that he did not have any. He was asked if they ever had a picture taken together and responded they had once, but he does not have one. The panel finds that the claimant has not established his identity as a homosexual. (TA6–02210, 5)

Despite the claimants' testimony that they were both in long-term same-sex relationships, the adjudicators assigned to these cases questioned the lack of physical proof they believed necessary to substantiate the claims.

The expectation of corroborating evidence sends mixed messages to claimants. On one hand, it suggests that genuine relationships require a public element. This is particularly evident when claimant testimony included discussions of long-term relationships; in the obtained decisions, a lack of correspondence between couples often raised suspicion concerning the legitimacy of the relationship, and ultimately the individual's claim of sexual minority status. Written communication between individuals is typically considered private; however, it becomes public when used as a way to gain state recognition. Commentary in the above decisions therefore suggests that a public component to the claimant's relationship narrative can potentially enhance the legitimacy of the testimony.

On the other hand, claimants are often criticized for having their homosexuality discovered, the expectation being that sexual minorities should know better to keep their sexual orientation hidden in order to avoid situations of discrimination and abuse. In a decision involving a lesbian claimant from Nigeria, the adjudicator commented, "The fact that Nigeria is a homophobic society ... suggests that the claimant, as a lesbian, could not be unaware of the continuing peril she faced" (TA6–00989, 5). This was echoed in another decision involving a Nigerian man – specifically his account of getting caught kissing another man at his place of employment – when the validity of the claimant's testimony was questioned by the assigned adjudicator: "I asked the claimant why he and his friend would have started kissing and hugging in the store in view of passers by, knowing how much homosexuality is rejected by Nigerian society" (MA4–06500, 4). Similarly, in a case involving a claimant from Moldova, the adjudicator stated, "The claimant agreed that he knew Moldova was homophobic. It is unreasonable for the claimant and his older lover not to have been extremely careful and not to have carelessly forgotten to close the door" (TA4–03989, 3–4). In these decisions, the claimants' failure to remain in the closet called their claims of persecution into question, the assumption being that legitimate sexual minorities living in homophobic countries avoid being caught engaging in nonheterosexual acts because those who are never caught are never accused of being homosexual.

Enforcing a paradoxical understanding of sexuality-based persecution, sexual minority refugee claimants are simultaneously expected to prove they are victims of sexuality-based persecution and to make sure their sexual orientation remains private in order to pass as heterosexuals. As such, it is challenging for a claimant to substantiate a claim of sexual persecution when getting caught in a homosexual act is often used to ascertain whether a claim is well-founded. This task is further complicated when claimants are then expected to provide a paper trail that verifies their relationship narrative. Sexual minority refugee claimants are placed in a no-win situation. Claimants are criticized for getting caught or for not having proof of their nonheterosexual relationships, proof that could inevitably lead to them getting caught. The reliance on physical proof as evidence for one's relationship history is therefore contradictory and establishes vague expectations for sexual minority refugee claimants.

Future Considerations and International Response

A reliance on relationship patterns highlights how queer claimants can be simultaneously accused of not living up to stereotypes that paint them as promiscuous beings and penalized for not engaging in long-term same-sex relationships. Relationship patterns can also be used to assess the true sexual orientation of bisexual claimants, ultimately determining whether claimants can pass as heterosexuals or require protection from the Canadian state. Inconsistent assessment of one's relationship patterns makes it difficult for sexual minority refugee claimants to have their sexual orientation taken seriously, let alone obtain access to Canadian borders.

Relationship patterns are also used to reproduce Western conceptions of sexuality and reproduce certain sexual stereotypes. While a single homogeneous understanding of Western sexuality does not exist, Mohanty contends that "it is possible to trace a coherence of effects resulting from the implicit assumption of 'the West' (in all its complexities and contradictions) as the primary referent in theory and practice" (2003, 17–18). Canada's refugee program relies on an understanding of the Western sexual minority in order to assess the non-Western sexual minority, a process developed by "us" to help "them." Sexual minority refugee claimants constitute a universal victimized group in need of liberation that only the Canadian state can provide. The IRB thus fails to account for the reality that individuals – both inside and outside Canada – do not experience or express their sexuality in uniform fashion.

Using one's relationship patterns as proof of sexual orientation often makes it difficult for sexual minority refugee claimants to meet adjudicators' assessment expectations. Considering that sexual minorities seek refugee status in order to flee the homophobic climate of their home country, the obligation to prove that a relationship pattern does exist through the provision of physical proof is unrealistic for many claimants. Moreover, those who provide proof are often accused of being careless, subjecting their testimony to further scrutiny. The question then remains: How can there be a reliance on relationship patterns when the expectation is that nonheterosexual relationships remain hidden? Contradictory expectations make it difficult for sexual minority refugee claimants to prove that their sexual orientation and the persecution they experience as a result is consistent with adjudicators' assumptions about sexual orientation and identity.

Critics took issue with the UNHCR's 2008 *Guidance Note,* citing the document's failure to provide a comprehensive analysis of determination processes for sexual minority refugee claimants. In addition to guidance notes that lacked legislative muscle, primary queer rights stakeholders, activists, and experts were excluded from the drafting process (LaViolette 2010, 177). In response, the UNHCR released a more substantive framework in 2012, providing legislative guidance to decision makers and policy practitioners responsible for carrying out sexual minority refugee determinations. While the UNHCR has traditionally implemented an understanding of sexual orientation similar to *Ward,* that of being fixed and unchangeable, the guidelines signify a shift by cautioning that a claimant's sexual identity could still be evolving. As such, the UNHCR interprets self-identification as the following:

Self-identification should be taken as an indication of the individual's sexual orientation. While some applicants will be able to provide proof of their status, for instance through witness statements, photographs or other documentary evidence, they do not need to document activities in the country of origin indicating their different sexual orientation or gender identity. Where the applicant is unable to provide evidence as to his or her sexual orientation, and/or there is a lack of sufficiently specific country of origin information, the decision-maker will have to rely on that person's testimony alone. If the applicant's account appears credible, he or she should, unless there are good reasons to the contrary, be given the benefit of the doubt. (UNHCR 2012, Principle 11)

The main premise of this definition of self-identification is that individuals should have the capacity to declare and confirm their sexual orientation without external confirmation. While external evidence can support a claimant's application, the legitimacy of one's claim of sexual minority status should not be determined by third-party confirmation alone. This is not to suggest that a claim of persecution should be made without evidence; rather, self-identification refers to claimants not having to satisfy adjudicators that they are in fact a sexual minority. Evidence would therefore be used to evaluate claims of persecution. In this light, adjudicators would be convinced that a claimant is a sexual minority by their declaration alone.

As the UNHCR states, a limited interpretation of sexual orientation disregards the reality that "not all applicants will self-identify with the LGBTI [lesbian-gay-bisexual-transgender and/or intersex) terminology and constructs as presented by them [decision-makers] or may be unaware of these labels" (2012, Principle 11). To ameliorate this, the guidelines encourage decision makers to avoid determination assessments based on "superficial understandings of the experiences of LGBTI persons, or on erroneous, culturally inappropriate or stereotypical assumptions" (2012, Principle 4). Self-identification therefore requires an element of public recognition in the form of adjudicators recognizing alternative terminologies and constructs. The extent to which this is possible under current Canadian determination practices is unclear in the guidelines; current methods of assessment for sexual minority refugee claims thus need to be revisited in order to ascertain how the Canadian state understands self-identification and whether this interpretation is consistent with UNHCR's guidelines (Gaucher and DeGagné 2016; LaViolette 2014; Hersh 2015). Indeed, there needs to be a conversation – both nationally and internationally – regarding these proposed flexible boundaries for sexual minority refugee claimants and the implications they present for claimants and decision makers.

As a refugee-receiving country, it is essential that "we bear in mind that the stakes in refugee determinations are immense" (Rehaag 2009, 429).

Sexual minorities seek refugee status in order to flee from violently oppressive practices in their countries of origin; negative and wrongly decided claims result in claimants being deported to situations where they will potentially face persecution, torture, and death. It is therefore imperative that determination processes for sexual minority refugee claimants are able to consistently accommodate differentiation within this group of potential claimants. As this chapter demonstrates, IRB adjudicators' evaluations of relationship evidence are often unevenly applied, complicating claimant assessment. Moreover, intimate relationship patterns are used to reinforce sexual stereotypes. As a result, current refugee determinations ignore the lived experiences of homosexual and bisexual refugee claimants. This reliance on sexual stereotypes and an assessment of a sexual minority refugee claimant's relationship pattern is used to assess a claimant's deviation from the conjugal nuclear family, which is then used to assess whether the claimant is, in fact, a sexual minority in need of state protection. These trends in assessment suggest that even in an individualized process like refugee assessment, relationships play a role in the provision of citizenship. Adjudicators work under the assumption that upon obtaining entry, refugees will either start a family here or start the process of sponsoring family members from abroad (Interviews). Interestingly, it is not until a refugee becomes a permanent resident that they can apply to sponsor family members. Refugees are therefore assessed according to their future family formations without the guarantee of family reunification. Relationship history is used to filter sexual minority refugee claims and assess potential claims for citizenship despite the fact that claimants apply for status as individuals, and refugee status is not a necessary or sufficient condition for future family development.

Legal precedence has paved the way for state treatment of homosexual refugee claimants; however, there has not been a similar path provided to bisexuals seeking refuge. Consequently, this has resulted in bisexual claimants being assessed according to preconceptions of homosexuality and heterosexuality. Ultimately, methods of assessment for both homosexuals and bisexuals are flawed both in terms of the stereotypes that shape these policies and the mechanisms used to assess claimant testimony. Proper reform thus requires deconstructing sexual stereotypes, including the connection between relationship history and sexual orientation. These connections also need to be examined in relation to changes made to the IRPA with the passing of Bill C-31, granting ministerial authority over the safe country list and citizenship revocation. While determination processes are necessary, there is room within the current framework to make Canada's refugee system more accessible for sexual minorities. Institutionalized assumptions about sexual minorities and their relationship patterns make for policy that are both exclusionary to potential claimants and unresponsive to the lived experiences of sexual minorities in Canada and abroad.

4

An Education in Conjugality: Experiences of Common-Law Couples with Spousal Sponsorship

"It is the kind of thing that nobody asks you to define unless you are communicating with the state. So socially, we weren't going around identifying ourselves as common-law because it doesn't often naturally come up in conversation."

– INTERVIEWED COMMON-LAW COUPLE

After living together in Canada for two years, Juliet – a Canadian citizen – applied to sponsor her partner, Peter – a citizen of New Zealand – through the spousal sponsorship program. Peter's student visa was reaching its expiration date, forcing the couple, who had met in university, to examine their options to keep Peter in Canada and their relationship local. Following their lawyer's advice, Peter and Juliet applied as a common-law couple, the result being a lengthy application process that focused on the intimate details of their relationship. Peter and Juliet were required to prove to Immigration, Refugees and Citizenship Canada (IRCC) that their relationship was genuine – that it was not formed solely for the purpose of allowing Peter to remain in Canada. This meant providing IRCC with physical evidence that corroborated their narrative of legitimate pre-application conjugal living, used by IRCC to assess the continuousness of the relationship post-application.

While there are no publicly available statistics breaking down spouse/ partner sponsorship with respect to the percentage of married versus common-law couples, interviewed IRCC policy analysts confirm that similar to trends within Canada, common-law spousal immigration is on the rise (Interviews). What is unique about Peter and Juliet's experiences with the spousal sponsorship program – and the experiences of common-law couples more generally – is the requirement for assessing conjugality for common-law and married couples. As previously discussed in Chapter 2, state inclusion of common-law relationships transpired through the extension of marital benefits to unmarried cohabiting couples; common-law relationships were treated identically to marital relationships. As a result, the Canadian state implemented a one-size-fits-all approach to conjugal relationship recognition, an approach that is generally more visible in immigration policy than in other areas of policy in Canada. When it comes to spousal sponsorship, married and common-law couples are uniformly assessed according to a single understanding of conjugality, suggesting equal treatment; however, by treating all conjugal couples identically, the spousal sponsorship program presents obstacles to common-law couples seeking sponsorship, obstacles that for the most part have been unaccounted for.

In this chapter, I examine several implications the spousal sponsorship program presents for common-law couples. While common-law relationships within Canadian borders are typically defined by cohabitation, the criterion used by IRCC to assess common-law conjugality interprets common-law as synonymous with marriage. My analysis highlights how IRCC's treatment of conjugal relationships as a universal group fails to account for differences between married and common-law relationships. I contend that despite its neutral phrasing, the current spousal sponsorship program favours married couples, and I explore how this favouring of marital conjugality results in a program accessible only to those common-law couples capable of providing a similar relationship narrative to married couples.

My examination relies primarily on interviews with seventeen common-law and married couples – both same-sex and opposite-sex – that successfully applied for spousal sponsorship.[1] For all interviewed couples, sponsorship took place between 2001, after the passing of the IRPA, and 2011. Lasting approximately two hours in length, interviews focused on the following key areas: (a) the couple's overall experience with spousal sponsorship; (b) any advice the couple received from immigration officers, lawyers, or consultants that shaped their application; (c) perceptions of how their conjugal status impacted their application; and (d) challenges the couple faced during the application process.[2] Two methodological considerations are worth nothing. First, this descriptive account of spousal sponsorship is one-sided. I was only able to interview couples whose applications for spousal sponsorship were accepted; therefore, my analysis does not include interviews with couples who were denied access. In light of this, I have compared trends inherent in positive applications as illuminated by the interviewees to the content obtained through the discourse analysis portion of this research, as well as to my interviews with policy stakeholders. Second, the small sample size of interviewed couples can be attributed to the sensitivity of the issue. Discussions with individuals working in the fields of immigrant settlement and integration highlighted the possibility that immigrants would be hesitant to volunteer, fearful that any discussion concerning their application could potentially harm their current status in Canada, particularly individuals whose applications were refused and who might now be living in Canada illegally.[3]

Family Class Conjugal Immigration in Canada

The federal government's manual *OP2: Processing Members of the Family Class (OP2)* outlines what immigration officers should look for when assessing a marital or common-law relationship for the purposes of spousal sponsorship. When a Canadian citizen wishes to sponsor his/her spouse, the couple must prove that their relationship is genuine and was not entered into primarily for the purpose of immigration. While historically marriages were viewed with less suspicion, recent concerns regarding marriage fraud have placed both groups under heightened scrutiny (Interviews). As outlined in *OP2*, assessing the genuineness of conjugal relationships depends on whether the relationship is a marriage or a common-law relationship. Marriages are seen as "status based," meaning that the relationship exists from the day the marriage is legally valid until the day it is legally terminated through death or divorce. Common-law relationships are considered "fact based," which means that the relationship exists "from the day in which two individuals can demonstrate that the relationship exists on the basis of facts." In *OP2*, IRCC recognizes significant differences between married and common-law relationships; however, the department states that it chooses to focus on the similarities and attributes this to the "history of the recognition in law of common-law relationships and their definition" (Citizenship and Immigration Canada 2006, s 5.25).

According to *OP2*, the primary similarity between marriages and common-law relationships is conjugality. This is what separates legitimate relationships deserving of reunification from illegitimate relationships. As *OP2* outlines, conjugality does not solely refer to sexual partners; it symbolizes an intimate attachment between two people (2006, s 5.25). Basing its assessment of conjugality on *Molodowich v Penttinen*, *OP2* stipulates that all conjugal relationships, married or unmarried, should embody characteristics of interdependency to a certain degree. These characteristics are then validated through documentary evidence, particularly for common-law couples whose relationships are considered fact based. Acceptable documentary evidence includes proof of cohabitation (mortgage, lease), joint bank accounts and insurance policies, proof of joint large-item purchases (car, furniture), proof of continuous communication (emails, letters, long distance phone bills), testimonies from friends, family members, and community/religious leaders, and photographic evidence of trips and major events (birthdays, holidays, weddings, commitment ceremonies) (Citizenship and Immigration Canada 2006, s 10.1).

An exception to IRCC's privileging of conjugality is its treatment of fiancé(e)s. Individuals who are dating with the intent of marrying or cohabiting do not qualify as conjugal. The category of fiancé(e) is viewed as an illegitimate relationship category under Canadian immigration law; while the intent to marry exists, traditional views on engagement assume that the long-distance engaged couple has yet to establish a sexual relationship (Citizenship and Immigration Canada 2006, s 10.1). As Lois Harder points out, "Canada's definition of good sexual citizenship would thus seem to suggest that pre-marital sex is an immigration requirement" (2008, 10). This example highlights that it is imperative we account for differentiation within the category of conjugality, as it is not a monolithic concept.

Similar to other areas of federal policy, IRCC defines a common-law partner as a person who is "cohabiting in a conjugal relationship for a period of at least one year" (Citizenship and Immigration Canada 2006, s 6). While immigration officers are instructed to account for the possibility that continuous cohabitation might not be realistic – particularly when one party is living in Canada and trying to sponsor the other – common-law couples who are separated at the time of application must prove that (a) they have lived together continuously for a year (pre-break) and (b) they would still be living together in the absence of these extenuating circumstances. Ultimately, the longer a couple is living separately, the more challenging it is to ascertain that a conjugal relationship exists (Citizenship and Immigration Canada 2006, s 5.36). Up until this point, it appears that common-law couples seeking reunification are treated the same way as common-law couples requesting conjugal benefits within Canadian borders. Both rely on an understanding of common law that is primarily defined by permanent conjugal cohabitation. This, however, is where the similarities end. While the technical definition for common-law is the same, assessment of common-law couples seeking sponsorship highlights a differentiation in treatment between those with Canadian citizenship (inside family) and those whose citizenship status remains precarious (outside family).

Unlike previously discussed trends in domestic policy, cohabitation alone is insufficient for spousal sponsorship. While common-law status in Canada is defined as "conjugal cohabitation," couples are generally not obliged to prove that their relationship is, in fact, conjugal to obtain conjugal benefits. This logic fails to translate to common-law couples applying for sponsorship; the combination of cohabitation and seeking reunification does not automatically convince immigration officers that the common-law relationship is genuinely conjugal. When it comes to family reunification, the outside family must prove that their relationship is genuinely conjugal, while the inside family is given the benefit of the doubt so long as cohabitation requirements are met. For both types of families, conjugality matters; however, it matters in different ways.

Moreover, the weight accorded to conjugality in the assessment of spousal sponsorship applications demonstrates that the way conjugality is defined shapes how the genuineness of these relationships is evaluated. Both married and common-law couples undergo intense scrutiny in a comparison of spousal sponsorship to areas of domestic policy. Immigration officers are instructed to use the state's understanding of marriage to assess the genuineness of martial and common-law relationships and to refuse applications that fail to meet these criteria (Fleras 2015, 140), ultimately reinforcing the state's one-size-fits-all approach to conjugal relationship recognition.

Challenges for Common-Law Couples Seeking Sponsorship

It is important to reiterate that similar to IRB adjudicators' assessment of sexual minority refugee claimants, there is no single standard formula for assessing spousal sponsorship applications. *OP2* provides immigration officers with guidelines for evaluation; however, the assigned officer determines the amount of evidence required. Satzewich contends that in the name of bureaucratic efficiency, immigration officers "cannot afford to approach every application as a blank slate," and, as such, they often triage applications according to a series of macro- (e.g., broader understandings of migration) and micro- (individual understandings of "normality") level forces, focusing attention toward applications that come across as "less credible" through this process (2015, 140–41). In examining these micro-level forces, my interviews with IRCC employees and married/common-law couples underscored three trends. First, focus tends to be on the early stages of the relationship rather than on the state of the relationship at the time of application. Since common-law relationships are considered fact-based, couples must provide proof that documents the entire relationship from its beginning to current time. Second, considerable emphasis is placed on the presence or absence of a wedding. Finally, current reliance on evidence to prove that conjugality exists as well as the types of permissible evidence required ignore implications unique to common-law couples, particularly same-sex common-law couples.

Relationship Present vs. Relationship Past

Contrary to many marriages, common-law relationships tend to develop more organically (Bowman 2010). Quite often couples move in together with no intention of officially identifying as common-law but over time become increasingly interdependent with the fusion of finances, raising of children, and so forth. This was evident in *Molodowich v Penttinen* – whether or not Penttinen felt his relationship with Molodowich was "marriage-like," the relationship had become conjugal. Moreover, common-law relationships are typically undefined as common-law until the point when a couple establishes contact with an institution. For married couples, getting married means being automatically entitled to marital benefits provided by the state. Common-law couples, however, are not recognized as common-law until they seek those same benefits. While recognition is followed by access to benefits for the married, recognition and benefits are one and the same for common-law couples.

In contrast to domestic policy where common-law relationships are generally assessed on their present-day status, those applying for spousal sponsorship must provide a timeline of conjugality. Moreover, increased attention is paid toward the beginning of the relationship. In addition to the general family class application process, spouses/partners must complete the *Sponsored Spouse/Partner Questionnaire*. For this part of the application, couples are divided into two groups: partners currently living in Canada and partners living outside of Canada.[4] Both married and common-law couples are required to fill out the same questionnaire, supporting criticisms that the federal government has adopted a one-size-fits-all approach toward accommodating common-law relationships. The first section – titled "First Meeting" – includes the following questions:

- When and where did you first meet your sponsor in person?
- Did anyone (individual or organization) introduce you to your sponsor?
- Did you give your sponsor any gifts?
- Did your sponsor give you any gifts?
- Give any additional details describing the circumstance of your first meeting with your sponsor.[5] (Immigration, Refugees and Citizenship Canada 2017c)

The second section – titled "Development of Your Relationship" – asks the following:

- Describe how your relationship developed after your first contact/meeting with your sponsor and if you and your sponsor dated or went on any outings or trips together.
- Was your relationship known to close friends and family?
- Did your sponsor meet any of your close friends and family? (Immigration, Refugees and Citizenship Canada 2017c)

These sections are used to identify arranged marriages and to assess whether the relationship in question, arranged or not, is a relationship formed solely for the purpose of immigration, a "marriage of convenience" (Interviews). If an applicant answers "no" to any of the questions outlined in the second section, an explanation is required. These questions require applicants to provide a detailed account of how their relationship evolved into something conjugal. Moreover, when an applicant answers "yes" to any of these questions, evidence is required that supports the claims.

While both married and common-law couples must complete these two sections, it was interviewed common-law couples who expressed difficulty. Common-law couples generally found it challenging to provide concrete details that highlighted the early stages of their relationship and corroborated their claim of genuine conjugality. This was due in part to the fact that for the majority of common-law interviewees, they did not officially identify as common-law until they chose to apply for spousal sponsorship. As Peter and Juliet commented, "We didn't consider ourselves common-law, even after a year of living together" (Interviews). Couples felt added pressure to satisfy officers' doubts that their relationships qualified as common-law, particularly when they had not identified officially as common-law themselves pre-application.

This was compounded by the fact that, unlike marriage, the legal category of common-law is not a universal concept. An interviewee from Bosnia stated, "In Bosnia, there is not a direct translation for common-law status. It exists legally, but it is not part of colloquial understanding. So even in the translation, it was 'Latinized.' Friends and family in Bosnia were laughing that my parents were attesting that they knew their daughter was in a monogamous, exclusive, conjugal relationship" (Interviews). The cultural particularity of common-law status further complicates the application process for unmarried cohabiting couples. Without a common language of nonmarital conjugality, it can be challenging for applicants to provide an application that satisfies all conditions.[6] "I felt there was more pressure because we were common-law. At the same time, we know that even if we had been married, we could have still had to document that there was a relationship. So maybe there was not more pressure, but definitely more stress because the terms of common-law status are fuzzy compared to marriage" (Interviews). Ultimately, the ambiguous language of unmarried cohabitation, combined with the reality that common-law relationships tend to develop organically, puts pressure on common-law couples to produce a narrative consistent with Canadian standards of conjugality.

A related frustration with the application process was the expressed invasion of privacy. For married applicants, a marriage certificate provides a starting point for state identification of a legitimate conjugal relationship; evidence included in the application merely offers context that a genuine relationship existed pre-wedding and continues to exist post-wedding. In contrast, immigration lawyers and consultants advised common-law interviewees that their relationships lacked a finite starting point and, as such, required more evidence that the relationship was "genuine, monogamous, exclusive, and conjugal" (Interviews). This process was described as a "CSI investigation of our relationship because we had to prove a timeline of being common-law, as well as the awkward component of proving on paper that not only do we cohabitate, but we do so in a conjugal manner" (Interviews). Shared sentiment among interviewees, both married and common-law, was that with a marriage certificate, the "monogamous, exclusive, and conjugal" aspects of the relationship were assumed; ultimately, the only proof required was that which supported the applicants' claims that their marriages were not marriages of convenience. On the other hand, applying as common-law required proving that all four characteristics were present.

Marriage – Wedding = Common-Law

For both married and common-law couples, a significant amount of attention is directed toward the actual wedding. For married couples, a section in the questionnaire titled "Information about Your Marriage" requires details about the proposal, the engagement, and the wedding ceremony. Couples are asked to provide particulars about the wedding ceremony including date, location, number of attendees, family members in attendance, and religious component, confirming these details with photographic evidence.[7] In addition, couples are expected to provide analogous specifics about the wedding reception, as well as the honeymoon. Similar to other sections, answering "no" to any of these questions requires further explanation. Moreover, applicants must justify the absence of proof if they answer "yes" and are unable to provide details requested by IRCC. For example, if a couple got married without their family in attendance, they are required to explain why. This suggests that IRCC expects a wedding narrative that coincides with traditional Western notions of marriage and marital ceremony.

For immigration officers, the absence of a wedding or wedding traditions results in applications being red flagged (Interviews). As one immigration officer explained:

> If there is no actual ceremony, I want to know why. If no one attends the ceremony, I want to know why. If there are no photos of the event, I want to know why. Most couples that get married have a wedding, have their families there, eat cake, and dance, etc. So if I have an application and those details aren't there? That means I have to ask more questions to make sure it is not a marriage of convenience. (Interviews)

Another interviewed immigration officer justified IRCC's reliance on the wedding by referring to its universality, commenting, "Whether you're in an arranged marriage or a nonarranged marriage, both are typically celebrated with a ceremony of some kind. So this section of the questionnaire is not meant to distinguish between different kinds of marriages; it is meant to weed out the bad ones" (Interviews). By partaking in this normalized rite of social intimacy, a married couple's relationship is more likely to be viewed as genuine for the purposes of immigration.

The pressure not only to adhere to this narrative of the wedding ritual but also to observe it in a manner consistent with IRCC's expectations was expressed by one of the interviewed married couples. Having decided to get married at Toronto City Hall in lieu of a more documentable wedding ceremony, this couple then faced the challenge of explaining their decision in the questionnaire. In their account of the application process, they concluded that "the most difficult part was explaining the circumstances of our wedding [getting married at City Hall]. We had to explain why our parents were not there, why they were not invited, why we chose not to have a formal ceremony afterwards, and why we chose not to go on a honeymoon" (Interviews). On the surface, their reasoning was simple – they wanted to get married at city hall. When it came to completing the questionnaire, however, they were advised by their lawyer to overcompensate by providing more evidence that their relationship was genuine in order to counterbalance their nontraditional ceremony – "He told us that while a wedding at city hall wouldn't raise that many eyebrows, a wedding at city hall without our families, or a reception, or a honeymoon probably would" (Interviews). As such, the couple constructed a narrative claiming that the only reason they were married at city hall was financial; their financial status led to their choosing to hold a small service. Their response implied that if they had had the financial resources, they would have had a more traditional wedding. IRCC's focus on the wedding pressures married couples to justify either the absence of a public element to their conjugal relationship or a public element that is inconsistent with traditional expectations of the ceremony itself.

IRCC's focus on the presence or absence of a traditional wedding ceremony has implications for common-law couples as well. Considering that legitimacy seems to be more easily documentable when there is public recognition, common-law couples are asked in the questionnaire to discuss whether there was a formal ceremony to recognize/celebrate the relationship. Similar to wedding-related questions for married couples, common-law couples are required to provide details if there was a ceremony and an explanation if there was not. Moreover, couples must explain the absence of family members and friends if there was a formal ceremony. Like married couples, common-law couples are expected to justify the absence of public celebration.

In addition to having to answer questions regarding ceremony, common-law couples are obligated to explain why they are not married and if they intend on getting married in the future. A former policy analyst justified this question, claiming that it assists in their assessment of common-law couples because "most common-law couples end up getting married at some point" (Interviews). For several interviewed common-law couples, responding to this question required a careful answer. As one couple remarked:

> It is a loaded question. There are several ways you could answer that ... we object to the institution of marriage and the subjugation of women in this institution. That is not going to play well with bureaucrats. So

what we said was – and this is partially true – is that we're poor, and we are looking to get married in the future, but we're both away from our families and cannot afford a wedding. So we constructed that into a carefully worded paragraph. (Interviews)

This was echoed by another couple that explained in their application they had postponed getting married until they could marry in his home country in order for his ailing mother to attend (Interviews). From a policy perspective, the purpose of the questionnaire is for immigration officers to assess the likelihood of the relationship continuing post-sponsorship; however, in practice, continuousness for a common-law relationship is potentially confirmed through the promise of marriage. As one interviewed common-law couple commented:

There is a heightened sense of legitimacy to the act of marriage that if you are common-law, there is more of a burden to prove the genuineness and continuousness of a relationship. What is interesting is that there are couples who are in common-law relationships for years, couples who get married after a month, and there are couples in arranged marriages ...: all of which who are in genuine continuous relationships. So marriage and a continuous relationship are not necessarily one and the same. Even long-term marriages and continuous relationships are not one and the same. (Interviews)

These couples expressed feeling pressure to justify their decision not to marry, but to do so in a way that avoided suggesting aversion to the institution of marriage. In this light, a common-law relationship comes across as a transitional period between singledom and marriage, instead of a life choice in and of itself. Common-law couples felt they were faced with two choices – either defend their decision to choose a common-law relationship over marriage and potentially jeopardize their chances of being approved, or provide a misconstrued account of why a marriage has yet to take place and a promise of marital plans for the future.[8]

IRCC's focus on the wedding in its questionnaire highlights two important points. First, for both married and common-law couples, a significant amount of attention is paid to ceremony. Married couples are required to provide details of the ceremony, reception, and honeymoon; couples who do not have a wedding or opt for a nontraditional wedding must provide an explanation. Common-law couples are asked to provide similar details about the presence or absence of a commitment ceremony to publicly celebrate their relationship. Moreover, they are obligated to explain their choosing common-law over marriage – "Clearly a marriage is not always ubiquitous of what a good relationship is; however, it is from a bureaucratic point of view" (Interviews). While both married and common-law couples are scrutinized, they are assessed according to the state's interpretation of the ideal marriage and marital ceremony.

Ceremony-related questions in the questionnaire suggest that legitimacy is more easily recognizable with public acknowledgment; marriage provides IRCC with an important interrogation opportunity. As interviewed policy analysts and immigration officers confirmed, the details of a marriage story are a great place to spot fraud (Interviews). The normative force of marriage has made it an expeditious site for detection of false claims. The problem is that in their quest for expediency, IRCC has developed an application premised on a single understanding of conjugality and conjugal ceremony. While focus on the wedding has implications for both married and common-law couples, the framing of the questionnaire establishes a standard for conjugality that is more conducive to married couples, resulting in the unfair treatment of common-law couples. Instead of being defined primarily by cohabitation, common-law couples are required to justify their relationship decisions in reference to the presence or absence of ceremony, which in the case of Canadian conjugality is epitomized by the wedding.

Second, interviewees expressed pressure to provide an account of their relationship that corresponded with Western narratives of relationship patterns, as made evident in one couple's response:

> For me, a big wedding is not important, but our answer suggested that we were not married because we could not afford the big wedding that we want to have. But really, you can get married for one hundred bucks. So the fact that we were poor really has no significance if we were really committed to being married. The plausibility of our answer, however ... the woman who wants the big wedding ... our answer is really good and

did not raise any suspicion, even though it is partly true, but we have
many reasons why we are not actually married.[9] (Interviews)

This was echoed by several interviewed couples who claimed financial
status as their primary justification for either not having a traditional
wedding or not getting married at all. The decision to emphasize financial
constraint is an interesting one, as sponsors are also evaluated on their
ability to financially provide for their sponsored spouse or partner.
Canadian governments have been and continue to prioritize ensuring that
a sponsor has adequate funds to support their sponsored family members;
therefore, any weakness on that front could be considered a risky strategy.
Interviewed common-law couples who used this justification, however,
were encouraged by immigration lawyers to use financial status as their
primary reason to not marry. As one couple commented, "He [their immigration lawyer] asked us why we weren't married, and we gave a couple
reasons ... we had never discussed marriage, our families lived far away,
we couldn't afford a wedding. He stopped us right there and said, 'Yes.
That's it. Use the lack of money reason.' So we did" (Interviews). These
couples were under the impression that while mentioning financial weakness might be risky, the legitimacy of their relationship and its proximity
to the marital norm was a greater risk to a positive assessment. For couples
whose relationships were not marked by a public ceremony or were marked
by a nontraditional public ceremony, the challenge was to construct a
conceivable explanation that would not minimize the particular narrative
of conjugality engrained in Canadian society.

One could argue that this process is no different than in any other state
program that demands certain behaviours in order to qualify. Indeed, as
Chapter 2 suggests, domestic policy in Canada relies on a specific understanding of the conjugal family unit. What is different about conjugal
relationships in the context of immigration is that citizenship is at stake.
If Canadian citizens living within Canadian borders choose to get married
or to not get married, to live together or to not live together, their decisions
could result in the refusal of state recognition of their relationship; however,
their citizenship would not be revoked. At the end of the day, regardless
of the types of personal relationships they form, they remain citizens. For
the sponsorship-seeking couple, the provision of citizenship relies on the

genuineness of the relationship in question as determined by the assigned immigration officer. This is not to suggest that this power imbalance between immigration officers and spousal sponsorship applicants is avoidable or even unjustifiable; the very enforcement of physical borders requires some form of assessment protocol, meaning that power imbalances are inevitable. The question is whether these imbalances generate inequalities between families. While there are other state programs that require a specific type of behaviour in order to qualify, access to citizenship is not hanging in the balance and, as such, the appropriateness of these inequalities needs to be taken into consideration.

Proving Conjugality

IRCC's reliance on evidence to prove a conjugal relationship exists ignores the implications that these evidence requirements hold for common-law couples. IRCC's approach to assessing common-law applications as fact based means that conjugality is evaluated on the existence of factual evidence. Couples are expected to use evidence to support a timeline of conjugal living deemed worthy of immigration status by the assigned immigration officer. All interviewees – both married and common-law – discussed the tedious nature of this process, having to organize details in order to provide the immigration officer with a clear, comprehensive application. Comparatively speaking, however, common-law couples expressed more discomfort with the process than did their married counterparts. This discomfort was primarily equated with the perceived pressure to prove that in the absence of a marriage certificate, their relationships were, in fact, conjugal. This raises the question: If common-law conjugality is treated synonymously with marriage, what are the implications of the current fact based approach for common-law couples?

As previously discussed, interviewed common-law couples found it difficult to provide details about the early stages of their relationship that corroborated their claim of common-law conjugality, particularly because they did not seek state recognition prior to applying for spousal sponsorship. As Peter commented:

> I had come to Canada on a student visa, which was close to expiring, and was looking at my options post-graduation to work in Canada. I qualified

then as a federal skilled worker because of my research experience ... that was a really drawn out process. I went to a few information sessions about the immigration process and was told that I was looking at a minimum of two years to be assessed. We went to an immigration lawyer and found out that we could apply as common-law. I could be sponsored through Juliet. He [the lawyer] was saying, "Absolutely, go through common-law as it is much quicker ... as long as you can show evidence that proves your common-law status, then that is the way to go." (Interviews)

For Peter and Juliet, it was not until they applied for spousal sponsorship that they identified as common-law. While they had lived together for over two years at the time of application, their relationship had evolved without any official declaration to the state – "There were things we did consciously in 'common-lawliness,' but formally it was the immigration application" (Interviews). Other common-law interviewees provided similar narratives; they lived in conjugal relationships that were officially recognized by the state when one partner applied to sponsor the other.

As a result of cohabitation requirements, common-law couples must already be common-law in order to qualify. This is not to suggest that common-law couples are incapable of forming relationships of convenience; however, unless there are extenuating circumstances, a one-year cohabitation period is obligatory. This often leads immigration officers to assume that because common-law couples have lived conjugally for an extended period of time, they should be able to provide proof of conjugality similar to that of married couples (Interviews). Due to the less formal development of their relationships, interviewed common-law couples elaborated on the challenge of amassing evidence to substantiate their claims of being more than roommates. For some couples, not having planned to formally claim common-law status meant that they had not anticipated having to provide physical evidence of conjugal living. This is evident in the range of evidence provided by interviewees including train ticket receipts, photos, boarding passes, leases, bank statements, bills, etc. After being asked to prove that their relationship was conjugal and mon-ogamous, one couple included the receipt of a queen-sized bed they had co-purchased; another couple provided their immigration officer with intimate emails they had exchanged while apart. Both couples felt this was an extreme violation of their privacy – "Due to the personal nature of the emails, we felt our privacy was being violated, so we tried to weed out some of the more personal emails but were still trying to demonstrate that we were more than friends" (Interviews).

Married couples are required to prove that their relationship is genuine, while common-law couples must prove that their relationship is conjugal. To put it simply, married couples are considered conjugal until proven nonconjugal and common-law couples are considered nonconjugal until proven conjugal (Interviews). This differentiation in approach fails to translate into different expectations depending on the relationship in question. As such, the current program is not cognizant of the difference in starting points for married and common-law couples, resulting in frustrations for common-law couples with respect to the provision of evidence.

These frustrations were particularly evident for same-sex common-law interviewees. Comparatively speaking, the Canadian state has been favourable toward homosexual relationship recognition. This has been attributed to the institutional importance of the Supreme Court (Matthews 2005; Smith 2007), successful mobilization of gay and lesbian advocacy groups (Lahey and Alderson 2004), and a rights-supportive societal culture (Epp 1998). It is important to remember, however, that Canada is only one of a handful of countries that recognize same-sex marriage and same-sex domestic partnerships (common-law). One could assume that because obtaining immigration status as a common-law couple is not solely dependent on home state recognition, the Canadian state is conscious of the reality that same-sex, unmarried cohabiting couples do not have universal access to state recognition. What is concerning about this assumption is that while it clearly accounts for institutional homophobia, IRCC's reliance on physical evidence to assess conjugality ignores the very real possibility of societal homophobia.

After living together in Slovakia for two years, Sarah – a Canadian citizen – applied to sponsor her partner, Alena. While compiling their application, the couple found it difficult to collect physical evidence that proved their relationship was conjugal. In their account of the process, Sarah explained:

> We were living together in a relationship, but we were not public about it ... that is not something you do where we were. When we applied [for

spousal sponsorship], we had a hard time giving them proof that we were in a serious relationship ... we didn't have any photos, our family didn't know we were together ... we lived in a two-bedroom apartment. It was difficult to prove that we were more than roommates. (Interviews)

By neglecting the homophobic social climate of many countries, common-law, same-sex couples are expected to provide evidence that might be difficult to obtain. Required criterion assumes that same-sex and opposite-sex common-law couples are treated similarly. Moreover, it supposes that all same-sex couples are "out" to their friends, family, and community. For Sarah and Alena, providing physical evidence of their monogamous conjugal relationship was challenging as a result of their sexual orientation and geographical location, factors unaccounted for in the spousal sponsorship application. Identical evidence requirements for married and common-law couples thus have implications for common-law couples as a group, as well as those specific for same-sex couples.

Finally, in order to prove that their relationships are genuine, common-law couples require third-party validation – "You are officially advised to provide a list of people who can attest to having known you as a conjugal couple" (Interviews). When applying for common-law benefits within Canadian borders, a couple's declaration of their relationship to the state is theirs alone. In the case of spousal sponsorship, however, couples are asked to include testimony from friends, family members, and community/ religious leaders who can speak to the conjugal nature of their relationship, reinforcing the need for public validation of one's intimate relationships. Letters of relationship reference provide an element of public legitimacy that the state believes genuine conjugal relationships should possess.

This is particularly fascinating for several reasons. It suggests that our friends, family members, and community/religious leaders are fully aware of the intimate details of our personal relationships. By attesting to the conjugal nature of the relationship in question, these testimonies suggest that references assume that the relationship is monogamous, conjugal, and exclusive. While it is impossible to speak for all couples, I find it difficult to believe that all couples typically share these details with others, at least to the extent that renders these individuals qualified to speak to them for the purpose of immigration. Ultimately, these testimonies are based on assumptions, which questions their effectiveness in application assessment.

Second, returning to Sarah and Alena, it assumes that family members, friends, and community/religious leaders are willing to speak to the conjugal nature of these relationships. For this couple, acquiring references was challenging because they were not "out" to many. This challenge, however, is not limited to same-sex couples. Potential references might decline providing testimony if they have never met the partner, have only met the partner a few times, disapprove of the relationship for religious or cultural reasons, or are estranged from the couple. There are situations where these testimonies are difficult, if not impossible, to obtain. It is therefore misleading to assume that letters of reference are easily accessible.

When the issue of reference accessibility was brought up in my interviews with IRCC policy analysts, one interviewee explained that this is why IRCC has a "conjugal" category (Interviews). In addition to spouses and common-law partners, the IRPA recognizes conjugal partners that are unable to live together as a conjugal couple. In theory, couples like Sarah and Alena could apply under the conjugal category, and the state would assess their application accordingly. Interviewed immigration officers, however, told a different story. When asked about the conjugal category, one interviewee admitted that in the absence of cohabitation, success rates for couples applying under the conjugal category are low.[10] As one immigration officer commented, "In my twenty-five years as an immigration officer, I have maybe seen fifty conjugal applications, and in those fifty, I think I passed two" (Interviews). The conjugal category therefore does not guarantee same-sex common-law couples or noncohabiting opposite-sex common-law couples a fairer assessment process.

Finally, requesting third-party validation to assess the authenticity of a common-law conjugal relationship means that when it comes to spousal sponsorship, the process does not solely involve the applicant couple – "In a much more minimal way, it does entail other people ... it isn't just about us" (Interviews). State focus on the social element of one's intimate life underscores that the state is always in the bedrooms of the nation. Considering the stakes of this process, interviewees recognized they were asking their references to testify to IRCC that their relationship is monogamous, conjugal, and exclusive. Without third-party validation, applications are called into question, as officials "lack any account of social perception of either relationship" (Interviews). Common-law couples applying for benefits within Canadian borders do not require references to speak to the seriousness of their relationship; however, self-identification is insufficient for sponsorship-seeking couples. In order for these relationships to be considered genuine, someone outside of the relationship must corroborate the common-law couple's application. As such, not only is the state present in the bedrooms of the nation; it is bringing other people in as well.

Both married and common-law couples applying for spousal sponsorship are obliged to prove that their relationships are genuine and not solely formed for immigration. While all applications undergo scrutiny, they are assessed according to a series of criteria informed by the courts that, while vague, have been adopted by IRCC for the identification of genuine conjugality. As legal scholars have contended, the ideal conjugal relationship continues to be defined by the state's privileged narrative of marital standard, and this one-size-fits-all approach has implications for common-law couples. The current sponsorship program glosses over differences between married and common-law relationships, as well as between same-sex and opposite-sex relationships. By treating all conjugal relationships as a monolithic group, the program presents a series of challenges for common-law couples, as expressed by the interviewees. These challenges include providing evidence that substantiates a coherent narrative of one's relationship development despite the often casual nature of common-law relationship evolution, ignoring the presence of societal homophobia in other countries, and also providing sufficient third-party validation of the relationship in question. While assessment measures are required, it is imperative that we develop policy cognizant of the differences in our intimate relationships. Ultimately, conjugal criteria for spousal sponsorship should be accommodating of these variations.

My analysis of relationship recognition in Canada highlights how the similarity of treatment between married and common-law couples in Canadian law and policy presents unequal distinctions between inside conjugal couples (those with access to the Canadian state) and outside conjugal couples (those seeking access to the Canadian state), between married couples and common-law couples applying for spousal sponsorship, and between same-sex and opposite-sex common-law couples pursuing family reunification. This sheds light on the complexity of conjugality and draws attention to the inadequacies inherent in the Canadian state's current one-size-fits-all approach to its management of conjugal relationships both inside and outside its borders. The treatment of common-law as marriage-like in our immigration program has implications unique to common-law couples, resulting in a limited interpretation of what defines conjugal living. Moreover, this restricted definition of conjugality ultimately determines which spouses are awarded Canadian citizenship. Instead of ignoring these differences, it is therefore imperative that we account for differences within intimate relationships by developing policy reflective of these complexities.

My point here is not that policy architects should simply extend current immigration policy to be more accommodating of conjugal relationships. Rather, the key lesson is that we need to take a step back and re-evaluate what makes a conjugal relationship conjugal, and then examine how different types of intimate relationships reinforce and challenge the parameters of state-defined conjugality. Ultimately, policy communities need to have a discussion that should have taken place when the federal government officially recognized common-law conjugality. Since passing the *Modernization of Benefits and Obligations Act* (2000), governments at all levels have failed to have a meaningful discussion concerning policy and conjugality, as I have argued in this chapter, with regards to spousal sponsorship and have, in some cases, retreated to a stricter interpretation of marriage, as I will argue in the next chapter.

5

Canada's Anti–Marriage Fraud Campaign and the Production of "Legitimate" Conjugal Citizens

"If this is the kind of training that immigration officers are getting, one really has to wonder about the quality and competence of the officers who are making decisions that will make or break a family."

– AVVY GO, IMMIGRATION LAWYER

A national anti–marriage fraud commercial released by the government of Canada shows a tiered white wedding cake, topped with an ornamental white bride and groom of colour, the wedding march playing in the background. The music fades, and a voiceover begins: "Many Canadians marry people from other countries. Sometimes the marriage is a scheme to jump the immigration queue. Victims are left financially responsible if the sponsor goes on welfare." The ornamental groom disappears – "Being a sponsor is no cakewalk" (Citizenship and Immigration Canada 2011b). Part of IRCC's anti–marriage fraud campaign launched in 2011, this commercial exemplified the Harper government's commitment to combatting marriage fraud, an issue deemed a top priority in its 2011 Speech from the Throne (Johnston 2011). Under this government, marriages of convenience – marriages entered into primarily for the purpose of acquiring immigration status – became a catalyst for a series of immigration policy reforms.[1]

At the time of the campaign's launch, sponsored spouses were automatically granted permanent residency, complemented by a three-year commitment of financially accountability on the part of the sponsor regardless of the status of the relationship between the sponsor and the sponsored. Parliamentary Hansard highlights that while the topic of marriage fraud emerged in policy discussions in 2008 – particularly during meetings of the Standing Committee on Citizenship and Immigration – it was not identified as a policy target by the government until 2010. Then minister of citizenship, immigration, and multiculturalism Jason Kenney attributed this to a rise in reported cases of marriage fraud, advocating for a crackdown on marriages of convenience aimed at both preventing and stigmatizing the formation of relationships for the sole purpose of immigrating to Canada.

This chapter examines both the implications the government's anti-marriage fraud campaign presents for our spousal reunification program and the stakes in the Canadian state's regulation of "genuine" and "fraudulent" relationships. In the case of sponsorship-seeking couples, what is at stake is citizenship; for the government, it is the simultaneous prevention of fraud and preservation of a specific understanding of the conjugal family unit through a rhetoric of immigration system integrity. The impacts of such a campaign are therefore various and widespread. Using evidence generated from media coverage of the anti–marriage fraud campaign,[2] marriage fraud appeal decisions,[3] IRCC news releases, parliamentary debates,[4] and interviews with policy analysts and immigration officers, my analysis highlights how this crackdown on marriage fraud furthered the divide between inside and outside families, producing new elements in this discourse surrounding the ideal conjugal citizen. I contend that while the language of the campaign appeared neutral, the preliminary framing of this campaign targeted relationships along racialized, gendered, and sexualized lines. In addition to exploring how the targeting of certain groups allowed the government to reinforce a narrative of family class migration based on a normalized conception of the conjugal family unit, I question the government's motivations for this campaign. This chapter thus investigates the implications the anti–marriage fraud campaign had for current and future couples seeking reunification.

Definition of Marriages of Convenience

In *Chen v Canada*, Yo Long Chen's application to sponsor his second wife was refused on the grounds that the marriage was not genuine and was entered into primarily for his wife to gain admission to Canada.[5] Following the death of Chen's first wife in 2005, friends in China put Chen in touch with the woman – also married once before – who would eventually become his second wife. After a brief long-distance relationship, Chen travelled to China, and the couple were married in 2006. The assigned immigration officer expressed several concerns about the relationship, specifically the applicant's relationship with her ex-husband and her inability to recall important details including the date of the death of her sponsor's first wife. Despite the couple's consensual decision to marry and have Chen sponsor his wife, the officer concluded their relationship was disingenuous, and the couple was denied sponsorship. This case is one of hundreds of appeal decisions the Immigration Appeal Division of the IRB receives on a yearly basis. Aside from issues of criminality (the sponsored spouse having a criminal record), disingenuous conjugality is the primary justification for application refusal (Interviews).

IRCC defines a "relationship of convenience" as a marriage or common-law relationship that is not genuine and was entered into primarily for the purpose of acquiring any status or privilege under the IRPA (Citizenship and Immigration Canada 2006, s 6). Assessment of spousal sponsorship applications is thus twofold, as it is possible for a couple's relationship to be deemed genuine by an immigration officer but still considered to be primarily formed for sponsorship purposes and consequently denied.[6] The genuineness of one's relationship is ultimately only one part of the sponsorship process – "Immigration always plays *some* role in the reasons for the marriage. My job is to determine whether it was *primarily* for immigration" (as cited by an interviewed immigration officer in Satzewich 2015, 143; emphasis in original).

IRCC recognizes three different types of marriage fraud – marrying/sponsoring an individual in exchange for money; marrying in good faith and being abandoned upon the sponsored spouse's arrival in Canada; and "purchasing" relationships through an external organization (e.g., fake wedding photos, relationship testimonies). In light of my analysis of appeal decisions and IRCC documentation, I would add a fourth category – marrying for the purpose of immigration without monetary payback, malice, or ill-intent. This includes couples currently living in Canada who marry in order to avoid deportation and Canadian citizens who marry abroad in order to sponsor loved ones so they can immigrate. While both of these examples include loving relationships between two consenting adults, these relationships could be refused access. Unlike relationship patterns within Canadian borders, in the case of marriage fraud, the presence or absence of consent does not trump other factors. Instances of marriage fraud are not always detectable at the time of application; stories of Canadian citizens who successfully sponsored their spouse only to have them disappear when arriving in Canada shaped this anti–marriage fraud campaign. The government's approach to marriage fraud was therefore both proactive (cutting off marriage fraud at the source) and reactive (punishing those post-application).

Assessment of Marriages of Convenience

Immigration officers assess applications according to a "balance of probabilities," an interviewed immigration officer explaining that "my decision is based on a balance of probabilities. That is the key word – the balance of probabilities. That is how I interpret the law. I have the docs, and whatever is on the table, if there is a 51 percent chance that they are telling me the truth then I will give the ... doubt in favour of the applicant" (as cited by an interviewed immigration officer in Satzewich 2015, 143). Criteria used to assess the probability that the relationship in question is a marriage of convenience are similar in most respects to criteria used to assess the conjugality of a relationship, as discussed in previous chapters. When evaluating suspected marriages of convenience, immigration officers examine the following factors:

- Intent of the parties
- Length of the relationship
- Amount of time actually spent together
- Conduct at time of meeting, engagement, and/or wedding
- Behaviour subsequent to the wedding
- Knowledge of each other's relationship histories
- Levels of continuing contact and communication
- Knowledge of and sharing of responsibilities for care of children brought into the marriage
- Knowledge of and contact with extended families of parties
- Knowledge about each other's daily lives. (Interviews)

Similar to couples applying for spousal sponsorship, couples who choose to appeal a decision bear the responsibility of convincing the appeal officer that their relationship is conjugal. Moreover, couples who file an appeal experience further scrutiny regarding the personal details of their relationships. While initial assessment focuses on the structural components of a relationship (e.g., living arrangements, sharing of finances, public perception), an assessment of appeals evaluates the presence or absence of intimacy (e.g., sharing of personal information, knowledge of intimate details), the assumption being that couples in a genuine relationship should have more in common than just sponsorship (Interviews).

My analysis of appeal decisions suggests that while protocol requires officers to assess appeals according to this list of criteria, evaluation tended to rely primarily on two factors: compatibility – which is not included on the list of criteria – and relationship history. In fact, length of relationship and relationship history were the only two factors from the list above that officers explicitly considered in these obtained decisions.[7] Couple compatibility played an influential role in determining whether a relationship was genuine or manufactured for the purpose of sponsorship. As these decisions suggest, compatibility was measured in several ways, one being age. While age was only mentioned in one positive decision – *Yu v Canada* – appeal officers frequently commented on age differences between couples in negative decisions.[8] In *Brobbey v Canada* – a decision involving a female Canadian citizen and her Ghanaian husband – the officer remarked, "The applicant [the sponsored] is over eight years older than the appellant [the sponsor]. In light of this, I find that this is a non-genuine, immigration marriage."[9] Age difference was also mentioned in a decision involving a sponsored spouse from Bangladesh in *Begum v Canada* when the officer stated, "Also of concern is the difference between the ages of the couple."[10] The assigned officer in *Simpson-Lee v Canada* took issue with the eighteen-year age gap between the couple, questioning whether the couple had anything in common considering their age difference.[11] Age difference, particularly when cases involved younger women sponsoring older men, acted as a starting point for officers to assess compatibility.

A second measure of compatibility was education; differences in education levels acted as a red flag for marriages of convenience. This was evident in *Hung v Canada* where the officer commented, "The appellant is better educated and westernized, and the applicant is an accounting clerk."[12] Similarly, a Canadian citizen's appeal to sponsor her Chinese spouse was denied, the officer remarking, "I had a problem with their testimonies with regards to why they liked each other or why they found each other compatible and suitable ... The appellant graduated from the University of Toronto with a Bachelor in Business Administration, and the applicant is a hairstylist. He completed high school level education and did vocational schooling."[13] Compatibility with respect to educational background, which arguably translates to class compatibility, influenced assessment of spousal relationships, assuming that similar education levels translated to similar interests.

In addition to age and education, religion was also used to measure compatibility. Mentioned in both successful and unsuccessful appeals, religious consistency was viewed as a positive. In *Amaral v Canada* – a positive decision involving the sponsoring of a spouse from Mexico – the officer remarked:

> I must also take into account the fact that after having been married in a civil ceremony in Toronto, the couple were re-married in Mexico in a Roman Catholic Church. Both parties come from a Roman Catholic religious tradition and I am of the view that by choosing to be married in the Church, they have indicated that they wish their matrimonial bond to be blessed by their religion, which incidentally does not recognize divorce. To my mind, this is a strong indicator that the marriage is genuine.[14]

A lack of religious compatibility was discussed in *Chen v Canada*, the officer mentioning, "The appellant and applicant are not compatible in religion, as the appellant describes himself as a Christian and is obviously very involved in his church. The applicant, who knows of the appellant's religious faith, is not a Christian and has made no real effort to learn about Christianity."[15] This was echoed in *Huayra v Canada* – a negative decision involving a Canadian citizen and his Peruvian spouse – the officer commenting, "The panel also finds that in a genuine relationship, the appellant would have had an elaborate religious wedding in Peru, instead of the Spartan civil ceremony they underwent there, and would not wait to have a religious ceremony in Canada once they are united here."[16] In this light, religious compatibility worked in two ways. In addition to the couple being religiously compatible, there was the expectation that genuine marriages involve a ceremony consistent with the couple's religious beliefs.

Moreover, this suggests that some immigration officers conflate religious and cultural compatibility. In the previous chapter, interviewed common-law couples discussed the pressure to provide a relationship narrative consistent with cultural norms of relationship development and ceremony. Analysis of appeal decisions adds a new level of complexity to this discussion; comments about religious and cultural compatibility imply that couples were also expected to provide a relationship narrative the officer believed to be consistent with the cultural norms in the applicant's country of origin. Walton-Roberts (2004) contends that couples from India whose relationship narratives fail to correspond with cultural narratives and customs are "easily refused"; interviews conducted by Satzewich with immigration officers suggest that while there is some validity to this claim, immigration officers recognize culture is not static and "socio-economic and other externally driven circumstances might prompt individuals and families to selectively reject or modify certain rituals" (2015, 153–54). In my analysis, assigned immigration officers in 67 out of the 140 decisions assumed that if the couple is from the same country of origin, their relationship should follow a pattern of cultural compatibility coherent with assumptions about that particular culture. Therefore, as discussed above, a Peruvian couple is expected to provide a relationship narrative consistent with perceived Peruvian cultural norms. A lack of religious/cultural compatibility acts as a warning sign in the assessment of appealed spousal sponsorship decisions.

Like religion, cultural compatibility was also conflated with ethnicity. Officers provided positive commentary with couples described as "ethnic Chinese" *(Yu v Canada, Hung v Canada, Lin v Canada, Li v Canada)*, "Bangladeshi" *(Begum v Canada)*, "truly Ethiopian" *(Tadessa v Canada)*, and "devoted Mexicans" *(Amaral v Canada)*.[17] In all of these decisions, officers considered the fact that these couples were ethnically well-matched as positive. Recognition of ethnic compatibility, however, translated to the expectation that couples' actions would correlate with religious and cultural norms associated with their particular ethnic group. In *Begum v Canada*, a Bangladeshi couple was refused sponsorship, the officer remarking, "You didn't have a formal wedding and none of your family members attended that wedding ... The circumstances of your relationship are inconsistent with the norms, traditions, and expectations of your own culture." This was echoed in *Rathod v Canada* – a decision involving a sponsored spouse from India – in which the officer refused the appeal on the grounds that "the appellant and applicant had sexual relations prior to their marriage contrary to the cultural norms and customs of their community."[18] This suggests that either religious or ethnic compatibility only goes so far; a positive evaluation of cultural compatibility required that both of these components line up with the officer's expectations of cultural norms in a given country, a consequence of the IRB's conflation of these terms. Cultural compatibility was therefore reliant on traditional and static cultural norms that must be observed and performed.

Finally, officers used the presence or absence of common interests shared by couples to assess compatibility. In *Li v Canada,* the officer took issue with a lack of shared interests: "She [the applicant] did not for example speak to those things they had in common, what types of things they talk about, if he had a sense of humour, etc. Her answer in my view was very basic and void of any real information that would point to a genuine relationship."[19] Similar commentary was provided by the officer in *Li v Canada* (same name, different decision):

> When they asked what they had in common, what they both said was rather general. For example, the appellant, when she was first asked, the first thing that I heard was that he was handsome, then she said that he was honest and that he cares about people a lot, that they care about each other, that he and her make jokes, that they respect their elders and parents and that he likes to help people ... When he was asked, "what do you love about the appellant?" he indicated that she is very understanding, considerate, caring; he indicated that he loves her and he is very happy and content with her.[20]

In these decisions, the assumptions of shared interests were generally perceived to be predetermined by age, educational background, religion, ethnicity, and culture; couples considered incompatible according to these factors were assumed to have less in common. In Canada, where citizens are generally free to develop personal relationships as they see fit, it seems odd that something as subjective as common interests shapes the assessment of sponsorship-seeking couples. It is also troubling that in a self-declared multicultural society, sponsorship-seeking couples who were religiously, ethnically, and culturally compatible were deemed less suspicious than spouses that came from different backgrounds. While the state plays no role in the assessment of compatibility for couples living within Canadian borders, the IRB's reliance on compatibility to assess these marriage fraud appeal decisions is both conceptually flawed and normatively unsound.

The second factor used in the assessment of appeal decisions was the relationship history of both the sponsor and the sponsored. Several aspects of one's relationship history, including but not limited to previous marriages, relationship length, and sponsorship history, are considered red flags (Interviews). Sponsors who have applied to sponsor multiple spouses at different times are considered highly suspicious, as are individuals who are sponsored and then sponsor someone else quickly after their relationship with the initial sponsor has ended (Interviews).[21] While these accusations were not made in the obtained appeal decisions, relationship history was mentioned in eighty-seven decisions. In *Chen v Canada,* the applicant was described as a "44 year-old divorcee" who "still retained possession of her former matrimonial home with her first husband" and was owed "200,000 RMB by her former husband." For the assigned officer, these three factors aroused enough concern for her relationship with the sponsor to be deemed disingenuous. In her defence, the applicant claimed that "she had retained possession of the former matrimonial home and would not be giving up her interest in the property until she had received the payment of 200,000 RMB that was owed to her in the matrimonial settlement."[22] The officer neglected to account for gendered power imbalances in divorce settlements, ultimately penalizing the applicant for maintaining a connection to her first husband in order to receive what was owed to her.

The length of one's previous relationships as well as the length of the relationship in question were also evaluated. In *Li v Canada,* the officer was suspicious of the sincerity of the couple's relationship after finding out that prior to their brief courtship, both parties had been involved in long-term marital relationships. This was evident in the officer's remarks:

> When examining a marriage of two persons coming out of a long-term relationship and re-marrying in a short period of time, I am of the view

that there has to be some substance to the evidence. That is to say, there has to be some indication that the two people involved are able to talk about the relationship; that they are able to describe those things that attracted them to the other person in detail; that they can speak to those things that are annoying to the other person or difficult situations. In other words and especially in a situation where two people have not spent a great deal of time together prior to marriage, the marriage has to make some sense.[23]

In this decision, the officer assumed that because both parties had been in long-term relationships prior to marrying each other, they should be well aware of what a genuine relationship looks like. Moreover, they should be able to translate that knowledge to their shorter-term relationship if their intent to marry was sincere. In this light, the assigned immigration officer used relationship history to automatically disqualify applicants, like in *Chen v Canada*, and to generate unreasonable expectations to scrutinize the validity of relationships, like in *Li v Canada*.

A lack of couple compatibility has traditionally been overlooked when children are involved. For example, in *Aujla v Canada*, the initially assigned immigration officer refused the application, citing incompatibility with respect to age (there was a three-year difference between the couple), educational background (the appellant was more educated), and relationship history (this was the applicant's second marriage).[24] When the decision was appealed, the appeal officer agreed with the initial assessment of compatibility but ruled that the relationship was genuine because there were children involved. The presence of children as the exception changed following *Mansro v Canada*.[25] In this decision, the officer recognized that children were involved but took issue with the lack of communication between the applicant – who was living in Canada at the time of application – and his children, who were living with the appellant in India. While the appeal officer reversed the initial decision, the officer made it clear that the presence of children did not automatically confirm that a relationship was genuine, commenting, "Typically the existence of a child of a marriage is an important factor which must be considered, and would be indicative of a relationship of some substance. However, the existence of a child of the marriage is not determinative of the genuineness of the marriage."[26] This decision has since been used to refuse appeals that involve children. In the case of *Gill v Canada,* the officer made reference to *Mansro v Canada,* ruling that the relationship was illegitimate despite the fact that the couple had two children together:

> Based on the documentary evidence made available to the panel, it does not appear that the applicant has contributed to his wife's support while she was pregnant nor to the children's support since their birth. No *viva voce* nor documentary evidence was presented to provide the panel with any evidence as to the applicant's relationship with the children, accounting of course for the distance and their ages. Has their father seen them, be it via Skype or any other webcam method? How was the applicant told of their birth and when? What information passed between the spouses during the course of the appellant's pregnancy? There would surely be a plethora of such evidence, either oral or documentary, in a genuine marriage.[27]

In the assessment of sponsorship-seeking couples, it is no longer safe to assume that children will trump couple compatibility.

In these decisions, immigration officers primarily relied on compatibility and relationship history to distinguish between genuine spousal relationships and marriages of convenience, the apparent aim being to maintain the integrity of the Canadian immigration system. It is this discussion of system integrity that frames current discourse surrounding marriage fraud. In negative appeal decisions, couples were accused of "engaging public policy considerations involving the integrity of the immigration system" *(Kagayutan v Canada)* and of "undermining the integrity of the immigration system, which depends on the honesty of applicants" *(Huayra v Canada).*[28] Kenney (2010) prefaced a discussion of reform proposals with the following comments: "I think most Canadians intuitively understand that broad public support for immigration, and frankly diversity in our society, is contingent on having a well-managed, rules-based, fair immigration system. I think they understand that we all have a stake in maintaining such a system." Those who engage in marriage fraud were framed as a serious threat to the execution of a fair, well-balanced, and effective immigration system. The integrity of our immigration system therefore rests on the state blocking out external threats, begging the question of whether all couples seeking spousal sponsorship are fraudsters. The government committed to defending Canadians from this external threat in order to "protect the integrity of our immigration system" by introducing measures to "address marriage fraud – an abuse of our system that can victimize unsuspecting Canadians and vulnerable immigrants" (Johnston 2011). Marriage fraud was identified as a top priority of the Harper government's immigration policy mandate, raising the question: How do we explain this recent shift in focus toward marriage fraud?

Motivations for a Crackdown on Marriage Fraud

In an examination of parliamentary Hansard, the issue of marriage fraud did not receive much attention before the government's policy position was identified in 2010. Prior to 2010, individual Members of Parliament (MPs) who failed to receive any type of policy response called on the government to take marriage fraud seriously. Concerns about marriage fraud were framed in two ways: concerns about couples marrying for the purpose of spousal sponsorship and concerns about the Canadian state's allowance of common-law couples to apply for spousal sponsorship. Former Liberal MP Gurbax Malhi (1998) addressed the former, stating, "I draw attention of the House to the fact that some individuals are marrying Canadian citizens or permanent residents for the primary purpose of entering Canada as a member of the family class. Since fraudulent marriages cause pain to innocent spouses, we must take action." For Malhi, the harm, both current and potential, of marriage fraud for citizens and the government warranted attention. Canadian Alliance turned Conservative MP Leon Benoit (2001) addressed the latter with this comment:

> The department [Citizenship and Immigration Canada] is already dealing with the huge problem of verifying whether a marriage is a marriage of convenience to accommodate immigration or whether it is a genuine marriage. How on earth would we deal with that when we allow a common-law marriage to be used under the bill? It is an administrative impossibility and an administrative nightmare.

For Benoit, the extension of conjugal benefits to common-law couples was a potential catalyst for an increase in marriage fraud. Apart from these isolated discussions, marriage fraud was not on any government's agenda pre-2010.

From an electoral standpoint, the Harper government's focus on marriage fraud was a logical policy target for three reasons. First, a crackdown on marriage fraud coincided with the party's mandate of "keeping families strong" (Conservative Party of Canada 2011). When marriage fraud was brought up during a House debate in 2008, the Harper government was accused of failing to address the perceived seriousness of the issue. Former New Democratic Party (NDP) MP Olivia Chow – arguably the most vocal non-Conservative MP on issues of spousal sponsorship and marriage fraud – criticized the government's inconsistent treatment of marriage fraud. At the time, the marriage of a couple who lived in Canada and applied for spousal sponsorship could be temporarily considered a marriage of convenience and the sponsored spouse deported until IRCC assessed the application. Due to an application backlog, couples could be separated for two to three years. Moreover, IRCC could eventually rule that the relationship was a marriage of convenience and the application be denied. Chow argued that the government's handling of marriage fraud was misguided, as it focused on already established families living within Canadian borders. For Chow (2008), the state's approach toward marriage fraud was in need of reform, and this required the government to reassess its position on the protection of families – "For over a decade, minister after minister talked about supporting families and yet they failed to support loving couples. It is absurd and cruel to separate families, and cause untold emotional and financial hardship just because of a failure or a political will or because Parliament is not paying attention. I say it is time for fairness of immigrant families." Then parliamentary secretary to the minister of citizenship and immigration Ed Komarnicki (2008) defended the government's position, remarking, "We have established a fair and adequate process in this country which ensures people are protected ... while the majority of spousal applications are bona fide and in bona fide relationships, some do abuse our programs. This is why we must take that reality into consideration." Former Liberal MP Andrew Telegdi (2008) refuted Komarnicki's justification:

> I am shocked, and I am sure all the opposition parties are shocked, because for years we listened to that party stand in this House and defend

family values. How much more of a family value can we have than not splitting husband from wife, father from child, sons and daughters, or mothers from their children? That is what this whole issue comes down to. If the case were that somebody was found to have a relationship that was not bona fide and it was a marriage of convenience, nobody is arguing that this person be allowed to stay here.

For opposition parties, the government's position on marriage fraud was contradictory. On one hand, the Harper government boasted a pro-family platform; on the other hand, families living within Canadian borders were being separated.

In this particular debate, opposition parties were not dismissive of marriage fraud; rather, what was at stake was whom current policy was targeting. Couples already living in Canada were not the enemy; calls for attention focused on the outsider using marriage to gain access to the Canadian state. As such, the Harper government's anti–marriage fraud campaign arguably accomplished that. It allowed for the protection of Canadian families – a prominent focus of their policy mandate – and perceivably maintained the integrity of the immigration system by keeping out those believed to be taking advantage of the institution of marriage for immigration purposes. The objective of the campaign was therefore not solely to distinguish between conjugal and nonconjugal families, but also to distinguish between legitimate and illegitimate conjugal families. This was evident in Kenney's comments to the media – "While we want to keep the doors open for legitimate spouses or partners, we also want to make sure the doors are not open to those who would break our laws and exploit Canadians" (McKie 2010). This discourse furthered distinctions between legitimate and illegitimate conjugal families, permitting the government to enact policy reform consistent with their electoral promise of protecting Canadian families by refusing access to fraudulent immigrant families. Strategically speaking, framing the campaign as a way to keep the conjugal family intact was a rational policy tactic for the Conservative government.

A second reason why the Harper government's crackdown on marriage fraud can be perceived as strategically beneficial is that it was framed as a way to protect immigrants already living within Canadian borders. While

Kenney (2010) recognized that marriage fraud was not a new problem, he claimed that increases in marriage fraud predominantly affected foreign-born Canadians:

> I'll tell you, there are very few native-born Canadians who have ever raised the issue of bogus spousal sponsorship with me. I have held a series of public forums across the country, and hundreds of people have come out, in Brandon, Vancouver, Montreal and elsewhere. I think all, or almost all of them, are immigrants to Canada, and they have insisted that we find ways to tighten up both the rules and the enforcement of the rules to prevent bogus spouses from coming to Canada as permanent residents.

Individual MPs who addressed the issue of marriage fraud in Parliament tended to represent ridings with high foreign-born populations. Conservative MP Nina Grewal, former NDP MP Olivia Chow, former Liberal MP Ruby Dhalla, and former Liberal MP Gurbax Malhi – all four of them calling for attention to the issue of marriage fraud in Parliament – represented ridings composed of 27, 28, 37, and 28 percent immigrant populations respectively, the majority of immigrants in all four ridings coming from India and China (Statistics Canada 2012). The crisis of marriage fraud in Canada was framed as an immigrant issue, coinciding with the Conservative party's aggressive ethnic outreach strategy (Friesen and Sher 2011; Kenney 2012). Combatting marriage fraud thus complimented the Harper government's focus on the immigrant vote.

Finally, the campaign allowed the Harper government to discuss restrictions on family class immigration in a way that was consistent with public support for the maintenance of a fair and well-balanced immigration system. As discussed in Chapter 2, national public consultations conducted by IRCC in the early nineties highlighted general support for immigration so long as the bad egg, in this case the queue jumper, is denied access. Cracking down on marriage fraud was framed as a form of protection against system cheaters. This rhetoric speaks to the perceived fear that queue jumpers ultimately challenge the integrity of the Canadian immigration system, and, as such, the government is able to introduce barriers to immigration in the name of protecting the state and its citizens from bad eggs while simultaneously targeting specific families.

In terms of bureaucratic attention to marriage fraud, sponsorship breakdown was identified as a primary concern in IRCC's 1995 annual report to Parliament; however, this referred to the state holding sponsors financially accountable for their sponsored family members. The issue of marriage fraud specifically had received minimal attention prior to the campaign. This is generally attributed to two factors. There is a lack of finite statistics of rates of marriage fraud in Canada. In a 2007 parliamentary debate, former NDP MP Bill Siksay asked the government how many individuals had been deported or had their permanent residence status cancelled by IRCC for engaging in marriage fraud. Then minister of public safety Stockwell Day (2007) was unable to provide that information due to a lack of numbers:

> The CBSA [Canada Border Services Agency] recognizes that some Canadians and permanent residents are deceived by foreign nationals into marriage for the purpose of acquiring permanent residence. The scope of this issue is unclear, however, because our computer system does not track this information. The system only recognizes misrepresentation in general and does not allow for differentiation between specific types of misrepresentation, including fraudulent marriages and marriages of convenience. For this reason, it is not possible to identify the number of people who have been deported or who have had their permanent residence status cancelled by CIC [Citizenship and Immigration Canada], for reasons of fraudulent marriages or marriages of convenience.

A lack of statistics has made it difficult for IRCC to track reported marriage fraud, leaving marriages of convenience off the bureaucratic radar.

There is also a differentiation in priorities between IRCC and CBSA. While IRCC is responsible for processing applications for immigration to Canada, CBSA physically monitors who gets into the country. Both agencies deal with access; however, they have clearly expressed different priorities during discussions concerning the severity of marriage fraud. When questioned about the government's plan of action for tackling marriage fraud in 2008, then minister of citizenship and immigration Diane Finley (2008) responded that "CIC and CBSA are both concerned about marriages of convenience" and that both "departments are engaged in the investigation of these cases." This united front between IRCC and CBSA was questionable, however, considering comments made two months prior by CBSA regarding the prioritization of marriage fraud. At a Standing Committee on Citizenship and Immigration meeting, the CBSA director of inland enforcement identified marriage fraud as a low priority:

> Marriages of convenience are an issue. Because it is on our lower-priority scale for areas that we enforce, it's not an area we've put a lot of resources on, but it is an issue. The priorities for immigration enforcement activities are those who pose a risk to national security, so your terrorist types. Once we've looked after those people, we go after failed refugee claimants, and then all others – those who overstay, and those who work, study, or misrepresent themselves, including marriages of convenience – are our lowest priority. (Kramer 2008)

In 2011, Kenney publicly criticized CBSA's inaction toward marriage fraud, calling for its reprioritization – "It's not for me to dictate how many cases they take up. When they get complaints, we want them to follow up on those and, whenever they can build a credible case, bring charges for fraud against the person who is breaking our immigration laws" (McKie 2011). CBSA defended their agenda, stating that their priorities were not typically dictated by outside influences and reasserting that the agency "focuses its investigative efforts on high-priority cases where individuals pose a safety or security risk and where national security, organized crime, crimes against humanity, serious criminality and criminality are involved" (McKie 2011). This resistance was short-lived, however, as CBSA announced the commencement of "project honeymoon" three days later, which involved the reopening of three dozen investigations of marriage fraud and an inquiry into organized criminal involvement in arranging marriages of convenience. The disconnect between IRCC and CBSA made it difficult for IRCC to fully enact the government's crackdown on marriage fraud.

As to whether there was actually a significant increase in reported cases of marriage fraud, the numbers are vague. The government does not track the number of people who have been either deported or stripped of their permanent residency status because they were found guilty of engaging in a marriage of convenience (Interviews). The government monitors misrepresentation as a single category, therefore failing to differentiate between various types of misrepresentation. As such, those who are denied access due to marriage fraud are grouped in the same category as those deported for other forms of misrepresentation (e.g., failure to declare dependent children, criminal record, security concerns, medical issues). This made it difficult for the government to provide firm data supporting the claim that marriage fraud was on the rise in Canada. Pre-2010, there was no discussion of actual numbers regarding marriage fraud; when asked about rates, the then CBSA director of inland enforcement ambiguously responded that "they get complaints all the time" (Kramer 2008). When asked specifically to provide a numerical amount in Parliament, then minister of citizenship and immigration Finley (2008) remarked, "Quantifying the rate of marriage fraud is difficult as relationships can break down at any time, from the date of entry to Canada to several years into the marriage. The CIC takes all tips, complaints, and reports of alleged marriages of convenience seriously and investigates when there is sufficient information to do so." The conflation of various types of sponsorship misrepresentation made it impossible for the government to pinpoint the actual rate of marriage fraud, complicating the government's declaration that marriage fraud had reached a crisis point in Canada.

The anti–marriage fraud campaign sparked increased opposition and media pressure on the Harper government to produce numbers; however, even those numbers were inconsistent. Kenney (2010) claimed he had been contacted by hundreds of marriage fraud victims since taking on the position of minister. An investigation undertaken by CBC in 2010 concluded that out of the 49,500 spousal sponsorship applications filed in 2009, 10,000 (20 percent) were rejected for several reasons, including suspicions of marriage fraud (CBC News 2010). When asked what proportion of these rejected cases were labelled bad-faith marriages, IRCC's response was "many." Similarly, IRCC stated that in 2010, 9,250 (16 percent) of spousal sponsorship applications were refused for unspecified reasons (Curry 2011). When CBSA began compiling figures between 2008 and 2010 – following the announcement of "project honeymoon" – the agency stated that 39 out of 200 (19.5 percent) reports of marriage fraud warranted a formal investigation; out of these 39 investigations, charges were laid in 7 (4 percent) (CBC News 2011). IRCC's website states that one thousand fraudulent marriages are reported annually, challenging CBSA's claim of 200 reports of marriage fraud over two years. Concrete rates of incidents of marriage fraud put forth by Kenney, IRCC, and CBSA were varying at best. The empirical backing for the government's anti–marriage fraud campaign was therefore questionable, as it lacked a clear picture of the current state of marriage fraud – "The Harper Conservatives' approach to immigration, like their approach to family values and the criminal-justice system, was not affected by facts or expert opinion" (Jeffrey 2015, 231).

Another factor that muddles discussions about marriage fraud is the government's failure to distinguish between reports of marriage fraud and CBSA-ruled cases of marriage fraud. For those Canadians who wish to report an incident of marriage fraud, they can file their tip through CBSA's Border Watch line. Complaints are then triaged and investigated by CBSA and law enforcement bodies, a process that had been neglected according to Kenney, who remarked, "I told the President of CBSA that I didn't think it was acceptable that people who make complaints to CBSA haven't even got the courtesy of a response" (McKie 2010).[29] This discrepancy in institutional objectives between IRCC and CBSA highlights an important point – reported cases of marriage fraud are not the same as ruled cases of marriage fraud. When we talk about reported cases, the numbers are significantly higher than those cases where an individual has been found guilty and then penalized accordingly. The government's discourse around marriage fraud was therefore misleading, as these terms were conflated, often failing to distinguish between reported and ruled cases.

Aside from resource limitations, the primary challenge to investigating reported cases of marriage fraud is proving that the accused individual married their Canadian sponsor with the sole intent of immigrating to Canada. While applicants are denied sponsorship because they are suspected of marriage fraud, CBSA cannot deport immigrants post-sponsorship if they have only been accused. Unless there is actual proof (e.g., phone records, photos, emails, witnesses), investigations generally turn into a sponsor-said/sponsored-said battle (Interviews). The challenge of proof was used by the government to justify the small number of individuals who have actually been charged with marriage fraud, despite marriage fraud being touted as an area of national concern (Finley 2008). Furthermore, they have used the challenge of marriage fraud investigations to rationalize focusing on proactive measures aimed at preventing perpetrators of marriage fraud from gaining access to the Canadian state in the first place, as made evident by Kenney's remarks: "Because we need to be able to go to a court and prove that they entered into their marriage with bad faith, it's virtually impossible for us to get successful convictions on marriage fraud cases after the fact. Which is why we need additional screening tools" (CBC News 2011). As a result, the government directed their attentions primarily toward preventative courses of action, attempting to attack marriage fraud at its source.

Canada's Anti–Marriage Fraud Campaign

This focus on proactive measures was the foundation of the government's anti–marriage fraud campaign. The campaign commenced with the launching of a publicly accessible online consultation in 2010 that was open on IRCC's website for three months. In addition to announcing the survey's presence via news release, approximately fifty stakeholder organizations including private sector employees, chambers of commerce, immigration lawyers/consultants, professional associations, immigration service organizations, civil rights organizations, ethno-cultural organizations, and other nongovernment organizations at the national, provincial, and local levels were invited to participate (Citizenship and Immigration Canada 2011a). Prior to completing the survey, participants were asked to read a background document defining what constitutes a marriage of convenience and outlining the Harper government's approach toward preventing marriage fraud. The document explained that while there were no firm numbers on the extent of marriage fraud in Canada, it was an issue in need of national attention. The document stated that concerns about marriage fraud could only be remedied through amendments to section 4 – the section that deals specifically with bad faith marriages – of the IRPA. The document then provided a brief overview of measures undertaken in Australia, United States, New Zealand, and the United Kingdom to curb marriages of convenience.[30] The document concluded by recognizing that while the prevention of marriage fraud demands resources, the re-evaluation of current priorities in the name of maintaining the integrity of our immigration system was necessary (Citizenship and Immigration Canada 2011a).

Methodologically speaking, the execution of this survey was flawed. The background document that participants were asked to read prior to completing the survey explained that people are "abusing spousal sponsorship by entering marriages of convenience so that they can sidestep Canada's immigration law" and that these relationships "weaken our immigration system and make it harder for genuine immigrants to get through the system" (Citizenship and Immigration Canada 2011a). IRCC failed to provide firm numbers on rates of marriage fraud in this document other than claiming that in 2009, 20 percent of spousal sponsorship applications were refused, some of them because they were ruled marriages of convenience (Citizenship and Immigration Canada 2011a). The background document provided survey participants with a negative picture of the current state of marriage fraud in Canada; participants were therefore exposed to IRCC's position before completing the survey. Studies show that the attachment of an attitude or position to a respected individual or agency can bias survey responses; support is arguably increased compared to what it would be had the attitude or position not been revealed (Babbie 1999, 131). By stating their position on marriage fraud, IRCC potentially biased the results, as participants would be more likely to support measures aimed at combatting marriage fraud if IRCC claimed these measures were necessary. Moreover, in its discussion of measures adopted in other countries, IRCC provided no evidence that these measures have actually reduced rates of marriage fraud. This lack of information meant that respondents were therefore expected to provide an uninformed opinion as to whether Canada should replicate these initiatives. The survey was ultimately premised on a limited amount of information, information that was slanted toward government action.

After reading the attached document, participants were then asked to complete a ten-question questionnaire. The questionnaire aimed to gauge public concern about marriages of convenience and support for government action. In order to do so, the survey asked respondents to rate their opinion on the following issues:

- The seriousness of marriages of convenience
- Public awareness about marriages of convenience
- Sponsor responsibility

- Government action
- Longer processing times as a consequence of increased investigation into potential incidents of marriage fraud
- Sponsorship bars (limitations on how many spouses one can sponsor within a certain period of time and on sponsored spouses for future sponsoring)
- Conditional visas (probationary period in lieu of automatic permanent residency)
- Increased spending/resources for government action. (Citizenship and Immigration Canada 2010)

The questionnaire also provided additional space for those respondents who have been victims of marriage fraud to share their experiences. In its three-month period, the questionnaire generated 2,431 responses – 2,342 (96 percent) from the general public and 89 (4 percent) from self-identified stakeholders (Citizenship and Immigration Canada 2010). Out of the 2,342 respondents from the general public, 37 percent specified that they had sponsored a spouse to come to Canada, 11 percent identified themselves as victims of marriage fraud, and an additional 11 percent indicated that a Canadian citizen had sponsored them.

On the issue of the seriousness of marriage fraud, 77 percent of respondents indicated that marriages of convenience are a *very serious* or *serious* threat to Canada's immigration system. Not surprisingly, victims of marriage fraud identified this as a *very serious* threat more often than nonvictims did. When questioned about the ways in which marriage fraud poses a threat, respondents cited effects on the immigration system (longer wait times, system integrity), effects on individuals (financial, emotional), and effects on Canadian society (welfare, health care) (Citizenship and Immigration Canada 2010). A strong majority of respondents (77 percent nonvictims, 88 percent victims) supported the need for increased public awareness and education about marriage fraud. Interestingly, approximately 90 percent of respondents believed that a sponsor should bear either *a lot* or *a moderate degree* of personal responsibility for making sure that their relationship with the sponsored is genuine; however, 50 percent of those respondents stated that the government should be responsible for protecting Canadians from marriage fraud. The most supported government measures to curb marriage fraud were punitive (deportation, financial penalties) and preventative (conditional visas, public awareness) actions. Fifty-two percent of respondents indicated they were unwilling to tolerate longer processing times in order to investigate potential cases of marriage fraud, citing that the current application process was already too lengthy. Finally, approximately 58 percent supported diverting more federal resources to investigate reported cases of marriage fraud, while 32 percent were skeptical that devoting more resources would rectify the issue and believed that the government should not play a role in determining whether a marriage is genuine in the first place. Overall, participants in this online consultation expressed concern about marriages of convenience and considered marriage fraud to be a legitimate threat to the integrity of the Canadian immigration system. As such, participants supported some form of government action aimed at preventing and penalizing perpetrators of marriage fraud.

In addition to the online questionnaire, Kenney hosted town hall meetings in Brampton, Vancouver, and Montreal in 2010 to discuss marriages of convenience. This provided Kenney with the opportunity to meet victims of marriage fraud, an experience that inspired the anti–marriage fraud campaign, as made evident by Kenney's remarks:

> In town hall meetings I held in 2010 with victims of marriage fraud, I heard first-hand from victims who were still suffering the consequences years later. They implored me to do something to stop this from happening to others. The problem with marriage fraud is serious and will only get worse if we don't put measures in place that protect the integrity of our immigration system while deterring people from trying to use a marriage of convenience to cheat their way into Canada. (Citizenship and Immigration Canada 2012d)

Kenney made similar comments in another IRCC news release explaining, "I held town hall meetings across the country to hear from victims of marriage fraud. In addition to the heartbreak and pain that came from being lied to and deceived, these people were angry. They felt they had been used as a way to get to Canada" (Citizenship and Immigration Canada 2012b).

Following the online and town hall consultations, the government introduced two primary changes to the IRPA: residency requirements for permanent residency status and sponsorship bars. The first amendment was a mandatory two-year residence requirement for childless sponsorship-seeking couples who had been in a relationship for less than two years at the time of application.[31] According to Kenney, the objective of the measure was to "weed out people trying to use a phony marriage as a quick and easy route to Canada" (Citizenship and Immigration Canada 2012b). The second measure required sponsored spouses to wait five years from the day they are granted permanent residence to sponsor a new spouse. This gives CBSA time to investigate reported marriages of convenience before the sponsored spouse obtains permanent residency; the enactment of sponsorship bars would mean that CBSA had two years. Moreover, it prevents those who do marry in order to get into Canada from immediately sponsoring another spouse. By suspending permanent residency and sponsorship privileges, the government believed these measures would deter "fraudsters who lie and cheat to jump the queue" (Citizenship and Immigration Canada 2012c).[32]

These measures garnered much criticism, particularly from feminist scholars and activists. Studies have shown that because female migrants are more likely to come to Canada as dependent spouses (Abu-Laban and Gabriel 2002; Citizenship and Immigration Canada 2014), sponsored women often experience what is referred to as a *sponsorship debt*, defined as a "family behaviour pattern where a husband and his family emphasize that the sponsored wife owes them for bringing her to Canada and keeping her here" (Côté, Kerisit, and Côté 2001; Merali 2009, 323). Sponsored wives often find themselves in a vulnerable position upon arriving in Canada and are therefore more susceptible to domestic abuse (Merali 2009; Hrick 2012; Macklin 2014). Feminist critiques of residency requirements express concern for sponsored wives who are already in a precarious position and will choose not to report incidents of abuse in order to protect their immigration status (Go, Balakrishna, and Sharma 2011). This is not to suggest that sponsored spouses are less likely to be abused if they have permanent residency; rather, the argument is that abusive sponsors can hold permanent residency over their sponsored spouse's head for two years. The government responded to these concerns, claiming that the residency requirement would not apply in instances where there was evidence of abuse or neglect; however, critics feared that the vulnerable position of these sponsored women would result in them enduring abuse in order to obtain citizenship.

Parliamentarians also criticized these measures, citing differential treatment between relationships involving sponsored spouses and those involving Canadian citizens. As Don Davies – former NDP immigration critic – commented, "The plan is problematic because divorce rates in North American are so high – about 50 percent – within the first two years. The mere fact that a marriage doesn't work out within two years is not by itself an indication that the marriage wasn't legitimate" (Radia 2011). According to Davies, a residency requirement for immigrant families was inconsistent with the state's allowance of Canadian citizens to enter and exit conjugal relationships at their own discretion. For both groups of critics, these measures enacted by the government were both dangerous and unrealistic.

In addition to these legislative measures, the government enacted several changes that did not require amending the IRPA. The most significant of these changes was increased scrutiny of spousal sponsorship applications. In 2012, Kenney announced that immigration officers would undergo supplementary marriage fraud identification training and would be expected to be more diligent in their assessment of conjugal relationships (Citizenship and Immigration Canada 2012d). While the specifics of the training program were not revealed, discourses surrounding the anti-marriage fraud campaign foreshadowed the targeting of certain relationships in the name of deterring marriages of convenience. In an open letter to "ethnic Canadians" in April 2011, several Canadian immigration lawyers warned that the government's proposed policies would result in all sponsorship-seeking couples facing "additional, harsher, longer and more invasive scrutiny" (Radia 2011). The neutral phrasing of these measures suggested that scrutiny would be uniform; however, the actual enactment of these measures was far from neutral. By placing too much emphasis on trying to catch deviant applicants pre-application, certain relationships were targeted, and specific racialized, gendered, and sexualized discourses surrounding these relationships were reproduced.

Canadian Victim and Evil Foreign Queue Jumper

After marrying Fode Mohamed Soumah in Guinea in 2007, Lainie Towell – a Canadian citizen – sponsored Soumah at the end of that same year. Twenty-nine days after arriving in Canada, Soumah left Towell, claiming that Towell's personality changed once he arrived. Towell, a performance artist, charged that she had been duped into marrying Soumah so that he could immigrate to Canada. Donning her wedding gown with a red door strapped on her back and the words "Mr. Immigration Minister, it's getting heavy" written on the door, Towell walked to Parliament Hill, explaining that her performance symbolized the fact that her marriage was nothing but a doorway into Canada for Soumah (*National Post* 2012). In 2009, the IRB ruled that it lacked sufficient evidence to find Soumah guilty of engaging in a marriage of convenience, as the couple had a long romance in Guinea pre-marriage, and it was Towell who had proposed to Soumah. Interestingly, however, Towell provided the IRB with emails sent to Soumah suggesting he had fathered a child in Guinea with another woman. In light of this information, the IRB charged Soumah with "false representation" for failing to declare the existence of a dependent child in his application for sponsorship, and Soumah was subsequently deported.

Despite the fact that the IRB did not rule their relationship a marriage of convenience, Towell publicly branded herself a victim of marriage fraud and Soumah as a "marriage fraudster." Both Towell and Soumah became the poster children for the two main characters in this discourse of marriage fraud – Towell, the Canadian citizen who married for love only to be used and abandoned by her sponsored spouse, and Soumah, an evil foreigner who saw marriage as a one-way ticket to Canada. The language of victimization took centre stage in the anti–marriage fraud campaign, painting sponsors as helpless prey that fall victim to malicious sponsorship-seekers. While there are victims of marriage fraud, this distinction between "citizens as victims" and "noncitizens as evil queue jumpers" is misleading, as it ignores the complexity of spousal sponsorship.

The sponsorship process consists of a series of power dynamics between the sponsor and the sponsored. When discussing sponsorship with interviewed common-law and married couples, the consensus was that during the application process, the sponsor has all the power because without the sponsor's cooperation, the sponsored spouse would not gain access to the

Canadian state. The relationship changes once the sponsored spouse arrives in Canada; the sponsor is now financially responsible for the spouse regardless of whether the relationship stays intact. All relationships endure varying degrees of stress; however, couples seeking sponsorship face a unique tension that comes with the reality that when it comes to spousal sponsorship, citizenship is on the line. This was made evident by Juliet – whose common-law relationship was discussed in the previous chapter – commenting the following:

> This kind of process [the application process] could break people up because it is frustrating, time-consuming, annoying, and it has that aspect that all of a sudden I hold these cards and could impact Peter's life. Then, now [post-application], if Peter really wanted to, he could make my life miserable because now I'm legally responsible for him to apply for health care, prescription coverage, and social security. (Interviews)

When it comes to sponsoring a spouse, power belongs either to the sponsor or to the sponsored; it is never shared.

What is missing from this conception of power, and what this discourse of the Canadian victim and the evil foreign queue jumper highlights, is the issue of citizenship. Soumah's deportation shows that even with permanent residency, citizenship is not guaranteed. While the sponsor is financially responsible for the sponsored spouse, the sponsor is not without power. In this particular situation, Towell had the government on her side. The case of Towell and Soumah demonstrates that in circumstances of marriage fraud where the lines of citizenship have to be drawn, power imbalances between citizens, partial citizens, and noncitizens are reinforced. While the current system is by no means perfect, the Canadian citizen is not without agency. Citizenship is not a uniform status equally applied to all; there remain distinctions between Canadian-born and foreign-born citizens. This discourse fails to account for distinctions between citizens, potential citizens, and noncitizens.

Another interesting aspect of this dialogue is its racial component. In light of Towell's protest on Parliament Hill, CBC's *The Passionate Eye* released the 2010 documentary on marriages of convenience titled *True Love or Marriage Fraud? The Price of Heartache*. Using Towell's story as context, the film follows three Caucasian Canadian women as they apply to sponsor their Moroccan male spouses. While all three women were convinced that their husbands married them for love and not sponsorship, the film is premised on suspicion, inadvertently asking the women: You think you know ... but do you really know? This visual of the white Canadian woman who is naively marrying for love and the foreign male of colour who is using marriage to get into the country has been integral to the anti-marriage fraud campaign. The racialization of this dialogue does two things. It reinforces the eroticization of interracial relationships, casting these relationships as deviations from normalized conceptions of the traditional nuclear family (Yu 1998; Luibhéid 2002; Barnard 2004; Luibhéid and Cantù 2005). In between interviews with the women, scenes of the women exploring "exotic" Morocco – it is dusk, the markets are bustling, the air is sticky, and the women are receiving welcomed attention from men as they wander the streets – effectively capture the perceived naïveté of Canadian citizens that this dialogue aims to highlight; these women are innocently lured into this land of exotic romance, unable to think clearly about the intentions of their new husbands. This dialogue also recasts the man of colour as someone to be feared. The Canadian victim and the evil foreign queue jumper dialogue generates a culture of suspicion around foreign men – particularly foreign men of colour – suggesting that relationships between white Canadian women and foreign men of colour are less likely to be genuine. Framing marriage fraud along these lines establishes a narrative in which Canadian citizens are rendered helpless, and foreign sponsorship-seeking spouses are portrayed as immoral in comparison to the morally strong white Canadian citizen.

Countries of Suspicion

The anti-marriage fraud campaign targeted certain countries believed to be producing more marriages of convenience than others, specifically India and China. Singling out India as a country of concern, Kenney (2009) used a "wall of shame" metaphor – referring to a wall in the Canadian visa office in the Indian city of Chandigarh plastered with a selection of fraudulent documents ranging from fake death certificates to university diplomas, all of which are produced in exchange for a fee – to highlight a rise in organized marriage fraud. This rise was confirmed by an assistant deputy minister at IRCC, who remarked, "It's a trend we're starting to see, and the department is concerned that there's organized fraud taking place in India" (Deschênes 2009). China was also red flagged by IRCC – "What we found out from our office in Hong Kong is that, especially in the provinces of Guangdong and Fujian, there were groups that were organized to do exactly that [produce false documents for the purpose of spousal sponsorship]" (Deschênes 2009). In the case of organized marriage fraud, couples can obtain documents required for a spousal sponsorship application (wedding photos, third-party testimonies, marriage certificate) for anywhere from $15,000 to $60,000 (Interviews). According to IRCC, trends of organized marriage fraud were increasingly prominent in India and China, putting these countries at the top of the list in the government's anti–marriage fraud campaign.

The government provided minimal empirical data supporting their claim that rates of fraudulent applications were higher in India and China. While the refusal rate for spousal applications in China in 2009 was 50 percent, it is unclear what percentage were ruled marriages of convenience (Long 2009). Moreover, IRCC confirmed that a significant portion of the 50 percent refused won their appeals, further reducing the number of actual marriage fraud cases (Long 2009). IRCC believes that high refusal rates discourage fraudulent couples from applying, attributing the decline in marriage fraud – again, without any discussion of actual numbers – to the government's "constant vigilance" on this issue (Gilbert 2011b). In the case of India, the majority of marriages have been ruled genuine, with approximately 85 percent being approved (Gilbert 2011a). With only a 15 percent refusal rate and those refused not necessarily being marriages of convenience, it becomes difficult to accept justifications for increased attention paid toward this specific country. These numbers provide mixed messages as to the severity of marriage fraud committed in these countries and beg the question whether heightened scrutiny in India and China is warranted; this is further compounded by the fact there had been no discussion in Parliament or committee meetings comparing refusal rates in India and China to rates elsewhere. Both the government and IRCC failed to prove that marriage fraud is higher in these countries and that sponsorship-seeking couples from these countries were deserving of this level of suspicion.

As a result, assessment of spousal sponsorship applications in India and China became increasingly intensive. Canadian immigration officers working in these countries were instructed to be assiduous in their assessment of applications (Interviews). An anti-fraud unit was established at the visa office in New Delhi where trained officers were expected to prevent and detect marriages of convenience. As a former immigration officer explained, "Case assessment is entirely dependent on the area in which you're located. When I was stationed in London, cases were rarely refused. When I was stationed in Delhi, couples were considered guilty until proven innocent. Geographical location meant everything" (Interviews). In most countries, immigration officers have the authority to waive interviews with a couple if they are satisfied that the relationship is genuine based on the written application alone. In China, however, this was not the case; all sponsorship applicants had to be interviewed in order for concerns of fraud to be quelled (Gilbert 2011a). There was a strong bias among officers posted in these countries, as they were trained to assume that individuals here were more likely to use marriage as a ticket to immigrate to Canada.

Heightened scrutiny of applications, combined with high refusal rates, meant that wait times for family reunification in these countries were longer. At a Standing Committee on Citizenship and Immigration meeting in 2009, Elizabeth Long, an immigration lawyer, discussed the status of sponsorship wait times, specifically in relation to high refusal rates in China. The average wait time for processing a spousal sponsorship application in most countries was twelve months. Should the application be refused and the decision appealed, the average wait time for appeals was eighteen to twenty months. In China, where the refusal rate was more than 50 percent and appeal rates were high, you were looking at couples who had been separated for a minimum of three years. As Long (2009) remarked, wait times for couples applying through visa offices in China tended to be even longer, ranging from three to five years. In addition to the financial implications of applying for sponsorship, costs that are drawn out when wait times are extended, separated couples experience an emotional toll as well. As Olivia Chow (2009) commented in Parliament, "This unfair, cruel and mean-spirited practice is really asking that when Canadians fall in love and decide to get married, they should double-check to make sure the person is not of a precarious immigration status." This discourse unfairly vilified and penalized couples form certain countries, further distinguishing between the good and bad sponsored spouse.

In addition to certain countries being targeted, certain types of conjugal relationships – specifically arranged marriages – were overly scrutinized as well. Common in many countries, including India, long-distance matchmaking between Canadian citizens and their foreign spouses has long been a contentious issue. The anti–marriage fraud campaign had some Canadians with ties to South Asia concerned that arranged marriages were now more likely to be labelled marriages of convenience (CBC News 2010). In a traditional arranged marriage, the conjugal relationship typically begins post-wedding; for couples in a long-distance arranged marriage, the development of a conjugal relationship is often prolonged until the spouse is successfully sponsored. As Imran Qayyum, chair of the Canadian Migration Institute commented, "Spouses in arranged unions often don't get to know each other until after they've wed, which can raise red flags with immigration officials – even though such marriages are statistically more likely to hold together than romantic matrimonies" (CBC News 2010). As previously discussed, IRCC has accounted for the unique situation of couples in arranged marriages by assessing couples according to predetermined assumptions and stereotypes of cultural compatibility. Sponsored spouses in arranged marriages from India are therefore in a double bind, as their applications are automatically compromised by their geographical location and then further scrutinized to determine whether their relationships are consistent with the Canadian relationship narrative for arranged marriages.

For Kenney, what was at stake in the crackdown on marriage fraud was system integrity; those who immigrate to Canada under false pretenses undermine the legitimacy of our immigration system. Marriage fraud does affect a state and its citizens; however, the extent to which this is affecting the Canadian state and its citizens remains ambiguous. Without clear data on rates of marriage fraud, it was difficult for the Harper government to claim that marriage fraud had reached a crisis point in Canada. Moreover, the framing of this campaign and the discourses that it produced suggests there was more at stake than immigration system integrity. What connects this examination of the Harper government's anti–marriage fraud campaign with earlier discussions concerning the role of relationship history in the assessment of sexual minority refugee claims and the treatment of common-law couples under the current spousal sponsorship process is that in addition to maintaining system integrity, Canadian governments have developed and continue to develop immigration policy that protects both the conjugal family unit and the institution of marriage. Put simply, marriages of convenience are considered a threat to normalized under-standings of family and marriage. This campaign allowed the Harper government to protect the conjugal family unit and the institution of marriage in a way that restricted access to certain types of personal rela-tionships. By developing discourses that targeted certain couples, relation-ships that challenged traditional notions of family and marriage continued to be labelled deviant. The integrity of the Canadian immigration system is therefore reliant on more than simply preventing bad apples from getting in. It depends on the state limiting entry while simultaneously reinforcing particular understandings of family, marriage, and conjugality.

In addition to dictating which conjugal relationships are worthy of access to Canadian borders, this crackdown on marriage fraud also fur-thered the precariousness of those sponsored spouses living in Canada as permanent residents. Prior to the Harper government establishing resi-dency requirements, sponsored spouses were subjected to citizenship revocation if found guilty of misrepresentation. Residency requirements enhance the vulnerability of sponsored spouses by placing more power in the hands of the state and sponsors. Either way, citizenship is never a guarantee for sponsored spouses; rather, citizenship hangs in the balance, dependent on a couple's ability to reproduce state-defined conjugal values. Indeed, the sponsored spouse's individual citizenship status is contingent on the success of their conjugal family unit.

The consequences of immigration fraud should not be minimized; however, the Harper government's anti–marriage fraud campaign – without any clear empirical justification – warranted questioning. Even if a more rigorous analysis of rates of misrepresentation confirmed the government's claim that marriage fraud had reached a crisis point in Canada, their strategy of making spousal sponsorship more restrictive was not necessarily the answer. This is primarily due to the fact that these restrictions were not uniform; government scrutiny was and continues to be selective. Instead of focusing on how to keep people out, attention should be paid to examining how the arguably arbitrary nature of state-recognized conjugal compatibility lends itself to being easily replicated. Is conjugality as it is currently defined by the Canadian state an effective method of assessment for its immigration and refugee program? Is there an alternative way to monitor access to our borders? It is these questions I now turn my attention toward in the final chapter.

6

Rethinking Conjugality

"Through the legal recognition of personal adult relationships, the state has recognized and supported some relationships but failed to recognize others; as a result, people's choices are not being respected."

– LAW COMMISSION OF CANADA

In their article "What Is Marriage-Like Like? The Irrelevance of Conjugality," Brenda Cossman and Bruce Ryder (2001) contend that a trend exists in Canadian law – when it comes to outlining the boundaries of conjugality, the once important sexual component is becoming increasingly insignificant. With the court ruling in *Molodowich v Penttinen* that intimate relationships believed to be worthy of state recognition should be evaluated according to a set of functional attributes, the existence of a monogamous sexual relationship no longer held primacy in determining conjugality.[1] Interestingly, while the courts' understanding of conjugality became more expansive, answers to the question, "What is conjugality?" remained elusive (Cossman and Ryder 2001, 270). For Cossman and Ryder, state recognition of conjugal relationships consisting of a series of attributes means that less attention is paid toward whether the couple in question is sleeping together, and more attention is paid toward establishing whether a relationship of interdependency exists. As such, the irrelevancy of a sexual component further blurs the line between conjugal and nonconjugal relationships, the assumption being that if we take away the sexual component, a relationship traditionally identified as conjugal is now no different from relationships of interdependency between friends, family members, etc. It therefore becomes increasingly difficult for the state to uphold this distinction between conjugal and nonconjugal; Cossman and Ryder conclude that conjugality, as we understand it, has been reduced to a minimal role in state recognition of personal relationships.

The question of whether conjugality continues to be an effective access point for Canadian citizenship runs throughout this book. As my analysis suggests, the state retains a vested interest in conjugality depending on what is at stake, the result being the inconsistent treatment of conjugality in Canadian law and policy. Sexual stereotypes of queer relationship patterns are used to assess the legitimacy of one's sexual identity and whether that sexual identity is in need of state protection. In addition, the Canadian state's treatment of common-law conjugality as synonymous with marriage in family class sponsorship creates unfair and inconsistent expectations for Canadian citizens wishing to sponsor a common-law spouse. While common-law status is defined primarily by cohabitation within Canadian borders, cohabitation alone is insufficient for common-law couples seeking sponsorship. As such, couples applying for sponsorship must prove their relationships are conjugal and as my interviews with common-law couples suggest, the assumption of a sexual component is not immaterial to determining conjugality. Finally, the Harper government's crackdown on marriages of convenience encouraged an increasingly restrictive interpretation of conjugality for family class migration, targeting certain types of conjugal families. This suggests that even within the conjugal family unit, families receive differential treatment; Canadian state privileging of conjugality is not universal.

Returning to Cossman and Ryder's (2001) question: is conjugality irrelevant in Canadian law and policy? My answer is no. These three areas of Canada's immigration program highlight that while citizenship is individualized, the type of citizen the Canadian state seeks influences family formation. Citizenship is therefore not awarded to the conjugal family unit because this particular family formation best performs the functions of citizenship; rather, the provision of citizenship is predetermined by state conceptions of family, care, and interdependency. Like Cossman and Ryder, however, I too question whether this privileging of conjugal relationships best serves the objectives of the Canadian state. The question we should therefore be posing is not *does* conjugality matter, but *should* conjugality matter? If conjugality should not matter, how can we re-evaluate Canadian law and policy to make it more accommodating for our personal relationships, and what are the implications of such reassessment?

This chapter examines several policy frameworks capable of accounting for nonconjugal relationships. While these frameworks are a combination of theoretical and actual, none of them have been applied to immigration policy; an examination of the political implications such a transformation would entail is thus required. Through an examination of these frameworks, this chapter takes stock of theoretical debates surrounding the legal parameters of nonconjugality and provides a starting point for future discussion on immigration, family, and citizenship. In doing so, I aspire to establish a space for discussing the possibility of an immigration system in which the conjugal family unit no longer holds primacy.

Beyond Conjugality: The LCC and Nonconjugal Relationships

In 2001, the same-sex marriage debate inspired the Law Commission of Canada (LCC), an independent law reform body established in 1997 through the *Law Commission of Canada Act,* to conduct a study, titled *Beyond Conjugality,* focused on the state of legal recognition of intimate relationships. At the time, common-law status was available to both same-sex and opposite-sex couples; however, marriage remained a heterosexual privilege. Critical of the pro-marriage movement's limited focus, as well as of state treatment of relationship recognition more generally, the LCC saw this debate as an opportunity for a broader discussion regarding why the law relies on personal relationships as criteria for the distribution of rights, benefits, and burdens in the first place:

> Those debates about spouse invariably opened up debate about what the purpose of this challenge was and the poor fit between the definition of spouse and the purpose of those laws. While that was implicitly part of the litigation, it was not being explored with the same rigor we felt it should be. So while we were certainly not unsupportive of the fight for same-sex marriage, those of us involved with the LCC report felt it was

important to not let the broader question of the state's role in personal relationships slip away. It seemed to us to be a good moment to ask those broader questions because they were getting asked here and there in the court rulings and public debates, but they were not being pursued. So that was the driving force ... the sense that the conversation had been opened up but not in a way that would allow for sustained conversation. (Interviews)

Echoing this LCC member, the then president of the LCC commented, "It was at a time where the question of gay rights was prevalent, and there was a sense that there was still some ambivalence and ambiguity about how the law would respond to non-traditional sexual relationships. More widely, the big question was why?" (Interviews). In *Beyond Conjugality*, the LCC advocated for a more "comprehensive and principled approach" with respect to recognizing and supporting a wider range of personal relationships, necessitating a re-evaluation of what constitutes an intimate relationship in the first place (2001, ix). The LCC also took issue with the state's ambiguous definition of conjugality despite the fact that conjugality was so heavily relied on in policy and legal circles – "Conjugality lacks clarity, it is under-inclusive of the range of personal adult relationships that deserve recognition and it is at least potentially unduly intrusive of individual privacy" (Law Commission of Canada 2001, 34).

The LCC recommended that the government focus on addressing differences in legal treatment of conjugal and nonconjugal cohabitants and on providing citizens with the freedom to choose whether and with whom to form close personal relationships:

The value of autonomy requires that governments put in place the conditions in which people can freely choose their close personal relationships. The state must also avoid direct or indirect forms of coercive interference with adults' freedom to choose whether or not to form, or remain in, close personal relationships. While governments should do everything in their power to provide information and education and otherwise minimize the conditions that lead to the formation and continuation of abusive relationships, they should not create financial or other kinds of pressure to discourage relationships without reference to their qualitative attributes. (Law Commission of Canada 2001, 18)

The assumption is this – by privileging certain adult personal relationships over others, one's freedom of autonomy and equality is compromised. True autonomy requires that governments establish conditions for citizens to freely develop their personal relationships; true equality requires that governments promote equality between different types of relationships, as well as within relationships. In addition to governments needing to account for autonomy and equality when framing policy intended to acknowledge personal relationships, the LCC prescribed policy that seeks to improve personal security (economic, psychological, emotional, and physical), privacy (freedom from unwarranted state intrusion), religious freedom (recognizing the evolving nature of religion, particularly with respect to marriage), and coherency/efficiency in the development of policies (2001, 19–25).

The report proposed a new methodology for assessing existing/proposed laws dealing with close personal relationships, premised on four questions:

- Does the law pursue a legitimate policy objective? If the answer is no, then the law should be repealed.
- If we agree that the law's objectives are sound, are the included relationships relevant to these objectives? If not, then unnecessary references to relationships should be removed.
- If the relationships are relevant to these objectives and relationships do in fact matter, could the law in question allow individuals to choose which of their own personal relationships they want subjected? If the answer to this is yes, then the law should be revised to allow for self-determination of personal relationships.
- If relationships do matter but public policy requires that the law delineate the relevant relationships to which it applies, can the law be revised to more accurately include a more realistic range of relationships? Should this be possible, the law needs to be revised so that it embodies the appropriate combination of functional attributes and formal types of status. (Law Commission of Canada 2001, 31)

In order to accomplish this, Parliament had at minimum two options – develop a uniform functional definition for ascribing partnership that makes the sexual component of a relationship obsolete, or take a more contextual approach and tailor definitions for particular statutes. Favouring the latter, the LCC recognized that the appropriate level of relationship recognition varies across legal domains.

How does re-envisioning the relevancy of relationships in Canadian law and policy translate to immigration? In *Beyond Conjugality*, the LCC identifies family reunification as the primary objective of immigration legislation in Canada and takes the position that the concept of family itself is not the issue so long as we interpret family to be "deeply rooted relationships of interdependence" (Law Commission of Canada 2001, 43). Where the LCC takes issue is the exclusionary nature of the familial unit as currently dictated by law. In the report, the LCC examines the possibility for familial self-definition within the current immigration system, proposing three broader categories for family class applicants: (1) kinship through marital and offspring ties, recognizing spouses and dependent children as applicants; (2) extended kinship to include fiancé(e)s, parents, and grandparents; and (3) self-defined kinship giving sponsors the capacity to determine "who is the most important to them, and who is part of what they consider family in the broadest sense" (Law Commission of Canada 2001, 45). In this light, family becomes less about composition and more about interdependency. Accounting for potential abuse of this third category, the LCC stipulates that sponsors would continue to be financially responsible for whomever they choose to sponsor. Moreover, the sponsor must demonstrate that the sponsored individual is emotionally important to them. For the LCC, the application process itself does not have to be altered – applicants would continue to be expected to prove their relationship with their sponsor is genuine. What changes is the allowance of self-selection; individuals would have the capacity to dictate who composes their kinship network. Ultimately, the state would relinquish control over deciding who constitutes the "sponsorable" family member. These policy prescriptions are not meant to suggest that nonconjugal relationships can be easily assimilated into policy frameworks made for conjugal relationships (Cossman and Ryder 2001, 319). Regardless, the LCC contends that an understanding of how "personal relationships are negotiated and performed" through family reunification processes should not be shied away from due to a fear of logistical headaches (Law Commission of Canada 2001, 44).

Beyond Conjugality was met with resistance from several sides. Religious groups and right-wing organizations like REAL Women of Canada took issue with the LCC supporting family models that went beyond the traditional nuclear unit. While the Chrétien government was not vocally opposed to the policy prescriptions outlined in the report, its response was nevertheless underwhelming (Interviews). As the then president of the LCC explained:

> It [the report] was tabled and the government ... well, I think it was too scary of a report. In my conversations with the minister of justice at the time, they liked the report. This report was not designed to solve immediate problems of the government; it critiqued the knee-jerk approach to relationships. It was the first report that was a problem for them because they had to respond, but they responded very minimally and did not officially engage with it. (Interviews)

The reaction of the Liberal government to the report was ultimately indifference. In addition to the subject material of the report itself, interviewed former members of the LCC attributed this unresponsiveness to timing. While the LCC saw the same-sex marriage debate in Canada as an opportune time to address state treatment of personal relationships more generally, interviewees recognized the challenge of getting both the government and the public to discuss these broader questions of relationship recognition, with same-sex marriage topping the agenda – "The Liberal government was still consumed with the same-sex marriage debate and spent a lot of political capital on getting that passed" (Interviews). Pro–same-sex marriage activists were fearful that multiple relationship categories would scare away public support. Same-sex rights organizations such as Egale felt that the incorporation of nonconjugal relationships into Canadian law and policy prior to the legalization of same-sex marriage would result in same-sex relationships being subsumed within a nonconjugal category – "The report was about giving rights to tennis partners" (Interviews). These groups felt that by supporting nonconjugal relationships, the LCC had chosen not to support same-sex marriage. For the then president of the

LCC, this accusation ignored the fact that "this project was bigger than gay rights. The question was whether social policy should continue to be defined around conjugality as a proxy for interdependence" (Interviews). These organizations assured the LCC that a discussion of alternative relationships would follow once same-sex marriage was legalized (Interviews).

Fast-forward to 2018, same-sex marriage is now legal in Canada; however, this dialogue of alternative relationships has yet to materialize, and Canada remains a country that only recognizes and protects conjugal relationships (Cossman and Ryder 2017). This is due in large part to the Harper government's cessation of funding to the LCC in 2006. More importantly, however, the Canadian state is comfortable with a status quo in which conjugality is no longer discriminatory yet remains a privileged status, as a framer of *Beyond Conjugality* explains:

> My sense in Canada is that now that same-sex marriage has been legalized and most of the discrimination against gay and lesbian couples has been removed, that attention in the area has shifted. When it comes to the category of conjugality, it seems like the debate has moved on. I don't think that is true globally, and I don't think it is likely to remain that way indefinitely because the issues keep coming up, and jurisdictions that are currently grappling with the debate about same-sex marriage are inevitably having a discussion about why marriage matters and why conjugality matters. They are still in the thick of it, so to speak. I think it opens up space for a range of critical understandings of conjugality. (Interviews)

As this book suggests, there remains a need for revisiting the theoretical questions posed in *Beyond Conjugality,* and to explore the role conjugality plays in the creation of families and, consequently, the construction of citizens through our immigration and refugee program.

Beyond Conjugality: In Action

While *Beyond Conjugality* drew attention to state treatment of personal relationships within the context of Canada, academics and governments alike have addressed the prominent position of conjugality beyond Canadian borders as well. With the passing of the *Civil Partnership Act* in the United Kingdom, awarding civil unions to same-sex couples, legal scholars called for a conversation focused on distinguishing between the purpose and function of relationship recognition and the romantic ideology surrounding the family. Similar to Canada, the extension of conjugal benefits to same-sex couples was viewed as an opportunity to extend recognition to nonconjugal relationships:

> In the structure of the CPA [*Civil Partnership Act*], the omission of an express requirement for a sexual and monogamous relationship could, despite the partnership being otherwise almost identical to marriage overall, be said to provide some evidence of a shift from recognition of relationships based on their similarity to a conjugal, marital relationship, towards much more functional criteria and pragmatic concerns for legally recognizing relationships. (Barker 2006, 244)

Despite this possibility, Barker warns that while the framing of these debates appears promising for those advocating for state recognition of nonconjugal relationships, the push for legalizing same-sex relationships remains transfixed on conjugality. Echoing the LCC, Barker attributes this to the fact that motivations for legalizing civil unions remain in line with those for marriage (2006, 242). Scholars in the United States have used these discussions in Canada and the United Kingdom to advocate for the deconstruction of state recognition of conjugality altogether. As Martha Fineman contends, "We do not need marriage and we should abolish it as a legal category, transferring the social and economic subsidies and privilege it now receives to a new family core connection – that of the caretaker-dependent" (2006, 30). Similarly, Nancy Polikoff cautions that while extending legal rights and obligations to same-sex couples is a start, ceasing the extension of rights there is insufficient, as it continues to rely on the couple as the only type of family worthy of recognition (2008, 4). Another proposal is to have a nonconjugal regime for only nonfinancial policy areas (medical visits, immigration, etc.) in which the individual would have the capacity to assess the importance of their personal relationships (Walker 2001, 750). For these scholars, establishing a progressive regime of legally recognized relationships goes beyond same-sex marriage; rather, it is contingent on the realization that family is not synonymous with conjugality.

In addition to academics undertaking these debates, several governments have developed policies aimed at recognizing nonconjugal relationships including Tasmania's *Relationships Act,* Hawaii's *Act Relating to Unmarried Couples,* and Alberta's *Adult Interdependent Relationships Act* (AIRA). While the motivations behind these initiatives vary, all three provide an opportunity of recognition for nonconjugal relationships of care.[2] Enacted in 2003, the AIRA covers "a range of personal relationships that fall outside of marriage, including committed platonic relationships where two people agree to share emotional and economic responsibilities" (Alberta Ministry of Justice 2003). Relationships recognized by the AIRA involve two key elements: parties must be in an economically and emotionally interdependent relationship and must be cohabiting in this interdependent relationship for a minimum of three years. Unlike legislation in Tasmania and Hawaii, the AIRA is a personal agreement between two individuals; there is no central registry process. Furthermore, these have been situations where the status of adult interdependent partners is ascribed after three years regardless of a formal agreement existing or not between the parties involved. Under the AIRA, partners are entitled to the following: financial support from each other, the right to register together for coverage under the Alberta Health Care Insurance Plan, spousal insurance coverage, access to the deceased partner's estate, the right to sue for wrongful death, and the right to health care decision making. While it is possible to opt out of some of these statutes, it is not possible to opt out of all of them. The AIRA remains intact; however, same-sex marriage is now provincially recognized as well.

The AIRA drew criticism for its conservative intentions to continue reserving marriage for heterosexual couples. Glennon contends that these initiatives were taken in response to the proposed extension of some conjugal rights to same-sex couples, the reaction being to give these rights to all relationships in order to avoid giving "special recognition" to same-sex relationships (2005, 157). For Glennon, this reinforces the heteronormative nature of marriage by limiting the use of "spouse" to married couples and ascribing spousal rights to a range of conjugal and platonic relationships. By recognizing everyone, these governments were arguably recognizing no one. While the motivations for passing the AIRA were undoubtedly strategic, to momentarily sidestep legalizing same-sex marriage, it is important to recognize the possibilities these acts present for state recognition of nonconjugal relationships. In this light, one could argue that these acts present "a radical (if less threatening because less sexual) challenge to the presumed naturalness and ensuring privilege of the heteronormative married family" (Harder 2009b, 634). This is particularly possible in the context of the AIRA, as same-sex marriage is now legal, rendering initial motivations for the AIRA irrelevant. The AIRA provides a starting point for state recognition of nonconjugal relationships – "Canada will achieve even greater justice for families if the law embraces the principles of the *Beyond Conjugality* report and considers the Alberta *Adult Interdependent Relationships Act* a model from which to build other projects for nonconjugal relationships" (Polikoff 2008, 115).

Policy initiatives like the AIRA highlight the ability of the state to recognize adult personal relationships beyond the realm of the conjugal couple. It is important to note, however, that in these examples, legislation was enacted at either the provincial or state level and applies only to those living within these borders. It is therefore difficult to look at these policies and fully comprehend the repercussions should these policies be enacted at the national level and incorporate immigration rights. This raises the question: If we were to consider the LCC's recommendations for family reunification and entertain the possibility of nonconjugal sponsorship, what are the implications?

Beyond Conjugality: Implications

While implications are multiple, there are three primary tensions encapsulated within discussions of state relationship recognition and the reconceptualization of family reunification to include nonconjugal relationships. First, examining the politics of relationship recognition highlights the complexity of these discussions, including the logistical debate concerning the connection between recognition through ascription (the automatic attribution of a particular status to a relationship) versus recognition through registration (the act of individuals applying for relationship status). Deliberations about who controls admission complicate the provision of recognition. The second tension emerges with the potential insurgence of new migrants and state capacity to accommodate this potential influx. The third and final tension addresses attachments, both political and social, to the nuclear family; the implementation of these policy recommendations not only has implications for nonconjugal relationships, but for conjugal relationships as well. If we are to take these policy initiatives seriously and re-evaluate what constitutes family in Canada's immigration program, it is imperative that we recognize and account for these challenges.

Politics of Relationship Recognition

A common argument for state recognition of nonconjugal relationships is that as sexual intimacy becomes increasingly irrelevant in the legal assessment of conjugality, it becomes rather difficult to distinguish between conjugal and nonconjugal relationships. Advocates for nonconjugal relationship recognition claim that due to the interdependent nature of these relationships, extending state recognition would ultimately not change the substance of these relationships. This is misleading, as it neglects the reality that with state recognition comes responsibility – "A movement that seeks public recognition of its personal relationships concedes that the power to bestow value on them lies in the public ... and a movement that seeks state recognition of its personal relationships concedes that the power to evaluate and rank them lies in the state" (Halley 2001, 99). Recognition enhances state power by placing nonconjugal relationships under the same microscope already used to appraise the legitimacy of conjugal relationships. One could argue that state recognition of nonconjugal relationships undermines the very crux of critiques against state privileging of conjugality, the idea that the state should have no place in one's personal relationships. If the issue is state intrusion into the private details of our lives, then enhancing state power through a policy framework that recognizes nonconjugal relationships appears paradoxical. As such, what would change with recognition is that nonconjugal relationships would no longer be free from the gaze of the state.

Further, the LCC is not proposing that all relationships merit state acknowledgment, leaving the state to establish criteria for assessment. In *Beyond Conjugality*, the LCC stipulated that involved parties must prove their relationships are genuinely interdependent. In doing so, the state would now be responsible for establishing what constitutes a legitimate relationship, creating a new hierarchy of relationship recognition and ultimately new forms of exclusion. Cossman's work on sexual citizenship suggests that if we look toward "processes of becoming" that turn the noncitizen into a Canadian citizen, we must recognize that citizenship "becomes part of the present" (2007, 9). The fact that citizenship is in constant flux means that extending state discretion to the assessment of nonconjugal relationships will result in the redrawing of the boundaries of citizenship in line with the state's view of legitimate and illegitimate nonconjugal relationships. Is it therefore desirable to have this type of arrangement for all of our personal relationships? One could argue that the state is already present. In its privileging of conjugal relationships for the purpose of migration, the state controls family formation through negotiations of citizenship. In doing so, those whose relationships fall outside the current framework are excluded and denied access. Nonconjugal relationships are therefore already politicized. In this light, so long as the state has a role in evaluating our personal relationships, there will continue to be relationship inequality.

State recognition also changes the substance of relationships from within, particularly at the point of dissolution. Individuals are participants in a variety of relationships from which they can walk away without consequence; state recognition of nonconjugal relationships could complicate this. State recognition of nonconjugal relationships would submit the parties involved to similar accountabilities for conjugal couples. While all benefits wrapped up in state recognition are perceived as positive, this is arguably not the case (Boyd and Young 2003). The extension of state recognition to nonconjugal relationships has implications with respect to how we develop and foster our personal relationships, an action made increasingly difficult with state interference. State recognition of one's personal relationships comes at a cost. With recognition comes symbolic value and access to rights; however, the relationship is then open to state intrusion. Private lives are made increasingly public and assessed in terms of their legitimacy as dictated by the state. There are, however, many who desire recognition and feel that current state treatment suggests their relationships are less important and interdependent than conjugal relationships. These tensions speak to the complexity of recognition and caution against conceptualizing the inclusion of nonconjugal relationships as either wholly beneficial or wholly problematic.

If we are to agree that the state should recognize nonconjugal relationships and, for the most part, that individuals desire that recognition, a more logistical discussion about whether recognition should be ascribed (the automatic designation of recognition) or registered (individuals seeking formal acknowledgment from the state) must transpire. The federal government, as well as the majority of provincial governments, ascribe common-law status to couples living in a conjugal cohabiting relationship for a fixed period of time. Through ascription, governments are "able to convey benefits and duties on couples regardless of whether the parties to a relationship are willing to take on these obligations" (Harder 2007, 162). This reliance on ascription stems from the Supreme Court's approach toward recognizing common-law relationships in order to protect vulnerable and dependent partners at the point of dissolution, concluding that the state's interest is to "facilitate stability and certainty in relationships ... [by] providing citizens with mechanisms to ... meet their needs should they suffer a sudden deprivation of emotional and economic support resulting from death, illness, injury or the breakdown of their relationships (Law Commission of Canada 2001, 15). Canadian state reliance on ascription therefore accounts for the reality that relationships of interdependency do not necessarily evolve or dissolve by choice, as made clear in *Molodowich v Penttinen*. One could therefore argue that ascription would be desirable in order to avoid one party benefiting from the relationship at the expense of the other party involved.

While the ascription of recognition to nonconjugal relationships would arguably accomplish similar objectives, that being the protection of vulnerable parties, the automatic ascription of relationship status to all nonconjugal relationships is undesirable in certain situations. Returning to the spouse in the house rule in the Harris government's welfare legislation, the amendment captured numerous relationships not considered conjugal, making hundreds of single mothers ineligible for social assistance as a sole support parent. Ascribing recognition to nonconjugal relationships could potentially have a similar impact; by broadening the range of state-recognized relationships to include nonconjugal partnerships, the state inevitably acknowledges relationships that individuals do not necessarily want recognized. Moreover, as made evident by the spouse in the house rule, recognition has the potential to target certain individuals marked by, for example, race, class, and gender.

In the case of immigration, the debate between ascription and registration is different, as parties vying for sponsorship would still need to prove to immigration officers that their nonconjugal relationships are, in fact, genuine. This is due primarily to the fact that these relationships will not be formally recognized in their home countries, a problem experienced by many common-law couples seeking family reunification. When common-law couples apply for reunification without formal recognition of their relationship in the sponsored spouse's home country, they are evaluated according to the Canadian state's understanding of what constitutes a legitimate conjugal relationship. The implications of extending recognition to nonconjugal relationships, whether ascribed or registered, are therefore similar to those experienced by common-law couples. A lack of recognition in one's home country would put the Canadian state in a position of authority to assess the genuineness of their nonconjugal relationship that the individual wants recognized for the purpose of reunification. In applying for sponsorship, the Canadian model of relationship recognition is ascribed to involved parties; nonconjugal relationships would be assessed according to a list of characteristics defined by the Canadian state for relationships within Canadian borders. Should nonconjugal relationships be formally recognized, it is imperative that these power imbalances be addressed.

Increased Immigration and the Numbers Game

Another tension inherent in this discussion of nonconjugal relationship recognition involves perceived threats such recognition would present for immigration itself. These concerns often take the shape of a slippery slope argument in terms of what expanding family reunification would mean both from the outside (those who want to get into Canada) and from the inside (the impact inclusion would have on Canadian society at large). Liberal theorists contend that there is little justification for states to maintain restrictive borders – "Borders should generally be open and people should normally be free to leave their country of origin and settle in another, subject only to the sorts of constraints that bind current citizens in their new country" (Carens 1987, 251). Consistent with liberal theories of citizenship discussed in Chapter 1, this position is grounded in the belief that if our institutions are to remain neutral with respect to conceptions of the good life, then it becomes difficult to rationalize restricting one's movement from one country to another.

Recognizing that immigration controls are at times necessary, qualifications have been added. Restrictions are therefore consistent with liberal principles so long as international controls are absent (Heath 1997) or control is necessary for the protection of cultural groups against external pressures (Kymlicka 1989). On the other hand, communitarian theorists take issue with the claim that states have a moral obligation to make their borders universally accessible, the assumption being that if the cultural integrity of a community is considered an intrinsic good, immigration controls are acceptable if the goal is to secure this shared conception of the good (Walzer 1984). From a theoretical standpoint, this debate highlights the difficulty in establishing a starting point when it comes to discussing the further opening of state borders, as liberal and communitarian theorists justify minimal and maximum limits respectively.

This is not to suggest that the extension of immigration rights to nonconjugal relationships means abolishing all migration controls; the LCC's framework attempts to work within the Canadian immigration system, not to eliminate it altogether. There are, however, parallels between general fears of unrestricted immigration and the inclusion of nonconjugal relationships in our family reunification program – if we extend family reunification rights to nontraditional family arrangements, then what is next? While current guidelines for family reunification establish distinctions between those who have a legitimate claim to Canadian citizenship and, consequently, those who do not, the allowance of nonconjugal sponsorship would perceivably disrupt these boundaries. The critique here is that a legitimate claim for sponsorship would no longer be as easily identifiable, as the relationship in question lacks a clear starting point present in conjugal relationships (Interviews).

What is misleading about this argument is its suggestion that when it comes to conjugal relationships, legitimacy relies solely on a clearly identified moment when the relationship is formally recognized by the state, either through the provision of a marriage certificate or the declaration of common-law status. As demonstrated, discretion exercised by immigration authorities to assess the genuineness of a conjugal relationship highlights that a clear starting point does not necessarily translate to a successful application. Moreover, common-law couples often face the challenge of proving that a legitimate conjugal relationship exists, as they often lack formal state recognition at the time of application. The assumption that the current spousal sponsorship process is unambiguous is therefore flawed; claiming that extending family reunification to include nonconjugal relationships would challenge the clear-cut nature of the current program ignores the reality that the current program is anything but unequivocal.

Public support for changes in immigration and refugee policy typically wanes when the proposed changes perceivably make the system vulnerable to abuse (Interviews). This is compounded by government initiatives like the anti–marriage fraud campaign; the panic surrounding marriage fraud was used to bolster arguments that the assessment of conjugality needs to be even more restrictive in order to prevent system abuse. Interviewed policy analysts discussed how extending family reunification to nonconjugal relationships would mean that individuals could bring in whomever they wish. This expressed concern had racial undertones – the question was not *how many* Canadian citizens would take advantage of nonconjugal sponsorship, but rather *which* Canadian citizens. A former policy analyst expressed this sentiment:

> Immigrants from the United States and Western Europe would not be sponsoring a ton of people because they [those living in the afore-mentioned countries] probably do not want to immigrate, and if they did, they probably would not need nonconjugal sponsorship to do so. The people who would use the system would be those from developing countries who would try to sponsor anyone they possibly could. With conjugal sponsorship, you know you are only getting one [immigrant], but with nonconjugal sponsorship, the number is unknown. (Interviews)

Changes to Canada's immigration and refugee program, as well as resistance toward those changes, are not racially neutral. Critiques on extending recognition to nonconjugal relationships are premised on the fear that the weakening of migration controls will result in the flooding of sponsorship applications from undesirable applicants. Uneasiness with proposals like *Beyond Conjugality* stem from the fear that if nonconjugal relationships are recognized, the state will have less control over who has access to our borders – the assumption being that a decrease in state control has negative consequences for both the state and its citizens. Apprehension is therefore not grounded in concerns for what this would mean for the state; it is about protecting both the Canadian nation and the Canadian family from unwanted outsiders.

Implications for Conjugal Relationships

Social conservatives in Canada have been vocally opposed to the extension of state recognition to any intimate relationship that strays from the heterosexual definition of marriage. This resistance was evident following the release of *Beyond Conjugality;* right-wing organizations like REAL Women of Canada accused the LCC of devaluing marriage (Interviews). From this standpoint, the extension of state recognition to nonconjugal relationships further undermines the traditional nuclear family model. Critiques of non-heteronormative relationship recognition rely on a romanticized nostalgia of family life, ignorant of the reality that a single traditional family unit is a myth (Coontz 1992). In actuality, what constitutes family is in constant flux. This was the LCC's response to conservative critics, that families in all their forms are already recognized by the state in some way; therefore, there is a need for policy that facilitates equal and just recognition – "Speaking about under-inclusiveness or over-inclusiveness of the law is an important aspect of the institution of law reform. That is the job. The job is to look at whether the job we think we're doing is the job we're actually doing" (Interviews). For the LCC, the main objective of *Beyond Conjugality* is not to undercut marriage; rather, it is to advocate for equal treatment of all relationships under the law.

Proposals for the recognition of nonconjugal relationships during the same-sex marriage debates were criticized for reducing same-sex conjugal relationships to friendships (Lahey 1999; Boyd and Young 2003; Glennon 2005). In this light, state recognition of nonconjugal relationships would arguably minimize the work of those involved in the pro–same-sex marriage movement. While same-sex marriage is now legal, same-sex couples continue to be disadvantaged in certain respects. Same-sex couples remain unable to enjoy social recognition to the same extent opposite-sex couples do in many parts of the country, despite the fact that same-sex marriage has now been legal for over ten years. The inclusion of sexual orientation in the Charter's section 15 equality rights and provincial human rights acts and the establishment of hate crime laws have assured gay and lesbian citizens serious and much-needed protections (Warner 2002); however, formal rights and protections fail to fully address or eliminate all forms of systemic oppression (Janoff 2005; Sears 2007). Relational equality among conjugal relationships therefore remains an ongoing project and, as such, makes it difficult to focus on substantive equality when formal equality has yet to be fully achieved.

Continued challenges for sexual minorities are evident in Canada's current immigration and refugee program. As examined in Chapter 3, relationships play an influential role in the assessment of sexual minority refugee claimants; one's relationship pattern is used to evaluate one's claim as a sexual minority. Chapter 4 investigated how the current spousal sponsorship program's reliance on the heteronormative nuclear marriage model has made it difficult for same-sex common-law couples to prove that their relationships are legitimate. In these cases, distinctions were made between opposite-sex conjugal couples and same-sex conjugal couples, suggesting that even from within, conjugality remains an unevenly applied status. For gay and lesbian rights advocates critical of policy recommendations like those in *Beyond Conjugality,* the extension of recognition to nonconjugal relationships would further these distinctions (Gaucher 2014b). Moreover, it would eliminate any difference between nonconjugal relationships and their conjugal counterparts (Interviews).

For supporters of *Beyond Conjugality,* the uneven application of conjugality is precisely the issue. The aim of the report was to question the role of conjugality in legal process and to challenge its prominence in shaping the state's approach toward differentiating between legitimate and illegitimate relationships. As such, the purpose of nonconjugal relationship recognition is not to minimize same-sex or opposite-sex conjugal relationships; rather, it is to address inequalities generated by our current system of relationship recognition between nonconjugal and conjugal relationships, as well as among conjugal relationships. Another option then is to eliminate state recognition of relationships altogether instead of extending recognition to nonconjugal relationships. Supporters of this position claim that "marriage drags along with it certain historical assumptions about the institution and its members that limit the coherent development of family policy" (Fineman 2006, 30). Furthermore, they take issue with the fact that while Western states promote developing and maintaining a diverse secular society, only one family unit is considered worthy of state protection. When it comes to state recognition of familial relationships, family should not be defined by marriage; relationships of care do not necessarily dictate a specific family form. This is not to suggest that the symbolic dimension of conjugality would disappear; it would simply no longer exist as a legal category. If the objective is to protect relationships of interdependency and vulnerable parties within those relationships, solely privileging conjugal relationships does not allow the state to fully realize this goal. State objectives and motivations for the privileging of conjugal relationship therefore need to be re-evaluated.

The problem lies not necessarily with marriage but with conjugality being the sole focus of relationship recognition in Canada. How are we to reconcile the disconnect between the state's reliance on conjugality as a marker of legitimacy and the realities of family formation? These tensions highlight that state privileging of conjugality runs deeper than the protection of interdependent relationships; conjugal privilege is driven by state desire to (re-)produce a particular version of the family. Resistance toward extending family reunification rights to nonconjugal relationships is not solely about logistical concerns; it is rooted in an affective attachment to conjugality, and it is that attachment that acts as an access point for Canadian citizenship.

The LCC's proposed framework in *Beyond Conjugality* demonstrates not only that it is possible to rethink state recognition of relationships, but also that there is no one-size-fits-all framework. Focusing on the substance of adult interdependent relationships, this framework exhibits the need to evaluate the Canadian state's current approach toward understanding relationship recognition in Canadian immigration law and policy. While recommendations made in *Beyond Conjugality* were dismissed in 2001, Canada's immigration and refugee program remains reliant on intimate relationships as a primary marker for access to citizenship. It is time to revisit the LCC's theoretical musings and explore the state's objectives for trusting conjugality as an organizing principle of families and, inadvertently, future citizens.

Conclusion

"Are you seriously saying ... we should never be able to revoke citizenship from somebody?"

– STEPHEN HARPER

In a keynote address to the Canadian Club in March 2014, then minister of citizenship and immigration Chris Alexander stated that family reunification continued to be a top priority for the Harper government, claiming that families are better together than separated (Alexander 2014). This prioritization of family reunification was contradicted by the reality that family class migration consistently decreased after the Harper government took power in 2006. While family class migration dominated our immigration program pre-2006, it accounted for less than 20 percent of Canada's total immigrant intake (Metro Toronto Chinese and Southeast Asian Legal Clinic 2014). This was compounded by the fact that the Harper government implemented a quota of five thousand applications – not acceptances – for the sponsorship of parents and grandparents (Citizenship and Immigration Canada 2014). Curbing the sponsorship of extended family members established a family class migration system where the conjugal family unit continued to hold precedence. Yet even this privileged status remained precarious, as the government continued to enforce a particular understanding of conjugality. Moreover, enhanced ministerial autonomy allowed for families reunited in Canada to be separated once again, as was the case with the Harper government's crackdown on marriages of convenience.

Families were subjected to intense scrutiny regarding the intimate details of their family's life pre-access to reunification and continued to live under the threat of deportation post-arrival. Citizenship was therefore becoming more difficult to obtain and easier to lose. Former minister Alexander's championing government focus on reuniting families was contradicted by the implementation of policies that continued to "whittle away at family reunification as a priority" (Fleras 2015, 100).

Similar patterns emerged in the refugee program; while Canada touted itself internationally as a refugee-receiving country, the number of accepted refugees dropped by 25 percent between 2006 and 2011 (Canada Border Services Agency 2017). In addition to a decline in refugee acceptance, deportation and detention rates continued to increase, with over eighty-three thousand deportations during this same time period (Behrens 2012). With the passing of the *Refugee Exclusion Act* in 2012, the minister of citizenship and immigration now has the authority to designate countries to a safe country list, making persecuted individuals living in these countries ineligible for asylum. This has serious implications for sexual minority refugees, as Western conceptions of sexuality are used to assess the level of security in non-Western countries (Gaucher and DeGagné 2016). Despite Canada's refugee program becoming increasingly restrictive, the Harper government continued to promote its "progressive" agenda abroad. Launching an initiative to reach out to gay and lesbian refugees in Iran, the government provided links to media reports covering the government's efforts to protect sexual minority refugees. Critics accused the government of "pinkwashing" its policy activity in an effort to make their government sound friendlier to sexual minorities than it actually was (McGregor 2012). As such, there was a disconnect between the Canadian state's message abroad and the realization of this message within its own borders.

The Harper government's agenda for migration reform relied on mixed messaging, framing its agenda as more progressive than it actually was. Despite claims to the contrary, Canada's immigration and refugee program had become increasingly restrictive. Using a discourse of security, these alterations were framed as measures to eradicate future threats to the Canadian state and to penalize those who come to Canada under the guise of misrepresentation. The Harper government then used this language of border control to sell these changes to immigrant and nonimmigrant voters alike, allowing the government to implement these measures while continuing to promote Canada's immigration and refugee program as both advanced and accessible.

Restrictive measures rely on the government's continued privileging of the conjugal nuclear family. One's intimate relationships are assessed according to this ideal of family used to differentiate between desirable and undesirable newcomers. While a sexual minority refugee claimant's relationship history is used to assess the claimant's deviation from this specific family form and, consequently, whether the claimant's narrative of sexuality-based persecution is genuine, sponsorship-seeking couples are obligated to provide a narrative consistent with this family form in order to avoid suspicion. As such, this language of security aims to protect the state from both external and internal threats – undesirable immigrants and refugees perceivably pose a threat to our immigration system as well as to the Canadian conjugal nuclear family.

While neoliberal and security frameworks have been applied to analyses of the relationship between the state, immigration, and family, the integral role of citizenship is typically lost in these explanations. State reliance on a specific understanding of family shapes one's claim for citizenship; however, discussions of family remain outside the Canadian conversation. Mainstream scholarship on Canadian citizenship relies on the individual as the primary unit of analysis, disregarding the role family plays in the provision of citizenship and reinforcing the perceived position of family as apolitical. Incorporating family into this framework thus highlights the work of governing that family performs in state management of immigrants and refugees, ultimately challenging the longstanding assumption that citizenship is purely individualist. Using Dhamoon's matrix of meaning-making, family acts as a site of reproduction for specific meanings, values, and beliefs that shape the unequal distribution of power across populations. Therefore, the ways in which the state defines family play a role in defining one's interaction with the state as a citizen, partial citizen, or noncitizen.

Why Family Matters

This book commenced with a proposal to reconsider the Canadian conversation so as to identify the ways in which the conjugal family unit acts as a point of access for immigrants and refugees. This, I have contended, requires reconceptualizing our understanding of family, recognizing that conjugality does not necessarily dictate the development of relationships of care and interdependency. State privileging of the conjugal family unit in Canada's immigration program not only narrows the scope of what constitutes family, but also constructs the noncitizen in a way that conjugality continues to define the parameters of their permissibility. Moreover, the inconsistent and ambiguous treatment of the conjugal family unit calls into question its effectiveness in distinguishing between legitimate and illegitimate families. By contrast, my approach shifts the focus from the individual – the core of the Canadian conversation – to the family and its role in the provision of citizenship and, consequently, identity formation. As I argued in previous chapters, the provision of citizenship to desirable individuals (Chapter 3) and families (Chapters 4 and 5) goes beyond protecting the state and its citizens from system abuse; the integrity of the Canadian immigration system depends on state-limited entry while simultaneously reinforcing a specific understanding of family, marriage, and conjugality.

In my final chapter, I examined the possibilities for rethinking conjugality in Canadian law and policy, focusing specifically on the implications that state recognition of personal relationships – conjugal or nonconjugal – holds for both the state and its citizens. While the state claims to have no place in the bedrooms of our nation, the politicization of conjugality reinforces a hierarchy of legitimate relationships deserving of state recognition; extending recognition to nonconjugal relationships runs the risk of establishing new hierarchies. Policy reform therefore requires stepping back from this conjugal/nonconjugal dichotomy and re-evaluating the state's role in the regulation of one's personal relationships. As Fineman contends, "The theoretical availability of marriage interferes with the development of other solutions to social problems" (2006, 30). The Canadian state's reliance on the conjugal family unit ignores the reality that, quite often, it is the root of social issues that governments are continuously attempting to rectify, including, among others, poverty, elder care, and child care. Instead of focusing on relationships of care more generally, the state's reliance on the conjugal family unit has impeded our understanding of the ever-changing dynamics of family and of citizenship.

This is particularly evident in the state's handling of the family class. In the name of maintaining the integrity of the Canadian immigration system, sexual minority refugee claimants are assessed according to their relationship patterns, using past relationships to evaluate both their identification as a sexual minority and the persecution experienced as a result of that identity; common-law conjugality is defined as synonymous with marital conjugality, establishing unfair expectations for sponsorship-seeking common-law couples; and marriage fraud was used by the Harper government to eradicate foreign threat to the institution of marriage. In all three cases, the state responded to weaknesses in the immigration program by enacting further restrictions. As such, those families seeking access to the Canadian state (outside families) are expected to develop their familial relationships in a way that is consistent with the state's version of legitimate conjugality, a version that those families living within Canadian borders (inside families) are generally not expected to abide by. Family composition plays a key role in the provision of citizenship.

Moreover, state reliance on the conjugal family unit ignores the reality that interdependency takes on many forms. While Canadian legal treatment of conjugality suggests the adoption of a framework that accounts for the interdependent nature of personal relationships, conjugality continues to define relationship recognition. Conjugality's stronghold on state recognition has become increasingly flexible for inside families; however, it continues to define access for outside families. This suggests that the state's understanding of family is defined by *form*, not *function*. The integrity of the Canadian immigration system is therefore reliant on more than simply addressing and remedying weaknesses; it depends on the state limiting entry by refusing access to deviant individuals and families that challenge traditional notions of family and marriage.

Interactions between conjugality and policy highlight why we need to reject the notion that family is apolitical. Instead, we should turn our attention to understanding the role the conjugal family unit has been assigned and its effectiveness in that role. This is contingent on the realization that conjugality is not a necessary condition for interdependency. As Dorion Solot and Marshall Miller explain:

> Although marriage proponents often speak of marriage as the fabric of society, this fabric is actually woven of caretaking relationships of all kinds, with strands held by parents and children, sibling, spouses, part-

rs, friends, and neighbours. These human relationships – some simple and easy to understand, others "messy" and non-traditional – are what truly matter when it comes to ensuring that individuals, families, and communities are healthy and strong and receive the support they need. (2006, 100)

If family is about interdependency and care, then we must recognize that what constitutes family is broader than we admit. The complexity of care and the translation of this complexity to the development of our personal relationships warrant attention in citizenship discourse.

Implications

The findings outlined in this book present several practical implications. First, for policy and legal circles, my analysis provides a much-needed mapping of the inconsistent application of conjugality in Canadian law and policy. Conjugality plays an integral role in the development and management of Canadian policy programs used as a mechanism to organize access. As discussed in Chapter 2, the state has a history of inconsistently enforcing conjugality, depending on what is at stake. While conjugality has been used to dictate who is eligible for social assistance in Ontario, it has also been used to justify specific incidents of indecency in the name of maintaining healthy intimate relationships, as was the case in *R v Labaye*. This mapping has also highlighted that the parameters of conjugality are generally more flexible than the parameters used in Canada's immigration and refugee program. The inconsistent treatment of conjugality challenges the commonly held assumption that the conjugal family unit is part of Canadian common sense – that conjugality is just the way that Canadians do family. Mapping the state's reliance on conjugality calls attention to the political motivations for enforcing it in certain policy situations and for ignoring it in others. Conjugality is therefore part of the Canadian political agenda; however, it manifests itself in inconsistent and contradictory ways.

The boundaries of Canadian conjugality continue to be contested. The extension of conjugal rights and responsibilities to common-law and same-sex couples has significantly altered the institution of marriage. Recent discussions regarding the constitutionality of the state's ban on polygamy, as exemplified by the legal treatment of Bountiful, have questioned the effectiveness and relevance of current polygamy laws. The emergence of planned lesbian and gay families in Canadian legal discourse challenges traditional parameters of legal parentage, advocating for a legal system capable of recognizing three-parent families and creating a more equitable process specifically for the parent who is not bound to the child through biological or conjugal means. As census data suggests, Canadians are pushing the boundaries of conjugal relationships in their everyday lives, opting for nontraditional arrangements (common-law, blended families, sole parent families, etc.) over marriage. Canadian history of relationship recognition would suggest that its system of conjugal privilege is not immune to change; its boundaries are in no way fixed. Posing questions to policy and legal circles regarding both the application and effectiveness of conjugality as an organizing principle is therefore unlikely to undo the very foundations of Canadian law and policy; rather, mapping these challenges sheds light on the work conjugality performs in the implementation of these programs and how policymakers approach these contestations.

In highlighting the inconsistent treatment of conjugality, my findings also have implications for the immigrant and refugee assessment process itself. Regardless of category – family class, skilled worker, or refugee – immigration officers work under the assumption that successful applicants will eventually apply to sponsor someone. Chapters 4 and 5 examine how sponsorship-seeking couples are obligated to provide a narrative consistent with IRB expectations of conjugal ceremony and substance. Chapter 3 also highlights how a sexual minority refugee claimant's relationship pattern is used to assess a claimant's deviation from the conjugal nuclear family, which is then used to assess whether the claimant is, in fact, a sexual minority in need of state protection. Current immigrant and refugee assessment process therefore relies on a specific understanding of family used to distinguish between desirable and undesirable future citizens. State treatment of family in its immigration and refugee program therefore warrants continued attention. If we are to continue relying on immigration as an important resource for Canadian welfare, then we need to be cognizant of the state's inconsistent and unfair expectations for those seeking access to the Canadian state, both present and future. This book provides a framework to accomplish exactly this – to discuss the normative and empirical implications the current system presents for those seeking access.

While this book focuses primarily on policy decision makers and legal interpreters, the findings may also benefit additional stakeholder groups with a vested interest in immigrant and refugee rights (advocacy organizations, lobby groups, etc.). An examination of why the state relies on the conjugal family unit as an access point for Canadian citizenship, as well as the execution of this reliance, might be of some utility to those organizations seeking to challenge future changes to the IRPA. In an address to the Standing Committee on Citizenship and Immigration, Audrey Macklin (2014) explained that "any policies that deter or make more difficult or delay the ability of families to be reunited has both deleterious social consequences and also ultimately damaging economic consequences as well." Reliance on the conjugal family unit as grounds for detention, deportation, and the granting or refusal of access is consistent with injustices taken up by these advocacy organizations. While this analysis does not focus specifically on the work of advocacy groups, a contribution worthy of further inquiry, it does make evident that the Canadian state has a vested interest in the intimate lives of current and future immigrants and refugees, establishing unfair and ambiguous expectations for those seeking access.

Finally, the findings in this book provide a framework for assessing current and future immigration policy decisions and controversies. In the days leading up to the 2016 federal election, the Liberal Party, under now prime minister Justin Trudeau, was critical of certain aspects of the Harper government's immigration mandate, specifically its election strategy of "pitting Canadians against Canadians" on issues such as the niqab debate and its proposed Barbaric Cultural Practices anonymous community tip line (Kennedy 2015). Immigration initiatives under the Trudeau government, since it came into power, highlight a focus on eliminating distinctions of substantive citizenship between immigrants, refugees, and Canadian citizens. Initiatives include the allowance of twenty-five thousand Syrian refugees, increasing the annual allowance of parent/grandparent sponsorship applications from five thousand to ten thousand, reviving the Francophone Temporary Foreign Workers Program, issuing an official apology for the *Komagata Maru* incident, promising to reduce processing times for family sponsorship applications, revoking the Harper government's two-tier citizenship system enshrined in the *Strengthening Canadian Citizenship Act* (Bill C-24), restoring full-coverage health care for refugees and asylum seekers, and promising a review of the both the Temporary Foreign Worker and Live-In Caregiver programs. Considering the Trudeau government only recently came into power, it is impossible to predict the direction its immigration mandate will take; however, this framework provides an opportunity to address how family is defined in Canada's immigration and refugee program and how it contributes to these distinctions, shifting away from simply maintaining the status quo.

Enforcing this narrative that family constitutes an undesirable migrant class was not a strategy solely employed by Conservative governments; as outlined in Chapter 2, Canada's treatment of family in its immigration and refugee program is historically fraught and not party specific. Unique to the Harper government was the party's simultaneous framing of the migrant family as a threat to the integrity of Canada's immigration system and as a champion of Canadian family values. While the Harper government is no longer in power, the party's immigration program remains largely intact, raising questions regarding which areas of focus will take priority under the Trudeau government. Considering the Liberal Party's track record with family class migration, cynicism as to whether the Trudeau government will deconstruct the socially conservative components of the current immigration and refugee program is warranted. There is a chance, however, to revisit the role that family plays in the provision of citizenship to immigrants, refugees, and, an area in need of further inquiry, temporary foreign workers (Preibisch and Hennebry 2012; Gaucher 2014a).

Families continue to matter as they play an integral role in accessing citizenship. The primary conclusion that can be drawn from this book is that incorporating family both broadens and enriches our understanding of Canadian citizenship. My research highlights how the conjugal family unit acts as a point of access for immigrant families seeking reunification and for refugees who could potentially seek reunification; moreover, it demystifies the perceived naturalness of the conjugal family unit, examining how family is used to further political agendas. In addition, it opens up avenues for discussions concerning the substance of citizenship, particularly the ways in which the so-called neutrality of citizenship impacts identity formation. In doing so, the Canadian conversation becomes more robust, accounting for the reality that the provision of citizenship is not solely dependent on the individual. Not only does incorporating family therefore theoretically enhance our understanding of citizenship; it also provides a starting point for navigating the lived experiences of families both inside and outside Canadian borders.

Notes

Introduction

1 Renamed Immigration, Refugees and Citizenship Canada (IRCC) in 2015 by the Trudeau government, the department responsible for policies on processing permanent and temporary residence, visa, refugee protection, and citizenship applications was previously named Department of Immigration, and Colonization (1917–36), Department of Mines and Resources (1936–50), Department of Citizenship and Immigration (1950–66), Department of Manpower and Immigration (1966–77), Department of State for Citizenship (1966–91), Department of Employment and Immigration (1977–91), Department of Multiculturalism and Citizenship (1991–94), and Citizenship and Immigration Canada (1994–2015). For the purpose of clarity, I am using the current departmental name throughout.

2 For the purposes of this book, the state is not defined as a hegemonic entity; rather, it is "the complex expression of the links between the rules for inclusion and exclusion, governing mentalities/rationalities, the law, and, ultimately the definitive articulations of stability – discourses of security and insecurity" (Abu-Laban and Nath 2007, 80). My book examines how actions taken by governments, bureaucratic agencies (e.g. Immigration, Refugees and Citizenship Canada, Immigration and Refugee Board of Canada, etc.), and individual gatekeepers are implicated in producing and reinforcing these links with respect to questions of citizenship.

3 During the tenure of the Harper government, four Members of Parliament (MPs) held the immigration portfolio: Monte Solberg (2006–07), Diane Finley (2007–08), Jason Kenney (2008–13), and Chris Alexander (2013–15).

4 Those documents I was unable to locate on the websites of either the Immigration, Refugees and Citizenship Canada (IRCC) or the Parliament of Canada were retrieved at Library and Archives Canada in Ottawa.

5 These interviews are not representative of these populations as a whole; rather, they suggest that "a single case can undoubtedly demonstrate that its features are possible

and, hence, may also exist in other cases and, even if they do not, must be taken into account in the formulation of general propositions" (Platt 1988, 11).

Chapter 1: The Invisibility of Family in the Canadian Conversation

1 Non/partial citizens can be defined as "those who are excluded from without and those who are excluded from within specific citizenship communities or nation-states" (Yeatman 1994, 80).

2 Aside from a temporary increase in parent/grandparent sponsorship in 2012–13, extended family sponsorship has consistently decreased from 20,015 (8%) in 2006 to 15,489 (5.7%) in 2015 (Immigration, Refugees and Citizenship 2015a).

3 Kernerman recognizes the paradoxical nature of the term, as multiculturalism (the goal of accommodating diversity) and nationalism (the goal of achieving unity) are typically positioned as conflicting concepts; however, he proposes that contestation of the term lies not in the concepts themselves, but rather in the contradictions outlined above (2005, 4–6).

4 I recognize the diversity within the "Canadian School" and the "Critical School" – labels borrowed from Kernerman (2005) – in that the scholars who identify with these two schools of thought are not homogeneous in their theoretical viewpoints. There is variation within these groups, and it would be misleading to assess this dialogue without theoretically situating the primary scholars appropriately. Therefore, I am in no way suggesting that the ideas put forth by Kymlicka and Dhamoon are indicative of these ideological alignments as a whole; rather, I am focusing on their dialogue to illustrate two prominent frames of citizenship discourse in Canada.

5 For Carens, a contextual approach requires movement between theory and practice, recognizing that normative ideals of citizenship often have various outcomes on the ground. While not dismissing the value of general theoretical principles, Carens argues that "we do not really understand what general principles and theoretical formations *mean* until we see them interpreted and applied in a variety of specific contexts" (2000, 3; emphasis in original).

6 While the breadth of Kymlicka's work involves projects on liberal theory, liberal multicultural citizenship, Canadian multicultural citizenship, and, more recently, international models of multiculturalism, my focus will be on Kymlicka's Canadian citizenship projects. While these projects do not exist in isolation and there is significant overlap, the purpose here is to explore the implications Kymlicka's framing of Canadian citizenship hold for family reunification. Therefore, in the name of conceptual clarity, I am working from the distinction of Kymlicka as a liberal multiculturalist and as a Canadianist. Focusing on the latter (Léger 2011), Kymlicka's work as a Canadianist will inform the discussion laid out in this chapter.

7 Kymlicka recognizes the vagueness of his use of the term *immigrant* and acknowledges that in his discussions of cultural groups and integration, immigrant refers to newcomers and refugees, as well as to second-, third-, etc. generation Canadians. For Dhamoon (2009), Kymlicka's use of immigrant is synonymous with nonwhite. In this book, my focus on "newer" citizens refers to those who have immigrated to Canada; new simply means that I choose to focus on the process through which they gained access rather than on their experiences with integration.

8 Kymlicka defines *nation* as a "historical community, more or less institutionally complete, occupying a given territory or homeland, sharing a distinct language and culture" (1995, 11).

9 Dhamoon defines power as a "relation spread through the socio-political body instead of something possessed by the state ... it is productive, not just coercive ... it produces subjects and subjects are vehicles of power" (2009, 11–12).

10 Intersectionality theory attempts to theorize the ways in which multiple systems of oppression interact. By recognizing that these systems do not act independently of one another, intersectionality theory highlights how oppression and privilege can simultaneously exist (Crenshaw 1991).

11 Whiteness is a socially constructed term that is often used to identify structural privilege. While often described as invisible in that whiteness is the "unmarked norm against which other identities are marked and racialized," critical race theorists identify whiteness as a prominent organizer of power in the world (Rasmussen et al. 2001, 8).

12 Stevens (1999, 2010) shares a similar view in that the *state* and *nation* mutually reinforce each other. For Stevens, "the familial nation exists through practices and often legal documents that set out the kinship rules for particular political societies" (1999, 108). By shifting away from conceptualizing the two as separate, we can understand how migration rules shape and reproduce specific interpretations of sexuality via nationalist discourse.

13 I borrow the term gatekeepers from Bakan and Stasiulis, who claim that these individuals, organizations, etc., "interpret information and influence future policy changes that have a direct impact on the socially and politically constructed 'needs' and citizenship rights available to families" (2005, 63).

Chapter 2: Inside/Outside Families

1 *Molodowich v Penttinen* (1980), 17 RFL (2d) 376; [1980] OJ No 1904 (QL); 2 ACWS (2d) 486 [*Molodowich*].

2 *Nova Scotia (AG) v Walsh*, [2002] 4 SCR 325, 2002 SCC 83 [*Walsh*].

3 Ibid., *note* 42 at 102.

4 *Molodowich,* at para 30.

5 Ibid., at para 12.

6 The *Modernization of Benefits and Obligations Act* ((2000), S.C. 2000, c 12) extends benefits and obligations previously restricted to married couples to "all couples who have been cohabiting in a conjugal relationship for at least one year, in order to reflect values of tolerance, respect and equality, consistent with the *Canadian Charter of Rights and Freedoms.*" While cohabitation requirements vary across governments, couples qualify for provincial common-law benefits after living together for a period of one to three years.

7 Following the passing of the *Constitution Act* in 1982 – which included the *Canadian Charter of Rights and Freedoms* – a three-year moratorium was placed on the effective date of s 15. This was to allow all levels of government to assess the section's impact on policy development prior to formalizing who would be included and ultimately excluded.

8 These cases included *Egan v Canada* (1995), 2 SCR. 513 [*Egan*]; *Veysey v Canada (Correctional Services)* (1990), 109 NR 300 (FCTD) [*Veysey*] that challenged the denial of family visitation rights to homosexual inmates and their partners; *Haig and Birch v Canada* (1992), 9 OR 495 (OCA) [*Haig*] when the Ontario Court of Appeal read "sexual orientation" into the federal code; and *Canada (AG) v Mossop* (1993), 1 SCR 554 [*Mossop*] in which the Canadian Human Rights Tribunal ruled that the refusal of bereavement leave to homosexuals and their partners/partners' families qualified as discrimination on the basis of family status.

9 *Egan,* at 598, per Lamer CJ and La Forest J.

10 *M v H* (1999), 2 SCR 3 [*M v H*].

11 For a more detailed overview on Canadian legal treatment of same-sex marriage, see Gaucher (2014b).

12 In 2003, the Klein government introduced the *Adult Interdependent Relationships Act* (AIRA), which provided some (but not all) rights enjoyed by married couples to cohabiting pairs. Rather than providing special recognition to same-sex couples, the government opted to recognize all relationships, conjugal or nonconjugal. Ultimately, same-sex couples were to be absorbed within a new asexual legal category and were to be treated no differently than roommates, siblings, etc.; the nature of their relationships went from same-sex to no sex (Boyd and Young 2003). Quebec's civil union regime requires unmarried couples to register for recognition. In *Quebec (AG) v A* (2013), SC 5, 1 SCR 61, otherwise known as *Eric v Lola,* the Supreme Court ruled that the Quebec government is not legally obligated to provide unregistered common-law couples the same benefits as married couples.

13 This is not to suggest that cohabitation is the sole prerequisite for obtaining common-law status; cohabitation requirements are often reduced when a couple is already

living together with a child. Even with a child, however, cohabitation remains the focal point for common-law status.

14 *Falkiner v Ontario (Minister of Community and Social Services, Income Maintenance Branch)* (2002), 59 OR (3d) 481 (CA); 2003, [2002] SCCA 297 [*Falkiner*]; *R v Labaye* (2005), 3 SCR 728, 80 (SCC) [*Labaye*]; *Reference Re Section 293 of the Criminal Code of Canada* (2011), BCSC 1588 [*Section 293*].

15 Close to ten thousand Ontarians (the majority being single mothers) lost some or all of their benefits under the new legislation (CBC News 2004).

16 Past cases included *Towne Cinema Theatres Ltd v R*, [1985] 1 SCR 494 [*Towne Cinema Theatres*]; *R v Butler* (1992), 1 SCR 452; and *Little Sisters Book and Art Emporium v Canada (Minister of Justice)* (2000), 2 SCR 1120, 2000 SCC 69 [*Little Sisters*].

17 *Labaye*, at para 71, per McLachlin CJ.

18 Section 293 of the *Criminal Code of Canada* states,

> Every one who a) practices or enters into or in any manner agrees or consents to practice or enter into i) any form of polygamy, or ii) any kind of conjugal union with more than one person at the same time, whether or not it is by law recognized as a binging form of marriage, or b) celebrates, assists or is a party to a rite, ceremony or consent that purports to (i) or (ii), is guilty of an indictable offence and liable to imprisonment for a term not exceeding five years.

> Since its inclusion in the *Criminal Code,* there have only been two successful prosecutions of polygamy – *R v Bear's Shin Bone (1899)* and *The King v John Harris (1906)* (Drummond 2009). The first criminal investigation into Bountiful took place in 1990 (despite the community being established in the mid-1940s); however, authorities concluded they lacked sufficient proof and decided not to press charges.

19 *Section 293*, at para 5, per Bauman CJ.

20 *R v Blackmore* (2017), BCSC 1288 [*Blackmore*].

21 For more on Canadian state treatment of polygamy, see Gaucher (2016).

22 *Section 293*, at para 557, per Bauman CJ.

23 Refugees have to provide this list on their application for permanent residency.

24 A rough guideline for immigration officers used to be "no more than fifty percent"; however, the guideline has become increasingly difficult to respect with an ever-expanding family class (Hawkins 1989, 86).

25 Following a freeze on extended family sponsorship, IRCC now caps sponsorship for parents and grandparents to the first five thousand complete applications. After re-opening the program on January 4, 2016, IRCC closed the program three days

later because over fourteen thousand applications were received. Parents and grandparents can also apply for a "Super Visa" that allows them to stay in Canada for up to two years (rather than the six-month maximum of a regular visa) (Immigration, Refugees and Citizenship Canada 2017d).

26 Under the Mulroney government, immigration admittance went from less than 100,000 in 1986 to over 250,000 in 1993 (Citizenship and Immigration Canada 2012a).

27 Sponsorship breakdown is defined by IRCC as "when the sponsor, for whatever reason, fails to fulfill the commitments of the sponsorship agreement" (Citizenship and Immigration Canada 1994, 38).

28 *Alfonso v Canada (Minister of Citizenship and Immigration)* [2003] 2 FCR 683, 2002 FCT 1221.

29 This is enforced as a preventative mechanism to reduce rates of marriage fraud, suggesting that the category of spouse is being misused by same-sex couples seeking access to Canada (Citizenship and Immigration Canada 2011a).

30 Enacted in 1992, the Live-In Caregiver Program (LCP) aims to attract temporary domestic workers to come to Canada and reduce the demand for private live-in care of children, the elderly, and persons with disabilities. What distinguishes this program from the TFWP is that following their admittance to the LCP, applicants are permitted to apply for permanent residency after being employed as a full-time live-in caregiver for at least two years within the first four years of being part of the program. While often touted as a Canadian immigration "success" story, the LCP is not without fault, as the program is inherently gendered, fosters an environment for potential abuse, and glosses over the complexities of transnational care. For more on the LCP, see Parreñas (2001, 2008), Tungohan (2012, 2017), and Tungohan et al. (2015).

31 While the federal government has always been legally permitted to revoke citizenship, this was not a frequent occurrence. Between 1967 and 2011, only sixty individuals had their citizenship revoked; meanwhile, between 2011 and 2012, the Harper government was responsible for nineteen revocations, 3,139 investigations, and the flagging of five thousand permanent residents, and for twenty-five hundred recent arrivals being "closely monitored" (Jeffrey 2015, 229).

32 *R v Appulonappa* (2013), BCCA 79; *R v Appulonappa* (2015), 3 SCR 754, SCC 59; *Appulonappa v Canada (Citizenship and Immigration)* (2016), FC 914.

33 Marwah, Triadafilopoulos, and White refer to this balance as the "populist's paradox" (2013, 96).

34 The CPC's strategy of ethnic outreach proved successful, as sixteen of thirty ridings with the highest proportion of visible minority voters voted for the CPC, increasing the CPC's share of the ethnic minority vote from 9 percent in 2000 to 31 percent in

2011 and contributing to the Harper government's majority win (Saunders 2015; Omidvar 2016, 185). While CPC support among certain immigrant communities increased, Allison Harell contends the position of the CPC as the new champion of immigrant interests was grossly overstated and that minority voter support for the Liberal Party remained strong (2013, 141). The CPC's ethnic outreach strategy targeted older, socially conservative European groups, ultimately establishing a very narrow picture of the ethnic vote. Moreover, Harell points out that in their own electoral data, the CPC conflated immigrant voters with visible minority voters, reproducing longstanding problematic narratives about race, ethnicity, and citizenship.

Chapter 3: The Role of Relationships

1 I am adopting Rehaag's definition of *bisexual,* which refers to "a person whose sexual orientation, sexual identity, or sexual behaviour is not directed exclusively towards persons of one particular sex or gender" (2009, 417). While there have been several cases involving transgender claimants (see *Montoya Martinez v Canada [Citizenship and Immigration]* [2011], FC 13), I have chosen to examine only homosexual and bisexual refugee claimants for this project. I am by no means suggesting that transgender refugee claimants are any less important; this is an area of refugee studies in desperate need of further development.

2 Published decisions were obtained from the Canadian Legal Information Institute (CanLII) database (htpps://www.canlii.org). These decisions were obtained by reviewing cases found by the search terms: "refugee and: sexual minority, or homosexual or gay or lesbian or bisexual."

3 The access to information request was for one hundred sexual minority refugee claims from 2006 to 2014; data on the total number of sexual orientation–based claims reviewed by the IRB during that time period; the gender division of these claims; and the number of claims made by claimants who identified as bisexual. Using the search provided, the Access to Information office released the first one hundred decisions their search produced.

4 Equating current Canadian analysis of persecution with patriarchal notions of gender, LaViolette (2007) contends that traditional conceptualizations of the public-private divide shape claimant assessment, making it difficult for female applicants to satisfy requirements that rely on a public element of sexuality and sexual identity.

5 I use the term *sexual minority* with the objective of consistency, as the Canadian government uses this term to categorize nonheterosexual sexualities. I believe, however, that this language is limiting and inaccurate, as many queer-identified people do not consider themselves part of a sexual minority. Furthermore, current immigration policy recognizes sexual minorities as consisting of homosexuals and, more

recently, bisexuals. As a result, many individuals who identify as queer are rendered invisible under existing sexual minority refugee claimant assessment protocol.

6 This was recognized in *Adjei v Canada (Minister of Citizenship and Immigration)* (2007), IRB: TA5–14829. Joseph Adjei, a Ghanaian seeking UN Convention refugee status by reason of political opinion and his membership in the Trade Union Congress and the People's National Party, was denied entry on the grounds that he failed to provide an objective element to his claim of feared persecution in his home country. The Federal Court ruled that while the claimant must experience a subjective fear of persecution, the mere possibility of persecution is not considered a substantive ground for refugee status. It is the responsibility of the IRB to assess the claimant's subjective fear of persecution against characteristics of the claimant's home country that speak to the probability of their fear being realized (e.g., human rights record, political climate toward homosexuality, state of police force, existence of queer communities).

7 LaViolette (2009) contends that existing country documentation is insufficient due to a scarcity of information – a common struggle for nongovernmental organizations working on the ground to collect information concerning the treatment of sexual minorities in homophobic countries – as well as the use of inappropriate sources as substitutes for information by these organizations (e.g., gay tourism pamphlets). While LaViolette recognizes the importance of this documentation, she proposes that the IRB recognize the gaps in this information to avoid confusing silence with conditions suitable toward sexual minorities. Comparatively speaking, studies have shown that the IRB spends more money on information collection than do other immigration tribunal boards; however, there remains work to be done (Dauvergne and Millbank 2003, 311).

8 *Canada (AG) v Ward* (1993), 2 SCR 689 [*Ward*].

9 Ibid. at 739.

10 Ibid.

11 Ibid.

12 Dissatisfied with the polarizing nature of both theoretical perspectives, LaViolette (1997) proposes a middle ground, an approach that acknowledges both the innate and social factors responsible for constructing our sexual identities.

13 Dauvergne and Millbank's study involved analysis of 127 published sexual minority refugee decisions between 1994 and 2000. Rehaag continued this research by analyzing another 160 published IRB and Federal Court decisions from 2001 to 2004, as well as 1,351 unpublished IRB decisions from 2004.

14 *PWZ v Canada (Minister of Citizenship and Immigration)* (2000), CRDD involved the refusal of a claim made by a Colombian woman. The adjudicator concluded that because the claimant's physical presentation failed to match preconceived assumptions about lesbian women, the claimant was capable of "passing" as a heterosexual and therefore was not under threat of sexuality-based persecution.

15 Similar to *PWZ v Canada* (2000), *KQH v Canada (Minister of Citizenship and Immigration)* (2003), RPDD highlights assumptions of a "gay reality" that reinforce heteronormative assumptions about sexuality and sexual identity. This negative decision involved a man from Mexico who feared persecution because of his sexual orientation. In addition to these decisions upholding homosexual stereotypes, the presumption of a single "gay reality" is misleading, as it ignores intersections between sexual orientation and, among others, gender, race, class, geographical location, and immigration status (Rehaag 2008, 73).

16 UNHCR (2008) released this *Guidance Note* with the aim to recognize the unique obstacles sexual minority refugee claimants experience in the determination process. While guidance notes are considered less authoritative, they are often a first attempt at dealing with emerging legal issues. These decisions – TA–04080, TA4–13131 and TA5–02888 – were obtained in a study conducted by Millbank (2009). All three were copies of expedited reports from the IRB that were not intended for public release.

17 Interestingly, approximately 30 percent of the refused IRB decisions involved claims made by citizens of Mexico, all of which were denied by the IRB for similar reasons. For more information on queer Mexican migration, see Cantù, Luibhéid, and Stern (2005), Ramirez (2005), and Cantù, Naples, and Vidal-Ortiz (2009).

18 In many refused applications, a postponement between arriving in Canada and claiming refugee status was interpreted by adjudicators as challenging the seriousness of the claimant's experience of sexual persecution. Claim delay was identified as a "relative element" for assessing claimant credibility in *Huerta v Canada (Minister of Employment and Immigration)* (1993), 157 NR 225 (FCA), as it addressed the existence of a Convention refugee claim – a clarification outlined in *Cruz, Fernando Rodriguez v MEI* (1994) FCTD, no. IMM-3848-93, Simpson, June 16.

19 *Re K.O.C.* (2003), R.P.D.D.

20 *Christopher v Canada (Minister of Citizenship and Immigration)* (2008), FC 964.

21 *Gyorgyjakab v Canada (Minister of Citizenship and Immigration)* (2005), FC 1119.

22 *Re B.D.K.* (2000), CRDD No.72 (QL).

Chapter 4: An Education in Conjugality

1 Interviewed couples – all composed of one Canadian citizen or permanent resident and the sponsored spouse/partner – were recruited through immigrant settlement agencies in Kingston, Ottawa, Toronto, and Mississauga; immigrant rights organizations; queer community centres; and word of mouth. Scholars interviewing immigrants and refugees contend that community networking is one of the most effective ways to recruit these populations, who are often isolated and difficult to access (Pernice 1994; Merali 2009).

2 All questions were either open-ended or bidirectional to avoid assuming that any of the interviewees had had a negative experience. For example, questions about their

interactions with IRCC were framed in the following way: "Tell me about your experience applying for spousal sponsorship. In what way did these experiences shape your application?" I used this approach in order to maximize the probability that, positive or negative, the interviewees' responses would be a genuine account of their experiences with the program (Merali 2009, 327).

3 The sample of seventeen interviewed couples was made up of five homosexual and twelve heterosexual couples, of whom eight were married and nine were common-law.

4 In terms of length, the questionnaire is two pages for those living in Canada and six pages for those living outside of Canada. Those applicants living in Canada undergo less questioning about the details of their relationship, the assumption being that if the relationship has developed domestically, it is more likely to be consistent with Canadian values (Interviews).

5 The focus on gifts is primarily for the assessment of arranged marriages (Interviews). This suggests that IRCC has adopted a specific narrative for arranged marriages as well.

6 It is important to note here that a universal marriage language is also nonexistent; rather, a Canadian narrative of marriage is both encouraged and enforced.

7 As of 2015, IRCC no longer recognizes marriages conducted abroad via proxy, telephone, fax, internet, or any other type of ceremony where one or both parties are not physically present (Immigration, Refugees and Citizenship Canada 2015b).

8 It is important to reiterate that nothing from my research shows that common-law couples were less likely to be approved if they expressed dissatisfaction with the institution of marriage in their questionnaire. Due to the attention paid to the wedding in the questionnaire, however, interviewed common-law couples perceived this as a possibility. Considering what is at stake in this process, they were hesitant to provide any answers that might put their applications at risk. While it is possible that interviewed applicants could be wrong in their perspectives, their accounts reflect current critiques of Canadian legal treatment of common-law couples made by legal scholars (Holland 2000; Fineman 2001; Cossman and Ryder 2001; Cossman 2007).

9 The wedding as a form of gendered commercialization has been the focus for many feminist scholars. Freeman described the standard wedding as a "profound product of capitalism," attributing every aspect including "the veiled bride in a white satin dress, attendants in matching dresses, rings and bouquets, special music, showers, bachelor-bachelorette parties, large receptions, wedding gifts and a honeymoon" to the establishment of a relationship between intimacy and economic production (2002, 25–26).

10 Despite filing an access to information request for the number of couples applying under the conjugal category since the passing of the IRPA and asking interviewees about these numbers, I was unable to receive an actual number. The response to my request was that while IRCC tracks the number of successful spousal sponsorship applications, there is no differentiation between married, common-law, and conjugal couples.

Chapter 5: Canada's Anti–Marriage Fraud Campaign

1 This crackdown on marriages of convenience was not unique to Canada; other immigrant-receiving countries have introduced legislation aimed at reducing rates of marriage fraud. For more on these initiatives, see Charsley and Benson (2012), D'Aoust (2013), and Eggebø (2013). Although a marriage of convenience is one example of marriage fraud, IRCC uses the terms marriage fraud and marriage of convenience synonymously.

2 I obtained seventy-three articles dated 2008–12 from ten major newspapers: *Toronto Star* (14), *Winnipeg Free Press* (5), *Calgary Herald* (12), *The Gazette* (5), *Edmonton Journal* (9), *Globe and Mail* (8), *Leader-Post* (2), *Ottawa Citizen* (8), *Vancouver Sun* (6), and *National Post* (4). These articles were obtained using the search terms: "marriage of convenience," "relationship of convenience," "marriage fraud," and "fraudulent marriage." Articles were obtained using Newsstand.

3 I examined 140 published marriage fraud appeal decisions made between 2006 and 2012, including 76 decisions where the appeal was rejected (54%) and 64 where the appeal was successful (46%). This sample represents approximately 12 percent of all misrepresentation appeal decisions filed with the Immigration Appeal Division of the IRB between 2006 and 2012 (Immigration and Refugee Board of Canada 2017b). Neither the IRB or IRCC distinguishes between appeal decisions in their statistics; therefore, there are no set numbers outlining what percentage of the total number of filed appeals involve an accusation of marriage fraud. Appeal decisions, however, provide useful insight into the IRB's assessment of spousal sponsorship, as two officers examine these decisions – the initially assigned immigration officer and then an appeal officer. Appeal decisions therefore provide a detailed account of both decisions.

4 I conducted a general search of parliamentary Hansard between 2008 and 2012 on the Parliament of Canada website. In total, there were twenty-five mentions of marriage fraud; while these mentions primarily took place at Standing Committee on Citizenship and Immigration meetings (17), marriage fraud was also discussed in House of Commons Debates (7) and in the 2011 Speech from the Throne (1). These documents were complemented by eight interviews with former and current policy analysts and immigration officers from IRCC.

5 *Chen v Canada (Citizenship and Immigration)* (2010), TA6–14852.

6 This distinction was highlighted in *Ajaz v Canada (Public Safety and Emergency Preparedness)* (2011), TA9–13190. The appeal officer ruled that while the couple's relationship was genuine, it was a genuine relationship that was primarily for immigration purposes. The officer further acknowledged that it was rare for a conjugal relationship to be deemed genuine but then to be refused access, claiming that if a relationship between two citizens from different countries were genuine, it would make sense that the couple would seek reunification. Recognizing the rarity of the situation, the couple's appeal for sponsorship was granted.

7 References were made to relationship length in 36 of the 140 decisions.

8 *Yu v Canada (Citizenship and Immigration)* (2008), TA7–00735.

9 *Brobbey v Canada (Citizenship and Immigration)* (2006), TA4–01703.

10 *Begum v Canada (Citizenship and Immigration)* (2008), MA8–00393.

11 *Simpson-Lee v Canada (Citizenship and Immigration)* (2006), TA4–14172.

12 *Hung v Canada (Citizenship and Immigration)* (2009), TA7–09697.

13 *Li v Canada (Citizenship and Immigration)* (2011), TA9–06490.

14 *Amaral v Canada (Citizenship and Immigration)* (2011), TA8–08075.

15 *Chen v Canada (Citizenship and Immigration)* (2010), TA6–14852.

16 *Huayra v Canada (Citizenship and Immigration)* (2010), MA8–16540.

17 *Lin v Canada (Citizenship and Immigration)* (2011), TA8–05954; *Tadessa v Canada (Citizenship and Immigration)* (2009), TA7–12352.

18 *Rathod v Canada (Citizenship and Immigration)* (2008), TA7–02205.

19 *Li v Canada (Citizenship and Immigration)* (2011), TA9–05367.

20 *Li v Canada (Citizenship and Immigration)* (2011), TA9–06490.

21 Under the current spousal sponsorship program, sponsors are able to sponsor a new spouse/partner three years after their previous spouse/partner obtains becomes a permanent resident. Sponsored spouses/partners are able to sponsor a new spouse/partner five years after becoming a permanent resident (Immigration, Refugees and Citizenship Canada 2017d).

22 *Chen v Canada (Citizenship and Immigration)* (2010), TA6–14852.

23 *Li v Canada (Citizenship and Immigration)* (2011), TA9–06490.

24 *Aujla v Canada (Citizenship and Immigration)* (2008), TA7–03154.

25 *Mansro v Canada (Citizenship and Immigration)* (2008), VA6–01540.

26 Ibid.

27 *Gill v Canada (Citizenship and Immigration)* (2011), TB0–00040.

28 *Kagayutan v Canada (Public Safety and Emergency Preparedness)* (2011), TA9–21476.

29 Several immigration lawyers and former members of the IRB have come to CBSA's defense. While they recognize the department's shortcomings with respect to the handling of marriage fraud, they attribute this to a lack of financial resources (McKie 2010). Julie Taub, immigration lawyer and former IRB member, commented, "It is unfair to blame CBSA for these issues. They can't do the hiring. They don't control the budget. I believe they're doing the best they can with their limited staff and limited resources" (McKie 2010).

30 In Australia, New Zealand, and the United States, a sponsored spouse is prohibited from sponsoring a new spouse for five years from the time they are sponsored, and a conditional visa system is used in the United States, Australia, and the United

Kingdom granting permanent residency to sponsored spouses after a probationary period of generally two years. At the time, Canada had a sponsorship bar on Canadian citizens (they were unable to apply to sponsor another spouse for three years), but there was no similar bar on sponsored individuals, and there was no type of probationary system in Canada.

31 The Trudeau government reversed this residency requirement in 2017, claiming that, "while cases of marriage fraud exist, the majority of relationships are genuine and most spousal sponsorship applications are made in good faith" (Immigration, Refugees and Citizenship Canada 2017b).

32 Canadians Against Immigration Fraud (CAIF) and Canadian Marriage Fraud Victims Society were vocal supporters of both measures. Sam Benet, president of CAIF, stated, "We applaud Minister Kenney for taking bold steps to address the growing problem of marriage fraud and for protecting the integrity of our immigration system" (Citizenship and Immigration Canada 2012c). Interestingly, both organizations failed to provide any statistics on actual rates of marriage fraud on their websites either.

Chapter 6: Rethinking Conjugality

1 *Molodowich,* at note 19.

2 I recognize the institutional and constitutional differences between these three policy initiatives and am, therefore, not suggesting that they could easily be implemented at the Canadian federal level. The purpose of examining these initiatives is twofold: to demonstrate that state accommodation of nonconjugal relationships is possible and to examine the challenges of this type of recognition.

Works Cited

Abu-Laban, Yasmeen. 2009. "The Welfare State under Siege? Neoliberalism, Immigration, and Multiculturalism." In *Women and Public Policy in Canada: Neoliberalism and After?* edited by Alexandra Dobrowolsky, 146–65. Oxford: Oxford University Press.

Abu-Laban, Yasmeen, and Christina Gabriel. 2002. *Selling Diversity: Immigration, Multiculturalism, Employment Equity and Globalization.* Peterborough, ON: Broadview Press.

Abu-Laban, Yasmeen, and Nisha Nath. 2007. "From Deportation to Apology: The Case of Maher Arar and the Canadian State." *Canadian Ethnic Studies* 39, 3: 71–98.

Abu-Laban, Yasmeen, and Veronica Strong-Boag. 1998. "Keeping 'Em Out: Gender, Race, and Class Biases in Canadian Immigration Policy." In *Painting the Maple: Essays on Race, Gender and the Construction of Canada*, edited by Veronica Strong-Boag, Sherrill Grace, and Joan Anderson, 69–82. Vancouver: UBC Press.

Alberta Ministry of Justice. 2003. "Alberta's *Adult Interdependent Relationships Act* and You." https://web.archive.org/web/20070816234423/http://www.justice.gov.ab.ca/home/default.aspx?id=3550.

Alboim, Naomi, and Monica Boyd. 2012. "Managing International Migration: The Canadian Case." In *Managing Immigration and Diversity in Canada: A Transatlantic Dialogue in the New Age of Migration*, edited by Dan Rodriguez-Garcia, 123–50. Montreal: McGill-Queen's University Press.

Alexander, Chris. 2014. "Speaking Notes for Chris Alexander, Canada's Citizenship and Immigration Minister for a Keynote Address in Honour of International Women's Day." Canadian Club, Toronto, ON, March 7. https://www.canada.ca/en/news/archive/2014/03/speaking-notes-chris-alexander-canada-citizenship-immigration-minister-keynote-address-honour-international-women-day.html.

Anderson, Christopher. 2013. *Canadian Liberalism and the Politics of Border Control, 1867–1967.* Vancouver: UBC Press.

Anderson, Christopher, and Jerome Black. 2008. "The Political Integration of Newcomers, Minorities, and the Canadian-Born: Perspectives on Naturalization, Participation, and Representation." In *Immigration and Integration in Canada in the Twenty-First Century*, edited by John Locke, Meyer Burstein, and James Frideres, 45–75. Montreal: McGill-Queen's University Press.

Arat-Koç, Seref. 1989. "In the Privacy of Our Own Home: Foreign Domestic Workers as the Solution to the Crisis in the Domestic Sphere in Canada." *Studies in Political Economy* 28, 1: 33–58. https://doi.org/10.1080/19187033.1989.11675524.

–. 1997. "From 'Mothers of the Nation' to Migrant Workers." In *Not One of the Family: Foreign Domestic Workers in Canada*, edited by Abigail Bakan and Daiva Stasiulis, 53–80. Toronto: University of Toronto Press.

Arneil, Barbara. 2007. "Cultural Protections vs. Cultural Justice: Post-Colonialism, Agonistic Justice and the Limitations of Liberal Theory." In *Sexual Justice/Cultural Justice: Critical Perspectives in Political Theory and Practice*, edited by Barbara Arneil, Monique Deveaux, Rita Dhamoon, and Avigail Eisenberg, 50–68. New York: Routledge.

Babbie, Earl. 1999. *The Basics of Social Research*. Boston: Wadsworth.

Bailey, Martha. 2004. "Regulation of Cohabitation and Marriage in Canada." *Law and Policy* 26, 1: 153–75. https://doi.org/10.1111/j.0265-8240.2004.00166.x.

Baines, Beverley. 2012. "Polygamy and Feminist Constitutionalism." In *Feminist Constitutionalism: Global Perspectives*, edited by Beverley Baines, Daphne Barak-Erez, and Tsvi Kahana, 452–73. Cambridge: Cambridge University Press. https://doi.org/10.1017/CBO9780511980442.032.

Bakan, Abigail, and Daiva Stasiulis, eds. 1997. *Not of the Family: Foreign Domestic Workers in Canada*. Toronto: University of Toronto Press. https://doi.org/10.3138/9781442677944.

–. 2005. *Negotiating Citizenship: Migrant Women in Canada and the Global System*. Toronto: University of Toronto Press.

–. 2012. "The Political Economy of Migrant Live-In Caregivers: A Case of Unfree Labour?" In *Legislated Inequality: Temporary Labour Migration in Canada*, edited by Patti Tamara Lenard and Christine Straehle, 202–26. Montreal: McGill-Queen's University Press.

Bala, Nicholas. 2003. "Controversy over Couples in Canada: The Evolution of Marriage and Other Adult Interdependent Relationships." *Queen's Law Journal* 29: 41–102.

Bannerji, Himani. 2000. *The Dark Side of the Nation: Essays on Multiculturalism, Nationalism and Gender*. Toronto: Canadian Scholars' Press.

Barker, Nicola. 2006. "Sex and the Civil Partnership Act: The Future of (Non) Conjugality." *Feminist Legal Studies* 14, 2: 241–59. https://doi.org/10.1007/s10691-006-9029-7.

Barnard, Ian. 2004. *Queer Race: Cultural Interventions in the Racial Politics of Queer Theory*. Bern, Switzerland: Peter Lang.

Barton, Rosemary. 2015. "Canada's Syrian Refugee Plan Limited to Women, Children and Families." *CBC News*, November 22. http://www.cbc.ca/news/politics/canada-refugee-plan-women-children-families-1.3330185.

Basok, Tanya, and Marshal Bastable. 2009. "'Knock, Knock, Knockin' on Heaven's Door': Immigrants and the Guardians of Privilege in Canada." *Labour (Halifax)* 63: 207–19.

Bauder, Harald. 2008. "Dialectics of Humanitarian Immigration and National Identity in Canadian Public Discourse." *Refuge: Canada's Periodical on Refugees* 25, 1: 84–94.

Beale, Frances. 2008. "Double Jeopardy: To Be Black and Female." *Meridians: Feminism, Race, Transnationalism* 8, 2: 166–76.

Beck-Gernsheim, Elisabeth. 1998. "On the Way to a Post-Familial Family: From a Community of Need to Elective Affinities." *Theory, Culture and Society* 15, 3: 53–70. https://doi.org/10.1177/0263276498015003004.

Behrens, Matthew. 2012. "Taking Liberties: Canada's Booming Business of Detention and Deportation." *Rabble*, February 21. http://rabble.ca/columnists/2012/02/taking-liberties-canadas-booming-business-detention-and-deportation.

Bell, David, and John Binnie. 2000. *The Sexual Citizen: Queer Politics and Beyond*. London: Polity Press.

Benoit, Leon. 2001. *House of Commons Debates*. 37th Parliament, First Session, Vol 137, No 150, February 27, 12:55.

Berlant, Lauren. 1997. *The Queen of America Goes to Washington City: Essays on Sex and Citizenship*. Durham, NC: Duke University Press.

Bernhard, Judith, Patricia Landolt, and Luin Goldring. 2009. "Transnationalizing Families: Canadian Immigration Policy and the Spatial Fragmentation of Care-Giving among Latin American Newcomers." *International Migration* 47, 2: 3–31. https://doi.org/10.1111/j.1468-2435.2008.00479.x.

Bourbeau, Philippe. 2011. *The Securitization of Migration: A Study of Movement and Order*. London: Routledge.

Bowman, Cynthia. 2010. *Unmarried Couples, Law and Public Policy*. New York: Oxford University Press.

Boyd, Susan, and Claire Young. 2003. "From Same-Sex to No Sex? Trends towards Recognition of (Same-Sex) Relationships in Canada." *Seattle Journal for Social Justice* 1, 3: 757–93.

Brodie, Janine. 1997. "Meso-Discourses, State Forms and the Gendering of Liberal-Democratic Citizenship." *Citizenship Studies* 1, 2: 223–42. https://doi.org/10.1080/13621029708420656.

–. 2008. "The Social in Social Citizenship." In *Recasting the Social in Citizenship*, edited by Engin Isin, 20–43. Toronto: University of Toronto Press.

Brook, Heather. 2002. "Stalemate: Rethinking the Politics of Marriage." *Feminist Theory* 3, 1: 45–66. https://doi.org/10.1177/1460012002003001065.

–. 2007. *Conjugal Rites: Marriage and Marriage-Like Relationships before the Law.* New York: Palgrave Macmillan.

Butler, Judith. 2002. "Is Kinship Always Already Heterosexual?" *Differences: A Journal of Feminist Cultural Studies* 13, 1: 14–44. https://doi.org/10.1215/10407391-13-1-14.

Campbell, Angela. 2005. "How Have Policy Approaches to Polygamy Responded to Women's Experiences and Rights? An International, Comparative Analysis." In *Polygamy in Canada: Legal and Society Implications for Women and Children: A Collection of Policy Reports*, edited by Angela Campbell, Nicholas Bala, Katherine Duvall-Antonacopoulos, Leslie MacRae, Joanne J. Paetsch, Martha Baily, Beverley Baines, Bita Amani, Amy Kaufman, and The Alberta Civil Liberties Research Centre, 1–63. Ottawa: Status of Women Canada.

–. 2010. "Bountiful's Plural Marriages." *International Journal of Law in Context* 6, 4: 343–61. https://doi.org/10.1017/S1744552310000297.

Campion-Smith, Bruce. 2012. "PM Hints at Profound Immigration Changes." *Toronto Star*, December 22, 2012.

Canada Border Services Agency. 2017. "Asylum Claimants Processed by Canada Border Services Agency (CBSA) and Immigration, Refugees and Citizenship Canada (IRCC) Offices, January 2011–December 2017." Ottawa: Government of Canada. https://www.canada.ca/en/immigration-refugees-citizenship/services/refugees/asylum-claims/processed-claims.html.

Canadian Council for Refugees. 2007. *Families Never to Be United: Excluded Family Members*. Ottawa: Canadian Council for Refugees. http://ccrweb.ca/sites/ccrweb.ca/files/static-files/excludedfammembers.pdf.

Cantù, Lionel, Eithne Luibhéid, and Alexandra Minna Stern. 2005. "Well-Founded Fear: Political Asylum and the Boundaries of Sexual Identity in the U.S.-Mexico Borderlands." In *Queer Migrations: Sexuality, U.S. Citizenship, and Border Crossings*, edited by Eithne Luibhéid and Lionel Cantù, 61–74. Minneapolis: University of Minnesota Press.

Cantù, Lionel, Nancy Naples, and Salvador Vidal-Ortiz. 2009. *The Sexuality of Migration: Border Crossings and Mexican Immigrant Men.* New York: New York University Press.

Carens, Joseph. 1987. "Aliens and Citizens: The Case for Open Borders." *Review of Politics* 49, 2: 251–73. https://doi.org/10.1017/S0034670500033817.

–. 2000. *Culture, Citizenship, and Community: A Contextual Exploration of Justice as Evenhandedness.* Oxford: Oxford University Press.

–. 2003. "Who Should Get In? The Ethics of Immigration Admission." *Ethics and International Affairs* 17, 1: 95–110. https://doi.org/10.1111/j.1747-7093.2003.tb00421.x.

–. 2013. *The Ethics of Immigration*. Oxford: Oxford University Press.

Carlaw, John. 2015. "A Party for New Canadians? The Rhetoric and Reality of Neoconservative Citizenship and Immigration Policy." In *The Harper Record: 2008–2015*, edited by Teresa Healy and Stuart Trew, 105–28. Ottawa: Canadian Center for Policy Alternatives.

–. 2016. "Stuart Hall, Thatcherism and Kenneyism: Grasping Conservative Decade in Citizenship, Immigration and Multiculturalism." Presented at the Annual Meeting of the Canadian Political Science Association, Calgary, AB, June 1, 2016.

Carter, Sarah. 2008. *The Importance of Being Monogamous: Marriage and National Building in Western Canada to 1915*. Edmonton: University of Alberta Press.

CBC News. 2004. "Ontario Drops 'Spouse in the House' Appeal." *CBC News*, September 2. http://www.cbc.ca/news/canada/ontario-drops-spouse-in-the-house-appeal-1.481746.

–. 2010. "Arranged Marriages Risk Immigration Scrutiny." *CBC News*, May 3. http://www.cbc.ca/news/canada/toronto/arranged-marriages-risk-immigration-scrutiny-1.891890.

–. 2011. "Marriage Fraud Targeted by Canada Border Agency." *CBC News*, November 1. http://www.cbc.ca/news/politics/marriage-fraud-targeted-by-canada-border-agency-1.1003652.

Cere, Daniel, and Douglas Farrow. 2004. *Divorcing Marriage: Unveiling the Dangers in Canada's New Social Experiment*. Montreal: McGill-Queen's University Press.

Charsley, K., and M. Benson. 2012. "Marriages of Convenience or Inconvenient Marriages: Regulating Spousal Migration to Britain." *Journal of Immigration, Asylum and Nationality Law* 26, 1: 10–26.

Chow, Olivia. 2008. *House of Commons Debates*. 39th Parliament, Second Session, Vol 142, No 089, May 6, 10:05.

–. 2009. *House of Commons Debates*. 40th Parliament, Second Session, Vol 144, No 061, May 26, 10:20.

Citizenship and Immigration Canada. 1994. *Into the 21st Century: A Strategy for Immigration and Citizenship*. Ottawa: Government of Canada.

–. 1995. *A Broader Vision: Immigration and Citizenship Plan 1995–2000; Annual Report to Parliament*. Ottawa: Government of Canada.

–. 2005. *Annual Report to Parliament on Immigration 2005*. Ottawa: Government of Canada.

–. 2006. "OP2: Processing Members of the Family Class." *Operational Bulletins and Manuals*. Ottawa: Government of Canada. http://www.cic.gc.ca/english/resources/manuals/op/op02-eng.pdf.

–. 2010. "CIC Backgrounders: Marriage Fraud – Have Your Say." Ottawa: Government of Canada. http://www.cic.gc.ca/english/department/media/backgrounders/ 2010/2010-09-27.asp.

–. 2011a. *Consulting the Public on Marriages of Convenience*. Ottawa: Government of Canada.

–. 2011b. *Marriage Fraud: Stories from Victims*. Ottawa: Government of Canada. https://www.youtube.com/watch?v=FoyzsFaHk5g&t=21s.

–. 2012a. "Citizenship and Immigration Statistics Archives 1966–1996." Ottawa: Government of Canada. http://www.cic.gc.ca/english/resources/statistics/.

–. 2012b. "Conditional Permanent Residence Proposed to Deter Marriages of Convenience." Ottawa: Government of Canada. March 9. https://www.canada.ca/ en/news/archive/2012/03/conditional-permanent-residence-proposed-deter -marriages-convenience.html.

–. 2012c. "'The Jig Is Up on Marriage Fraud,' Says Minister Kenney." Ottawa: Government of Canada. October 26. https://www.canada.ca/en/news/archive/ 2012/10/jig-up-marriage-fraud-says-minister-kenney.html.

–. 2012d. "Minister Kenney Introduces Sponsorship Restriction to Address Marriage Fraud." Ottawa: Government of Canada. March 2. https://www.canada.ca/en/ news/archive/2012/03/minister-kenney-introduces-sponsorship-restriction -address-marriage-fraud.html.

–. 2014. "Evaluation of the Family Reunification Program." Ottawa: Government of Canada. http://www.cic.gc.ca/english/pdf/pub/e4-2013-frp.pdf.

Collins, Patricia Hill. 1993. "Toward a New Vision: Race, Class, and Gender as Categories of Analysis and Connection." *Race, Sex & Class* 1, 1: 25–45.

Conservative Party of Canada. 2011. "Here for Canada." https://www.conservative. ca/.

Coontz, Stephanie. 1992. *The Way We Never Were: American Families and the Nostalgia Trap*. New York: Basic Books.

Cossman, Brenda. 1994. "Family Inside/Out." *University of Toronto Law Journal* 44, 1: 1–39. https://doi.org/10.2307/825753.

–. 2002. "Sexing Citizenship, Privatizing Sex." *Citizenship Studies* 6, 4: 483–506. https://doi.org/10.1080/1362102022000041277.

–. 2007. *Sexual Citizens: The Legal and Cultural Regulation of Sex and Belonging*. Stanford, CA: Stanford University Press.

Cossman, Brenda, and Bruce Ryder. 2001. "What Is Marriage-Like Like? The Irrelevance of Conjugality." *Canadian Journal of Family Law* 18, 2: 269–326.

–. 2017. "Beyond *Beyond Conjugality*." *Canadian Journal of Family Law* 30, 2: 227–63.

Côté, Andrée, Michèle Kerisit, and Marie-Louise Côté. 2001. *Sponsorship ... for Better or for Worse: The Impact of Sponsorship on the Equality Rights of Immigrant Women*. Ottawa: Status of Women Canada.

Côté-Boucher, Karine. 2015. "Bordering Citizenship in 'an Open and Generous Society': The Criminalization of Migration in Canada." In *The Routledge Handbook on Crime and International Migration*, edited by Sharon Pickering and Julie Harn, 75–90. London: Routledge.

Cott, Nancy. 2000. *Public Vows: A History of Marriage and the Nation.* Cambridge, MA: Harvard University Press.

Cragnolini, Giulia. 2013. "Lesbian, Gay, Bisexual and Transgender Refugees: Challenges in Refugee Status Determination and Living Conditions in Turkey." In *Fleeing Homophobia: Sexual Orientation, Gender Identity and Asylum,* edited by Thomas Spijkerboer, 98–120. New York: Routledge.

Crenshaw, Kimberle. 1991. "Mapping the Margins: Intersectionality, Identity Politics and Violence against Women of Colour." *Stanford Law Review* 43, 6: 1241–99. https://doi.org/10.2307/1229039.

Curry, Bill. 2011. "Ottawa Moves to Curb Marriages of Convenience." *Globe and Mail*, October 26, 2011. https://www.theglobeandmail.com/news/politics/ottawa -moves-to-curb-marriages-of-convenience/article4182749/.

D'Aoust, Anne-Marie. 2013. "In the Name of Love: Marriage Migration, Governmentality and Technologies of Love." *International Political Sociology* 7, 3: 258–74. https://doi.org/10.1111/ips.12022.

Dauvergne, Catherine. 2005. *Humanitarianism, Identity, and Nation: Migration Laws in Canada and Australia.* Vancouver: UBC Press.

–. 2013. "How the Charter Has Failed Non-Citizens in Canada: Reviewing Thirty Years of Supreme Court of Canada Jurisprudence." *McGill Law Journal* 58, 3: 663–728.

–. 2016. *The New Politics of Immigration and the End of Settler Societies.* Cambridge: Cambridge University Press.

Dauvergne, Catherine, and Jenni Millbank. 2003. "Burdened by Proof: How the Australian Refugee Review Tribunal Has Failed Lesbian and Gay Asylum Seekers." *Federal Law Review* 31: 299–342.

Davis, Angela. 1981. *Women, Race and Class.* New York: Random House.

Dawson, Mary. 1993. "The Impact of the Charter on the Public Policy Process and the Department of Justice." In *The Impact of the Charter on the Public Policy Process,* edited by Patrick Monahan and Marie Finkelstein, 51–60. Toronto: York University Centre for Public Law and Public Policy.

Day, Richard. 2002. *Multiculturalism and the History of Canadian Diversity.* Toronto: University of Toronto Press.

Day, Stockwell. 2007. *House of Commons Debates.* 39th Parliament, First Session, June 8, 12:10.

Delgado, Richard. 1989. "Storytelling for Oppositionists and Others: A Plea for Narrative." *Michigan Law Review* 87, 8: 2411–41. https://doi.org/10.2307/1289308.

Delphy, Christine. 1996. "The Private as a Deprivation of Rights for Women and Children." Paper presented at the International Conference on Violence, Abuse and Women's Citizenship, Brighton, UK, November 11.

Denike, Margaret. 2014. "Polygamy and Race-Thinking: A Genealogy." In *Polygamy's Rights and Wrongs: Perspectives on Harm, Family, and Law*, edited by Lori G. Beaman and Gillian Calder, 142–69. Vancouver: UBC Press.

Deschênes, Claudette. 2009. "Evidence to House of Commons Standing Committee on Citizenship and Immigration." CIMM Number 037. Second Session, 40th Parliament. December 1.

Dhamoon, Rita. 2007. "The Politics of Cultural Contestation." In *Sexual Justice/ Cultural Justice: Critical Perspectives in Political Theory and Practice*, edited by Barbara Arneil, Monique Deveaux, Rita Dhamoon, and Avigail Eisenberg, 30–49. New York: Routledge.

–. 2009. *Identity/Difference Politics: How Difference Is Produced, and Why It Matters*. Vancouver: UBC Press.

–. 2010. "Security Warning: Multiculturalism Alert!" In *The Ashgate Research Companion to Multiculturalism*, edited by Duncan Ivison, 255–75. London: Ashgate.

Dhamoon, Rita, and Yasmeen Abu-Laban. 2009. "Dangerous (Internal) Foreigners and Nation-Building: The Case of Canada." *International Political Science Review* 30, 2: 163–83. https://doi.org/10.1177/0192512109102435.

Dobrowolsky, Alexandra. 2013. "Nuancing Neoliberalism: Lessons Learned from a Failed Immigration Experiment." *Journal of International Migration and Integration* 14, 2: 197–218.

Dobrowolsky, Alexandra, and Jane Jenson. 2004. "Shifting Representations of Citizenship: Canadian Politics of 'Women' and 'Children.'" *Social Politics* 11, 2: 154–80. https://doi.org/10.1093/sp/jxh031.

Drummond, Susan. 2009. "Polygamy's Inscrutable Criminal Mischief." *Osgoode Hall Law Journal* 47, 2: 317–69.

Eggebø, Helga. 2013. "A Real Marriage? Applying for Marriage Migration to Norway." *Journal of Ethnic and Migration Studies* 39, 5: 773–89. https://doi.org/10.1080/1369183X.2013.756678.

Epp, Charles. 1998. *The Rights Revolution: Lawyers, Activists, and Supreme Courts in Comparative Perspective*. Chicago: University of Chicago Press.

Fetner, Tina, and Carrie Sanders. 2011. "The Pro-Family Movement in Canada and the United States: Institutional Histories and Barriers to Diffusion." In *Faith, Politics and Sexual Diversity in Canada and the United States*, edited by David Rayside and Clyde Wilcox, 87–100. Vancouver: UBC Press.

Finch, Janet. 1989. *Family Obligations and Social Change*. Cambridge, UK: Polity Press.

Fineman, Martha. 2001. "Why Marriage?" *Virginia Journal of Social Policy and the Law* 9, 1: 239–79.

–. 2006. "The Meaning of Marriage." In *Marriage Proposals: Questioning a Legal Status*, edited by Anita Bernstein, 29–69. New York: New York University Press.

Finley, Diane. 2008. *House of Commons Debates*. 39th Parliament, Second Session, Vol 142, No 089, May 6, 13:10.

Fleischmann, Aldys, Nancy van Styvendale, and Cody Maccaroll. 2011. *Narratives of Citizenship: Indigenous and Diasporic Peoples Unsettle the Nation-State*. Edmonton: University of Alberta Press.

Fleras, Augie. 2015. *Immigration Canada: Evolving Realities and Emerging Challenges in a Postnational World*. Vancouver: UBC Press.

Foucault, Michel. 1979. *Discipline and Punish: The Birth of the Prison*. New York: Vintage Books.

–. 1988. "Technologies of the Self." In *Technologies of the Self*, edited by L.H. Martin, H. Gutman, and P.H. Hutton, 16–49. London: Tavistock.

Freeman, Elizabeth. 2002. *The Wedding Complex: Forms of Belonging in Modern American Culture*. Durham, NC: Duke University Press. https://doi.org/10.1215/9780822384007.

Friesen, Joe, and Julian Sher. 2011. "How Courting the Immigrant Vote Paid Off for the Tories." *Globe and Mail*, May 3. https://www.theglobeandmail.com/news/politics/how-courting-the-immigrant-vote-paid-off-for-the-tories/article578608/.

Gabriel, Christina. 2011. "Migration and Globalized Care Work: The Case of Internationally Educated Nurses in Canada." In *Feminist Ethics and Social Policy: Towards a New Global Political Economy of Care*, edited by Rianne Mahon and Fiona Robinson, 39–59. Vancouver: UBC Press.

–. 2017. "Framing Families: Neo-Liberalism and the Family Class within Canadian Immigration Policy." *Atlantis: Critical Studies in Gender, Culture and Social Justice* 38, 1: 179–94.

Gabriel, Christina, and Laura Macdonald. 2007. "Migration and Citizenship Rights in a New North American Space." In *Requiem or Revival? The Promise of North American Integration*, edited by Isabel Studer and Carol Wise, 353–70. Washington, DC: Brookings Press.

Gaucher, Megan. 2014a. "Family Women Need Not Apply: Intersections between Family and Citizenship in the Case of Canada's Foreign Domestic Worker." Paper presented at the Annual Meeting of the Canadian Political Science Association, St. Catharines, ON, May 29.

–. 2014b. "One Step Forward, Two Steps Back? Relationship Recognition in Canadian Law Post-Same-Sex Marriage." *Atlantis: Critical Studies in Gender, Culture and Social Justice* 36, 2: 61–72.

–. 2016. "Monogamous Canadian Citizenship, Constructing Foreignness, and the Limits of Harm Discourse." *Canadian Journal of Political Science* 49, 3: 519–38. https://doi.org/10.1017/S0008423916000810.

Gaucher, Megan, and Alexa DeGagné. 2016. "Guilty Until Proven Prosecuted: The Canadian State's Assessment of Sexual Minority Refugee Claimants and the Invisibility of the Non-Western Sexual Non-Citizen." *Social Politics* 23, 3: 459–81. https://doi.org/10.1093/sp/jxu029.

Giddens, Anthony. 1992. *The Transformation of Intimacy: Sexuality, Love and Eroticism in Modern Societies*. Cambridge, UK: Polity Press.

Gilbert, Rénald. 2011a. "Evidence to House of Commons Standing Committee on Citizenship and Immigration." CIMM Number 043. Third Session, 40th Parliament. February 15.

–. 2011b. "Evidence to House of Commons Standing Committee on Citizenship and Immigration." CIMM Number 046. Third Session, 40th Parliament. March 3.

Gitari, Eric. 2011. "You Are Not Gay Enough: Proving Sexual Orientation and Gender Identity within the Asylum Regime and the Credibility Challenge in Varying Cultural Expressions of Sex and Gender." Paper presented at the Fleeing Homophobia Conference, Amsterdam, NL, September 5.

Glennon, Lisa. 2005. "Displacing the 'Conjugal Family' in Legal Policy – A Progressive Move?" *Child and Family Law Quarterly* 17, 2 :141–63.

Go, Avvy Yao-Yao, Anita Balakrishna, and Atulya Sharma. 2011. "Marriage of Convenience." *Toronto Star*, April 6. https://www.thestar.com/opinion/editorial opinion/2011/04/06/marriage_of_convenience.html.

Goldring, Luin, and Patricia Landolt, eds. 2013. *Producing and Negotiating Non-Citizenship: Precarious Legal Status in Canada*. Toronto: University of Toronto Press.

Graveland, Bill. 2015. "Plan to Accelerate Acceptance of 20,000 Refugees Coming Soon, Kenney Says." *Globe and Mail*, September 16. https://www.theglobeandmail.com/news/politics/plan-to-accelerate-acceptance-of-20000-refugees-coming-soon-kenney-says/article26388855/.

Halley, Janet. 2001. "Recognition, Rights, Regulation, Normalization: Rhetorics of Justification in the Same-Sex Marriage Debate." In *Legal Recognition of Same-Sex Partnerships: A Study of National, European and International Law*, edited by Robert Wintemute and Mads Andenaes, 97–111. Portland, OR: Hart Publishing.

Harder, Lois. 2007. "Rights of Love: The State and Intimate Relationships in Canada and the United States." *Social Politics: International Journal in Gender, State and Society* 14, 2: 155–81. https://doi.org/10.1093/sp/jxm009.

–. 2008. "The Sexual Citizen of Neoliberalism: Reading the Rules of Conjugality in Canadian and U.S. Immigration Policy." Paper presented at the Annual Meeting of the International Political Science Association, Montreal, QC, May 31, 2008.

–. 2009a. "Neoliberalism's Agnosticism: Domestic and Immigration Policies in the Model Family in Canada and the United States." In *Post-Neoliberalism in the Americas: An Introduction*, edited by Laura Macdonald and Arne Ruckert, 215–30. New York: Palgrave Macmillan.

–. 2009b. "The State and the Friendships of the Nation: The Case of Nonconjugal Relationships in the United States and Canada." *Signs: Journal of Women in Culture and Society* 34, 3: 633–58. https://doi.org/10.1086/593331.

–. 2010. "'In Canada of All Places': National Belonging and the Lost Canadians." *Citizenship Studies* 14, 2: 203–20. https://doi.org/10.1080/13621021003594890.

–. 2015. "Does Sperm Have a Flag? On Biological Relationship and National Membership." *Canadian Journal of Law and Society* 30, 1: 109–25. https://doi.org/10.1017/cls.2014.24.

Harell, Allison. 2013. "Revising the 'Ethnic' Vote: Liberal Allegiance and Vote Choice among Racialized Minorities." In *Parties, Elections and the Future of Canadian Politics*, edited by Royce Koop and Amanda Bittner, 140–60. Vancouver: UBC Press.

Harper, Tim. 2014. "Jason Kenney Suspends Food Services Sector from Foreign Worker Program." *Toronto Star*, April 24, 2014.

Hathaway, James. 1991. *The Law of Refugee Status*. Toronto: Butterworths.

–. 1994. *Report of the National Consultation on Family Class Immigration*. Toronto: Centre for Refugee Studies, York University.

Hathaway, James, and Jason Pobjoy. 2012. "Queer Cases Make Bad Law." *International Law and Politics* 44, 2:315–89.

Hawkins, Freda. 1989. *Critical Years in Immigration: Canada and Australia Compared*. Montreal: McGill-Queen's University Press.

Heath, Joseph. 1997. "Immigration, Multiculturalism, and the Social Contract." *Canadian Journal of Law and Jurisprudence* 10, 2: 343–61. https://doi.org/10.1017/S0841820900001569.

Hersh, Nicholas. 2015. "Challenges to Assessing Same-Sex Relationships under Refugee Law in Canada." *McGill Law Journal* 60, 3: 527–71. https://doi.org/10.7202/1032678ar.

Hiebert, Janet. 2002. *Charter Conflicts: What Is Parliament's Role?* Montreal: McGill-Queen's University Press.

Holland, Winifred. 2000. "Intimate Relationships in the New Millennium: The Assimilation of Marriage and Cohabitation." *Canadian Journal of Family Law* 17, 1: 114–68.

Honig, Bonnie. 2001. *Democracy and the Foreigner*. Princeton, NJ: Princeton University Press. https://doi.org/10.1515/9781400824816.

Hrick, Pam. 2012. "A Dangerous Step Backwards: The Implications of Conditional Permanent Resident Status for Sponsored Immigrant Women in Abusive Relationships." *Dalhousie Journal of Legal Studies* 21: 1–30.

Hymowitz, Kay. 2006. *Marriage and Caste in America: Separate and Unequal Families in a Post-Marital Age*. Chicago: Ivan R. Dee.

Ignatieff, Michael. 2000. *The Rights Revolution*. Toronto: House of Anansi Press.

Immigration and Refugee Board of Canada. 2017a. "Assessment of Credibility in Claims of Refugee Protection." Ottawa: Government of Canada. http://www.irb -cisr.gc.ca/Eng/BoaCom/references/LegJur/Pages/Credib.aspx.

–. 2017b. "Refugee Appeal Statistics." Ottawa: Government of Canada. http://www. irb-cisr.gc.ca/Eng/RefApp/stats/Pages/index.aspx.

Immigration, Refugees and Citizenship Canada. 2015a. "Facts and Figures 2015: Immigration Overview." Ottawa: Government of Canada. http://open.canada.ca/ data/en/dataset/2fbb56bd-eae7-4582-af7d-a197d 185fc93?_ga=2.258720266. 1829355085.1511292851-675607745.1491767906.

–. 2015b. "Operational Bulletin 613 – June 11, 2015." Ottawa: Government of Canada. http://www.cic.gc.ca/english/resources/manuals/bulletins/2015/ob613.asp.

2017a. "Application Processing Times." Ottawa: Government of Canada. http://www. cic.gc.ca/ENGLISH/information/times/index.asp.

–. 2017b. "Notice – Government of Canada Eliminates Conditional Permanent Residence," Ottawa: Government of Canada. April 28. http://www.cic.gc.ca/english/ department/media/notices/2017-04-28.asp.

–. 2017c. "Relationship Information and Sponsorship Evaluation." Ottawa: Government of Canada. http://www.cic.gc.ca/english/pdf/kits/forms/IMM5532E.pdf.

–. 2017d. "Sponsorship Eligibility." Ottawa: Government of Canada. http://www.cic. gc.ca/english/immigrate/sponsor/spouse-apply-who.asp.

Janicek, Ainsley, Alan D. Wong, and Edward Ou Jin Lee. 2009. "Dangerous Shortcuts: Representations of Sexual Minority Refugees in the Post-9/11 Canadian Press." *Canadian Journal of Communication* 34, 4: 635–58.

Janoff, Douglas. 2005. *Pink Blood: Homophobic Violence in Canada*. Toronto: University of Toronto Press. https://doi.org/10.3138/9781442678491.

Janoski, Thomas. 2010. *The Ironies of Citizenship: Naturalization and Integration in Industrialized Countries*. Cambridge: Cambridge University Press. https://doi. org/10.1017/CBO9780511779206.

Javed, Noor. 2008a. "GTA's Secret World of Polygamy; As Toronto Mother Describes Her Ordeal, Imam Admits He Has 'Blessed' Over 30 Unions." *Toronto Star*, May 24. https://www.thestar.com/news/gta/2008/05/24/gtas_secret_world_of_polygamy. html.

–. 2008b. "I Do, I Do, I Do. The Last Taboo; It's Among the Last Taboos in a Society Where Little Shocks Us." *Toronto Star*, May 24. https://www.thestar.com/ news/2008/05/24/i_do_i_do_i_do_the_last_taboo.html.

Jeffrey, Brooke. 2015. *Dismantling Canada: Stephen Harper's New Conservative Agenda*. Montreal: McGill-Queen's University Press.

Jenson, Jane, and Martin Papillon. 2001. *The Changing Boundaries of Citizenship: A Review and a Research Agenda*. Ottawa: Canadian Policy Research Networks Inc.

Jenson, Jane, and Susan D. Phillips. 1996. "Regime Shift: New Citizenship Practices in Canada." *International Journal of Canadian Studies* 14: 111–36.

Johnson, Kecia R., and Karyn Loscocco. 2015. "Black Marriage through the Prism of Gender, Race, and Class." *Journal of Black Studies* 46, 2: 142–71.

Johnston, David. 2011. *Speech from the Throne*. First Session, 41st Parliament. June 3.

Joppke, Christian. 2010. *Citizenship and Immigration*. Cambridge, UK: Polity Press.

Kelley, Ninette, and Michael Trebilcock. 2000. *The Making of the Mosaic: A History of Canadian Immigration Policy*. Toronto: University of Toronto Press.

Kelly, Fiona. 2011. *Transforming Law's Family: The Legal Recognition of Planned Lesbian Motherhood*. Vancouver: UBC Press.

Kelly, James. 1999. "Bureaucratic Activism and the Charter of Rights and Freedoms: The Department of Justice and Its Entry into the Centre of Government." *Canadian Public Administration* 42, 4: 476–511. https://doi.org/10.1111/j.1754-7121.1999. tb02037.x.

Kennedy, Mark. 2015. "'No Election Win (Is) Worth Pitting Canadians against Canadians': Trudeau Says of Niqab Debate." *National Post*, July 10. http://nationalpost. com/news/canada/canadian-politics/no-election-win-is-worth-pitting-canadians -against-canadians-trudeau-says-of-niqab-debate/.

Kenney, Jason. 2009. "Evidence to House of Commons Standing Committee on Citizenship and Immigration." CIMM Number 037. Second Session, 40th Parliament. December 1.

–. 2010. "Evidence to House of Commons Standing Committee on Citizenship and Immigration." CIMM Number 036. Third Session, 40th Parliament. December 6.

–. 2012. "Speaking Notes." In *Minister Kenney News Conference at Victoria Hospital*. London Health Sciences Centre, London, Ontario, April 24.

Kernerman, Gerald. 2005. *Multicultural Nationalism: Civilizing Difference, Constituting Community*. Vancouver: UBC Press.

Komarnicki, Ed. 2008. *House of Commons Debates*. 39th Parliament, Second Session, Vol 142, No 089, May 6, 10:30.

Kramer, Susan. 2008. "Evidence to House of Commons Standing Committee on Citizenship and Immigration." CIMM Number 016. Second Session, 39th Parliament. March 10.

Kymlicka, Will. 1989. *Liberalism, Community and Culture*. Oxford: Oxford University Press.

–. 1995. *Multicultural Citizenship: A Liberal Theory of Minority Rights*. Oxford: Clarendon Press.

–. 2009. "Categorizing Groups, Categorizing States: Theorizing Minority Rights in a World of Deep Diversity." *Ethics and International Affairs* 23, 4: 371–88. https://doi.org/10.1111/j.1747-7093.2009.00229.x.

Lahey, Kathleen. 1999. *Are We 'Persons' Yet? Law and Sexuality in Canada*. Toronto: University of Toronto Press. https://doi.org/10.3138/9781442670952.

–. 2001. *The Impact of Relationship Recognition on Lesbian Women in Canada: Still Separate and Only Somewhat 'Equivalent.'* Ottawa: Status of Women Canada.

Lahey, Kathleen, and Kevin Alderson. 2004. *Same-Sex Marriage: The Personal and the Political*. Toronto: Insomniac Press.

LaViolette, Nicole. 1997. "The Immutable Refugees: Sexual Orientation in Canada (A.G.) v. Ward." *University of Toronto Faculty of Law Review* 55, 1: 1–41.

–. 2004. "Coming Out to Canada: The Immigration of Same-Sex Couples under the Immigration and Refugee Protection Act." *McGill Law Journal* 49: 969–1003.

–. 2007. "Gender-Related Refugee Claims: Expanding the Scope of the Canadian Guidelines." *International Journal of Refugee Law* 19, 2: 169–214. https://doi.org/10.1093/ijrl/eem008.

–. 2009. "Independent Human Rights Documentation and Sexual Minorities: An Ongoing Challenge for the Canadian Refugee Determination Process." *International Journal of Human Rights* 13 (2/3): 437–76.

–. 2010. "'UNHCR Guidance Note on Refugee Claims Relating to Sexual Orientation and Gender Identity': A Critical Commentary." *International Journal of Refugee Law* 22, 2: 173–208. https://doi.org/10.1093/ijrl/eeq019.

–. 2014. "Sexual Orientation, Gender Identity and the Refugee Determination Process in Canada." *Journal of Research in Gender Studies* 4, 2: 68–123.

Law Commission of Canada. 2001. *Beyond Conjugality: Recognizing and Supporting Close Personal Adult Relationships*. Ottawa: Law Commission of Canada.

Léger, Rémi. 2011. "Canada's French Fact – or Facts?" In *Against Orthodoxy: Studies in Nationalism*, edited by T. Harrison and S. Drakulic, 133–53. Vancouver: UBC Press.

Lenard, Patti Tamara, and Christine Straehle, eds. 2012. *Legislated Inequality: Temporary Labour Migration in Canada*. Montreal: McGill-Queen's University Press.

Lenon, Suzanne. 2015. "Monogamy, Marriage, and the Making of Nation." In *Disrupting Queer Inclusion: Canadian Homonationalisms and the Politics of Belonging*, edited by OmiSoore H. Dryden and Suzanne Lenon, 82–99. Vancouver: UBC Press.

Liew, Jamie. 2016. "The Ultrahazardous Activity of Excluding Family Members in Canada's Immigration System." *Ottawa Faculty of Law Working Paper* 16.

Liew, Jamie, Prasanna Balasundaram, and Jennifer Stone. 2017. "Troubling Trends in Canada's Immigration System via the Excluded Family Member

Regulation: A Survey of Jurisprudence and Lawyers." *Ottawa Faculty of Law Working Paper* 36.

Lister, Ruth. 1997a. *Citizenship: Feminist Perspectives*. New York: New York University Press. https://doi.org/10.1007/978-1-349-26209-0.

–. 1997b. "Citizenship: Towards a Feminist Synthesis." *Feminist Review* 57, 1: 28–48.

Little, Margaret. 2003. "The Leaner, Meaner Welfare Machine: The Ontario Conservative Government's Ideological and Material Attack on Single Mothers." In *Making Normal: Social Regulation in Canada*, edited by Deborah Brock, 235–58. Toronto: University of Toronto Press.

–. 2011. "The Increasing Invisibility of Mothering." In *A Life in Balance? Reopening the Family-Work Debate*, edited by Catherine Krull and Justyna Sempruch, 194–205. Vancouver: UBC Press.

Long, Elizabeth. 2009. "Evidence to House of Commons Standing Committee on Citizenship and Immigration." CIMM Number 032. Second Session, 40th Parliament. November 3.

Luibhéid, Eithne. 2002. *Entry Denied: Controlling Sexuality at the Border*. Minneapolis: University of Minnesota Press.

–. 2004. "Heteronormativity and Immigration Scholarship: A Call for Change." *GLQ: A Journal of Lesbian and Gay Studies* 10, 2: 227–35. https://doi.org/10.1215/10642684-10-2-227.

–. 2005. "Heteronormativity, Responsibility and Neo-Liberal Governance in U.S. Immigration Control." In *Passing Lines: Sexuality and Immigration*, edited by Brad Epps, Keja Valens, and Bill Johnson-Gonzalez, 69–104. Cambridge, MA: Harvard University Press.

–. 2008. "Sexuality, Migration, and the Shifting Line between Legal and Illegal Status." *GLQ: A Journal of Lesbian and Gay Studies* 14, 2–3: 289–315.

Luibhéid, Eithne, and Lionel Cantù. 2005. *Queer Migrations: Sexuality, U.S. Citizenship and Border Crossings*. Minneapolis: University of Minnesota Press.

Luxton, Meg. 1997. "Feminism and Families: The Challenge of Neo-Conservatism." In *Feminism and Families: Critical Policies and Changing Practices*, edited by Meg Luxton, 12–13. Halifax, NS: Fernwood Publishing.

Lyndon-Shanley, Mary. 2004. *Just Marriage*. Oxford: Oxford University Press.

Macfarlane, Emmett. 2008. "Terms of Entitlement: Is There a Distinctly Canadian 'Rights Talk'?" *Canadian Journal of Political Science* 41, 2: 303–28. https://doi.org/10.1017/S0008423908080451.

–. 2013. *Governing from the Bench: The Supreme Court of Canada and the Judicial Role*. Vancouver: UBC Press.

Macklin, Audrey. 1992. "Foreign Domestic Worker: Surrogate Housewife or Mail Order Servant?" *McGill Law Journal* 37, 3: 681–760.

–. 1996. "On the Inside Looking In: Foreign Domestic Workers in Canada." *In Maid in the Market: Women's Paid Domestic Labour,* edited by Winona Giles and Seref Arat-Koç, 13–39. Winnipeg, MB: Fernwood Publishing.

–. 2002. "Public Entrance/Private Member." In *Privatization, Law and the Challenge to Feminism,* edited by Brenda Cossman and Judy Fudge, 218–64. Toronto: University of Toronto Press.

–. 2007. "Who Is the Citizen's Other? Considering the Heft of Citizenship." *Theoretical Inquiries in Law* 8, 2: 476–508.

–. 2014. "Evidence to House of Commons Standing Committee on Citizenship and Immigration." CIMM Number 021. Second Session, 41st Parliament. April 9.

Malhi, Gurbax Singh. 1998. *House of Commons Debates.* 36th Parliament, First Session, Vol 135, No 184, February 18, 15:30.

Manfredi, Christopher. 2001. *Judicial Power and the Charter: Canada and the Paradox of Liberal Constitutionalism.* Toronto: University of Toronto Press.

Marwah, Inder, Triadafilos Triadafilopoulos, and Stephen White. 2013. "Immigration, Citizenship, and Canada's New Conservative Party." In *Conservatism in Canada,* edited by David Rayside and Jim Farney, 95–119. Toronto: University of Toronto Press.

Matthews, J. Scott. 2005. "The Political Foundations of Support for Same-Sex Marriage in Canada." *Canadian Journal of Political Science* 38, 4: 841–66. https://doi.org/10.1017/S0008423905040485.

McGregor, Glen. 2012. "Recipients of Kenney Missive Wondering How Government Knows Their Sexual Orientation." *Ottawa Citizen,* September 24.

McKie, David. 2010. "Marriages of Convenience Problems Persist." *CBC News,* November 8. http://www.cbc.ca/news/politics/marriages-of-convenience-problems-persist-1.876101.

–. 2011. "CBSA Urged to Act on Marriage Fraud Complaints: Immigration Minister Wants Border Agents to Build Credible Cases." *CBC News,* October 29. http://www.cbc.ca/news/politics/cbsa-urged-to-act-on-marriage-fraud-complaints-1.1003655.

Meilaender, Peter. 2001. *Toward a Theory of Immigration.* New York: Palgrave. https://doi.org/10.1057/9780312299118.

Merali, Noorfarah. 2009. "Experiences of South Asian Brides Entering Canada after Recent Changes to Family Sponsorship Policies." *Violence against Women* 15, 3: 321–39. https://doi.org/10.1177/1077801208330435.

Metro Toronto Chinese and Southeast Asian Legal Clinic. 2014. "Family Class Sponsorship." http://mtcsalc.org/en/publications/immigration/family-class-sponsorship/?p=02.

Millbank, Jenni. 2002. "Imagining Otherness: Refugee Claims on the Basis of Sexuality in Canada and Australia." *Melbourne University Law Review* 26: 144–77.

–. 2009. "'The Ring of Truth': A Case Study of Credibility Assessment in Particular Social Group Refugee Determinations." *International Journal of Refugee Law* 21, 1: 1–33. https://doi.org/10.1093/ijrl/een040.

Milne, David. 2005. *Asymmetry in Canada, Past and Present.* Kingston: School of Policy Studies, Queen's University, Asymmetry Series (5).

Ministry of Public Works and Government Services Canada. 1997. *Not Just Numbers: A Canadian Framework for Future Immigration.* Ottawa: Ministry of Public Works and Government Services Canada.

Mink, Gwendolyn. 1990. "Lady and the Tramp: Gender, Race and the Origins of the American Welfare System." In *Women, the State and Welfare,* edited by Linda Gordon, 92–122. Madison: University of Wisconsin Press.

Mohanty, Chandra Talpade. 2003. *Feminism without Borders: Decolonizing Theory, Practicing Solidarity.* Durham, NC: Duke University Press. https://doi.org/10.1215/9780822384649.

Morton, F.L., and Rainer Knopff. 1992. *Charter Politics.* Scarborough, ON: Nelson.

–. 2000. *The Charter Revolution and the Court Party.* Peterborough, ON: Broadview Press.

Murray, David. 2015. *Real Queer? Sexual Orientation and Gender Identity Refugees in the Canadian Refugee Apparatus.* London, UK: Rowman and Littlefield.

National Post. 2012. "Questions Linger about High-Profile 'Marriage Fraud' Case." May 13. http://nationalpost.com/2012/05/13/questions-linger-about-high-profile-marriage-fraud-case/.

–. 2013. "'Sometimes Marriage Is a Scam': Ottawa Launches Fresh Ad Campaign Targeting Immigration Fraud." March 20. http://nationalpost.com/2013/03/20/sometimes-marriage-is-a-scam-ottawa-launches-fresh-ad-campaign-targeting-immigration-fraud/.

O'Malley, Kady. 2007. "No Big Love Lost. Is British Columbia Finally Ready to Take On the Polygamists of Bountiful?" *Maclean's,* June 25. http://www.macleans.ca/politics/ottawa/from-the-macleansca-archives-no-big-love-lost-originally-posted-on-june-25-2007/.

Omidvar, Ratna. 2016. "The Harper Influence on Immigration." In *The Harper Factor: Assessing a Prime Minister's Policy Legacy,* edited by Jennifer Ditchburn and Graham Fox, 179–95. Montreal: McGill-Queen's University Press.

Ontario Law Reform Commission. 1993. *Report on The Rights and Responsibilities of Cohabitants under the Family Law Act.* Toronto: Ontario Law Reform Commission.

Pahl, Ray, and Liz Spencer. 2004. "Personal Communities: Not Simply Families of 'Fate' or 'Choice.'" *Current Sociology* 52, 2: 199–221. https://doi.org/10.1177/0011392104041808.

Palmer, Douglas L. 1996. "Determinants of Canadian Attitudes toward Immigration: More than Just Racism?" *Canadian Journal of Behavioural Science* 28, 3: 180–92. https://doi.org/10.1037/0008-400X.28.3.180.

Parreñas, Rhacel Salazar. 2001. *Servants of Globalization: Women, Migration, and Domestic Work*. Stanford, CA: Stanford University Press.

–. 2008. *The Force of Domesticity: Filipina Migrants and Globalization*. New York: New York University Press.

Pateman, Carole. 1988. *The Sexual Contract*. Stanford, CA: Stanford University Press.

Patten, Steve. 2013. "The Triumph of Neoliberalism within Partisan Conservatism in Canada." In *Conservatism in Canada*, edited by David Rayside and Jim Farney, 59–78. Toronto: University of Toronto Press.

Pernice, Regina 1994. "Methodological Issues in Research with Refugees and Immigrants." *Professional Psychology: Research and Practice* 25, 3: 207–13. https://doi.org/10.1037/0735-7028.25.3.207.

Pessar, Patricia. 1999. "Engendering Migration Studies." *American Behavioral Scientist* 42, 4: 577–600. https://doi.org/10.1177/00027649921954372.

Phillips, Nelson, and Cynthia Hardy. 2002. *Discourse Analysis: Investigating Processes of Social Construction*. London: Sage Publications. https://doi.org/10.4135/9781412983921.

Platt, Jennifer. 1988. "What Can Case Studies Do?" In *Studies in Qualitative Methods: A Research Annual*, edited by R.G. Burgess, 1–23. London: JAI Press.

Plummer, Ken. 2003. *Intimate Citizenship: Private Decisions and Public Dialogues*. Seattle: University of Washington Press.

Polikoff, Nancy. 2008. *Beyond (Straight and Gay) Marriage: Valuing All Families under the Law*. Boston: Beacon Press.

Preibisch, Kerry, and Jenna Hennebry. 2012. "Buy Local, Hire Global: Temporary Migration in Canadian Agriculture." In *Legislated Inequality: Temporary Labour Migration in Canada*, edited by Patti Tamara Lenard and Christine Straehle, 48–72. Montreal: McGill-Queen's University Press.

Privy Council Office of Canada. 2004. *Securing an Open Society: Canada's National Security Policy*. Ottawa: Privy Council Office.

Pryke, Sam. 1998. "Nationalism and Sexuality: What Are the Issues?" *Nationalism and Sexuality* 4, 4: 529–46.

Puar, Jasbir. 2007. *Terrorist Assemblages: Homonationalism in Queer Times*. Durham, NC: Duke University Press. https://doi.org/10.1215/9780822390442.

Radia, Andy. 2011. "Harper Government Set to Crackdown on Fake Marriages." *Canada Politics*, October 28. https://ca.news.yahoo.com/blogs/canada-politics/harper-government-set-crackdown-fake-marriages-145652382.html.

Rambukkana, Nathan. 2015. *Fraught Intimacies: Non/Monogamy in the Public Sphere*. Vancouver: UBC Press.

Ramirez, Horacio N. Roque. 2005. "Claiming Queer Cultural Citizenship: Gay Latino (Im)Migrant Acts in San Francisco." In *Queer Migrations: Sexuality, U.S. Citizenship, and Border Crossings*, edited by Eithne Luibhéid and Lionel Cantù, 161–84. Minneapolis: University of Minnesota Press.

Rasmussen, Birgit Brander, Eric Klinenberg, Irene J. Nexica, and Matt Wray, eds. 2001. *The Making and Unmaking of Whiteness*. Durham: Duke University Press. https://doi.org/10.1215/9780822381044.

Rayside, David. 2008. *Queer Inclusions, Continental Divisions: Public Recognition of Sexual Diversity in Canada and the United States*. Toronto: University of Toronto Press. https://doi.org/10.3138/9781442688896.

Razack, Sherene. 1998. *Looking White People in the Eye*. Toronto: University of Toronto Press.

Reddy, Chandan. 2005. "Asian Diasporas, Neoliberalism, and Family: Reviewing the Case for Homosexual Asylum in the Context of Family Rights." *Social Text* 23, 3–4: 101–19. https://doi.org/10.1215/01642472-23-3-4_84-85-101.

Rehaag, Sean. 2008. "Patrolling the Borders of Sexual Orientation: Bisexual Refugee Claims in Canada." *McGill Law Journal* 53: 59–102.

–. 2009. "Bisexuals Need Not Apply: A Comparative Appraisal of Refugee Law and Policy in Canada, the United States and Australia." *International Journal of Human Rights* 13, 2–3: 415–36.

Richardson, Diane. 2000. "Constructing Sexual Citizenship: Theorizing Sexual Rights." *Critical Social Policy* 20, 1: 105–35. https://doi.org/10.1177/026101830002000105.

–. 2005. "Desiring Sameness? The Rise of a Neoliberal Politics of Normalisation." *Antipode* 37, 3: 515–35. https://doi.org/10.1111/j.0066-4812.2005.00509.x.

Roseneil, Sasha, and Shelley Budgeon. 2004. "Cultures of Intimacy and Care beyond 'the Family': Personal Life and Social Changes in the Early 21st Century." *Current Sociology* 52, 2: 135–59. https://doi.org/10.1177/0011392104041798.

Rubin, Gayle. 1984. "Thinking Sex: Notes for a Radical Theory of the Politics of Sexuality." In *Pleasure and Danger: Exploring Female Sexuality*, edited by Carole Vance, 267–310. Boston: Routledge and Kegan Paul.

Salter, Mark. 2013. "Citizenship, Borders, and Mobility: Managing the Population of Canada and the World." In *Canada in the World: Internationalism in Canadian Foreign Policy*, edited by Heather Smith and Claire Turenne Sjolander, 146–65. Toronto: Oxford University Press.

Samers, Michael. 2010. *Migration*. London: Routledge.

Sapiro, Virginia. 1990. "The Gender Basis of American Social Policy." In *Women, the State and Welfare*, edited by Linda Gordon, 36–54. Madison: University of Wisconsin Press.

Satzewich, Vic. 1993. "Migrant and Immigrant Families in Canada: State Coercion and Legal Control in the Formation of Ethnic Families." *Journal of Comparative Family Studies* 24, 3: 315–38.

–. 2015. *Points of Entry: How Canada's Immigration Officers Decide Who Gets In.* Vancouver: UBC Press.

Saunders, Doug. 2015. "How Tories Win Immigrant Votes Using Anti-Immigrant Messages." *Globe and Mail*, October 9. https://www.theglobeandmail.com/opinion/tories-gain-from-anti-immigrant-messaging-among-immigrants-what-gives/article26749675/.

Sears, Tom. 2007. "Sex after Marriage? The Future of Queer Liberation." Paper presented at the Historical Materialism Conference, London, UK, November 9.

Sempruch, Justyna. 2011. "Beyond the 'Cultural' Landscape of Care: Queering Childcare, Caregiving and Work." In *A Life in Balance? Reopening the Family-Work Debate*, edited by Justyna Sempruch and Catherine Krull, 147–69. Vancouver: UBC Press.

Simmons, Alan. 2010. *Immigration and Canada: Global and Transnational Perspectives*. Toronto: Canadian Scholars' Press.

Smart, Carol. 2000. "Stories of Family Life: Cohabitation, Marriage and Social Change." *Canadian Journal of Family Law* 17, 1: 20–53.

Smart, Carol, and Bren Neale. 1999. *Family Fragments?* Malden, MA: Polity Press.

Smith, Miriam. 2007. "Framing Same-Sex Marriage in Canada and the United States: Goodridge, Halpern and the National Boundaries of Political Discourse." *Social and Legal Studies* 16, 1: 5–26. https://doi.org/10.1177/0964663907073444.

Solot, Dorion, and Marshall Miller. 2006. "Taking Government Out of the Marriage Business." In *Marriage Proposals: Questioning a Legal Status*, edited by Anita Bernstein, 70–105. New York: New York University Press.

Soroka, Stuart, Fred Cutler, Dietlind Stolle, and Patrick Fournier. 2011. "Capturing Change (and Stability) in the 2011 Campaign." *Policy Options* 32, 6: 70–77.

Stacey, Judith. 2004. "Cruising to Familyland: Gay Hypergamy and Rainbow Kinship." *Current Sociology* 52, 2: 181–97. https://doi.org/10.1177/0011392104041807.

Statistics Canada. 2012. *Canada Year Book, 2012.* Ottawa: Government of Canada. https://www.statcan.gc.ca/pub/11-402-x/11-402-x2012000-eng.htm.

–. 2017. *Families, Households and Marital Status: Key Results from the 2016 Census.* Ottawa: Government of Canada. http://www.statcan.gc.ca/daily-quotidien/170802/dq170802a-eng.htm.

Status of Women Canada. 2005. *Polygamy in Canada: Legal and Social Implications for Women and Children.* Ottawa: Government of Canada.

Stevens, Jacqueline. 1999. *Reproducing the State.* Princeton, NJ: Princeton University Press.

–. 2010. *States without Nations: Citizenship for Mortals.* New York: Columbia University Press.

Strong-Boag, Veronica. 2015. "From Tragic Little Boys to Unwanted Young Men." *ActiveHistory.ca.* October 9. http://activehistory.ca/2015/10/from-tragic-little-boys-to-unwanted-young-men/.

Stychin, Carl. 2000. "'A Stranger to Its Laws': Sovereign Bodies, Global Sexualities, and Transnational Citizens." *Journal of Law and Society* 27, 4: 601–25. https://doi.org/10.1111/1467-6478.00169.

Telegdi, Andrew. 2008. *House of Commons Debates.* 39th Parliament, Second Session, Vol 142, No 089, May 6, 11:00.

Thobani, Sunera. 2000. "Closing Ranks: Racism and Sexism in Canada's Immigration Policy." *Race and Class* 42, 1: 35–55. https://doi.org/10.1177/030639600128968009.

–. 2007. *Exalted Subjects: Studies in the Making of Race and Nation in Canada.* Toronto: University of Toronto Press.

Tolley, Erin. 2017. "Political Players or Partisan Pawns? Immigrants, Minorities, and Conservatives in Canada." In *The Blueprint: Conservative Parties and Their Impact on Canadian Politics*, edited by J.P. Lewis and Joanna Everitt, 101–28. Toronto: University of Toronto Press.

Touzin, Caroline. 2006. "Laetitia en a Assez d'attendre: Adolescente menacée d'expulsion à cause de son père polygame." *La Presse Montréal*, November 22. https://www.usherbrooke.ca/sodrus/fileadmin/sites/sodrus/documents/Immigration/polygamie29.pdf.

Tully, James. 1995. *Strange Multiplicity: Constitutionalism in an Age of Diversity.* Cambridge: Cambridge University Press. https://doi.org/10.1017/CBO9781139170888.

Tungohan, Ethel. 2012. "Debunking Notions of Migrant 'Victimhood': A Critical Assessment of Temporary Labour Migration Programs and Filipina Migrant Activism in Canada." In *Filipinos in Canada: Disturbing Invisibility*, edited by Roland Sintos Coloma, Bonnie McElhinny, Ethel Tungohan, John Paul C. Catungal, and Lisa M. Davidson, 161–80. Toronto: University of Toronto Press.

–. 2013. "Reconceptualizing Motherhood, Reconceptualizing Resistance: Migrant Domestic Workers, Transnational Hyper-Maternalism and Activism." *International Feminist Journal of Politics* 15, 1: 39–57. https://doi.org/10.1080/14616742.2012.699781.

–. 2017. "Temporary Foreign Workers in Canada: Reconstructing 'Belonging' and Remaking 'Citizenship.'" *Social & Legal Studies.* https://doi.org/10.1177/0964663917746483.

Tungohan, Ethel, Rupa Banerjee, Wayne Chu, Petronila Cleto, Conely de Leon, Mila Garcia, Philip Kelly, Marco Luciano, Cynthia Palmaria, and Christopher Sorio. 2015. "After the Live-In Caregiver Program: Filipina Caregivers' Experiences of Graduated and Uneven Citizenship." *Canadian Ethnic Studies* 47, 1: 87–105. https://doi.org/10.1353/ces.2015.0008.

United Nations General Assembly. 1951. *Convention Relating to the Status of Refugees,* 28 July 1951, United Nations, Treaty Series, vol. 189, p. 137. http://www.refworld.org/docid/3be01b964.html.

United Nations High Commissioner for Refugees [UNHCR]. 2008. *UNHCR Guidance Note on Refugee Claims Relating to Sexual Orientation and Gender Identity*. Geneva: UNHCR/Division of International Protection Services. http://www.refworld.org/pdfid/48abd5660.pdf.

–. 2012. *Guidelines on International Protection No. 9: Claims to Refugee Status Based on Sexual Orientation and/or Gender Identity within the Context of Article 1A(2) of the 1951 Convention and/or Its 1967 Protocol Relating to the Status of Refugees*, 23 October, HCR/GIP/12/01. http://www.refworld.org/docid/50348afc2.html.

van Walsum, Sarah. 2003. "Family Norms and Citizenship in the Netherlands." In *Social Construction of Diversity: Recasting the Master Narrative of Industrial Nations*, edited by Christiane Harzig and Danielle Juteau, 212–26. New York: Berghahn Books.

–. 2008. *The Family and the Nation: Dutch Family Migration in the Context of Changing Family Norms*. Newcastle upon Tyne, UK: Cambridge Scholars Publishing.

Walker, Kristen. 2001. "United Nations Human Rights Law and Same-Sex Relationship: Where to From Here?" In *Legal Recognition of Same-Sex Partnerships: A Study of National, European and International Law*, edited by Robert Wintemute and Mads Andenaes, 743–58. Portland: Hart Publishing.

Walton-Roberts, Margaret. 2004. "Rescaling Citizenship: Gendering Canadian Immigration Policy." *Political Geography* 23, 3: 265–81. https://doi.org/10.1016/j.polgeo.2003.12.016.

–. 2014. "Responsibilizing Immigration Intermediaries through Canadian Immigration Policy." Paper presented at Transnational Migration and the Changing Canadian Citizenship Regime Workshop, Ottawa, April 11.

Walzer, Michael. 1984. *Spheres of Justice: A Defense of Pluralism and Equality*. New York: Basic Books.

Warner, Michael. 1999. *The Trouble with Normal: Sex, Politics and the Ethics of Queer Life*. New York: The Free Press.

Warner, Tom. 2002. *Never Going Back: A History of Queer Activism in Canada*. Toronto: University of Toronto Press.

Watson, Scott D. 2009. *The Securitization of Humanitarian Migration: Digging Moats and Sinking Boats*. London: Routledge.

Webber, Jeremy. 1994. *Reimagining Canada: Language, Culture, Community, and the Canadian Constitution*. Montreal: McGill-Queen's University Press.

Weeks, Jeffrey. 1998. "The Sexual Citizen." *Theory, Culture and Society* 15, 3: 35–52. https://doi.org/10.1177/0263276498015003003.

Weeks, Jeffrey, Catherine Donovan, and Brian Heaphy. 2004. *Same-Sex Intimacies: Families of Choice and Other Life Experiments*. London: Routledge.

Weston, Kath. 1991. *Families We Choose: Lesbians, Gays, Kinship*. New York: Columbia University Press.

White, Stephen, Antoine Bilodeau, and Neil Nevitte. 2015. "Earning Their Support: Feelings towards Canada among Recent Immigrants." *Ethnic and Racial Studies* 38, 2: 292–308. https://doi.org/10.1080/01419870.2013.859289.

Wingrove, Josh. 2014. "Ottawa to Revise Foreign-Worker Rules as Employers Complain of Delays." *Globe and Mail*, January 27.

Wintemute, Robert. 2004. "Sexual Orientation and the Charter: The Achievement of Formal Legal Equality." *McGill Law Journal* 49: 1143–80.

Wood, Linda, and Rolf Kroger. 2000. *Doing Discourse Analysis: Methods for Studying Action, Talk and Text.* London: Sage Publications.

Yanow, Dvora. 2000. *Conducting Interpretive Policy Analysis.* London: Sage Publications. https://doi.org/10.4135/9781412983747.

Yeatman, Anna. 1994. *Post-Modern Revisionings of the Political.* London: Routledge.

Young, Jessica. 2010. "The Alternative Refuge Concept: A Source of Systemic Disadvantage to Sexual Minority Refugee Claimants." *University of New Brunswick Law Journal* 60: 294–337.

Yu, Henry. 1998. "Mixing Bodies and Cultures: The Meaning of America's Fascination with Sex between 'Orientals' and Whites." In *Sex, Love, Race: Crossing Boundaries in North American History*, edited by Martha Hodes, 444–64. New York: New York University Press.

Zilio, Michelle. 2017. "Senate Passes Bill that Repeals Many Conservative Citizenship Changes." *Globe and Mail*, May 3. https://www.theglobeandmail.com/news/politics/senate-passes-bill-that-would-repeal-many-many-conservative-citizenship-changes/article34890037/.

Cases Cited

Adjei v Canada (Minister of Citizenship and Immigration) (2007), IRB: TA5–14829.

Ajaz v Canada (Public Safety and Emergency Preparedness) (2011), TA9–13190.

Alfonso v Canada (Minister of Citizenship and Immigration) (2003), 2 FC 683, 2002 FCT 1221.

Amaral v Canada (Citizenship and Immigration) (2011), TA8–08075.

Appulonappa v Canada (Citizenship and Immigration) (2016), FC 914.

Aujla v Canada (Citizenship and Immigration) (2008), TA7–03154.

Begum v Canada (Citizenship and Immigration) (2008), MA8–00393.

Brobbey v Canada (Citizenship and Immigration) (2006), TA4–01703.

Canada (Attorney General) v Mossop (1993), 1 SCR 554.

Canada (Attorney General) v Ward (1993), 2 SCR 689.

Chen v Canada (Citizenship and Immigration) (2010), TA6–14852.

Christopher v Canada (Minister of Citizenship and Immigration) (2008), FC 964.

Cruz, Fernando Rodriguez v MEI (1994), FCTD no. IMM-3848–93, Simpson, June 16.

Egan v Canada (1995), 2 SCR 513.

Falkiner v Ontario (Ministry of Community and Social Services) (2002), 59 OR (3d) 481 (CA); 2003, [2002] SCCA 297.

Fitton v Hewton Estate (1997), 38 BCLR (2d) 78.

Gill v Canada (Citizenship and Immigration) (2011), TB0–00040.

Gostlin v Kergin (1986), 3 BCLR (2d) 264.

Gyorgyjakab v Canada (Minister of Citizenship and Immigration) (2005), FC 1119.

Haig and Birch v Canada (1992), 9 OR 495 (OCA).

Huayra v Canada (Citizenship and Immigration) (2010), MA8–16540.

Huerta v Canada (Minister of Employment and Immigration) (1993), 157 NR 225 (FCA).

Hung v Canada (Citizenship and Immigration) (2009), TA7–09697.

Kagayutan v Canada (Public Safety and Emergency Preparedness) (2011), TA9–21476.

KQH v Canada (Minister of Citizenship and Immigration) (2003), RPDD.

Li v Canada (Citizenship and Immigration) (2011), TA9–05367.

Li v Canada (Citizenship and Immigration) (2011), TA9–06490.

Lin v Canada (Citizenship and Immigration) (2011), TA8–05954.

Little Sisters Book and Art Emporium v Canada (Minister of Justice) (2000), 2 SCR 1120, 2000 SCC 69.

M v H (1999), 2 SCR 3.

Mansro v Canada (Citizenship and Immigration) (2008), VA6–01540.

Miron v Trudel (1995), 2 SCR 418.

Molodowich v Penttinen (1980), 17 RFL (2d) 376; [1980] OJ No 1904 (QL); 2 ACWS (2d) 486.

Montoya Martinez v Canada (Citizenship and Immigration) (2011), FC 13.

Nova Scotia (Attorney General) v Walsh (2002), 4 SCR 325, 2002 SCC 83.

PWZ v Canada (Minister of Citizenship and Immigration) (2000), CRDD.

Quebec (Attorney General) v A (Eric v Lola) (2013), SCC 5.

R v Appulonappa (2013), BCCA 79.

R v Appulonappa (2015), 3 SCR 754, SCC 59.

R v Blackmore (2017), BCSC 1288.

R v Butler (1992), 1 SCR 452.

R v Labaye (2005), 3 SCR 728, 80 (SCC).

Rathod v Canada (Citizenship and Immigration) (2008), TA7–02205.

Re B.D.K. (2000), CRDD 72 (QL).

Re K.O.C. (2003), RPDD.

Reference Re Section 293 of the Criminal Code of Canada (2011), BCSC 1588.

Simpson-Lee v Canada (Citizenship and Immigration) (2006), TA4–14172.

Tadessa v Canada (Citizenship and Immigration) (2009), TA7–12352.

Towne Cinema Theatres Ltd v R, [1985] 1 SCR 494.

Veysey v Canada (Correctional Services) (1990), 109 NR 300 (FCTD).

Yu v Canada (Citizenship and Immigration) (2008), TA-700735.

Legislation Cited

Adult Interdependent Relationships Act (2002), S.A. 2002, c A-4.5.

Citizenship Act (1985), R.S.C. 1985, c C-29.

Civil Marriage Act (2005), S.C. 2005, c 33.

Criminal Code of Canada (1985), R.S.C. 1985 c C-46.

Immigration and Refugee Protection Act (2001), S.C. 2001, c 27.

Modernization of Benefits and Obligations Act (2000), S.C. 2000, c 12.

Index